COMPETENCY BASED LEARNING:
Technology, Management, and Design

COMPETENCY BASED LEARNING:
Technology, Management, and Design

IVOR K. DAVIES

Professor of Education, Indiana University

McGRAW-HILL BOOK COMPANY
New York   St Louis   San Francisco

07 084420 8

Published in Great Britain under the title **The Management of Learning** © 1971

PRINTED AND BOUND IN GREAT BRITAIN

Preface

Teaching is a highly skilled professional activity, and a great deal of what teachers and instructors do, both within and outside the classroom, involves making decisions of one kind or another. In the past, many of these decisions have been made as a matter of expediency on a short-term basis, from moment to moment, or incident to incident. This approach is now no longer possible, and both short- and long-term decisions are becoming characteristic of the teaching process. These decisions, furthermore, are increasingly subtle and complex in character, and the factors involved are often shifting and ill defined. All of this demands a renewed degree of professionalism from the teacher, as well as a framework within which decision-making can be made.

Many books on education and training set out, in effect, to tell teachers and instructors how they should do their job. This book has *not* been written from this standpoint. It is not a cookbook of recipes for all occasions and all seasons. The aim of this book on the management of learning is to give teachers and instructors useful and valid criteria against which *they* can choose alternative courses of action in the light of the assumptions *they* make about the nature of teaching, the objectives to be realized, the resources available, and the character of the students involved. In this sense, the book is designed to cater for the needs of lecturers, teachers, and administrators (who control the purse strings), working in the area of secondary and tertiary education; instructors involved in industrial and military training programmes; and staff working in management training. Students undergoing teacher-training and postgraduate courses in education and educational technology will also find the material particularly relevant to their studies.

In writing the book, I have made three basic assumptions:

1. Many teachers and instructors have a tendency to overteach. They overmanage the learning situation, define their students' role too narrowly, and tend to make far too many decisions on their behalf.

2. Problems of student motivation are more likely to result from the way that learning is organized than from a simple unwillingness of students to work harder.

3. Student behaviour in a teaching and learning situation is *always* sensible

v

to the student involved. If a teacher wishes to understand why a student behaves as he does, it is necessary to look at the environment in the same way that he looks at it.

In other words, we are not using students to their full capacity. We have tended to design learning tasks in such a way that we are taking advantage of only the minimum performance that students are capable of investing. The powerful motivating force of learning itself has been obscured. Learning tasks, which are often organized so that most of the challenge has been removed, need to be enriched and revalued if learning potential is to be fully and effectively realized.

While no panacea for all ills is available, behavioural science is at last beginning to yield a number of clues which suggest effective courses of action for teachers and instructors to consider. For this reason, this book is essentially based on research. There have been many times as an author when I have wished to fill in some of the gaps in the argument on the basis of my own teaching experience, but I have tried to resist the temptation if evidence has not been available or has not been suggested by the data at present available.

In preparing the book, I have also attempted to practise the tactics and strategies which I have been describing. There is a minimum of theory, and the approach is essentially practical in nature as will be seen from the actual wording of the chapter titles Each chapter begins with a statement of learning objectives. The subject matter has been structured in the way described in the first part of the book, and the tactics and strategies employed in teaching the material are those detailed in the sections on organizing and leading. The book has also been 'reader-tested' in order to determine whether or not the text successfully realized its objectives, and the material was then rewritten, and again rewritten, on the basis of these evaluations.

Many people have helped in the preparation of the manuscript, and I am deeply grateful and indebted to them for their assistance and advice. Finally, my wife missed none of the agonizing process peculiar to authorship, and I would like to acknowledge her assistance, patience, and endurance.

Ivor K. Davies.

For my son, Simon –

more teacher than pupil

Foreword

To many people, the expression 'instructional systems' is intimidating. Somehow, it brings forth images of cold, mechanical construction of instructional units, without regard for the 'warmth' of human beings, without regard for that never defined thing called humanism.

Of course, if you look at some of the complicated intertwining of boxes and arrows that some of our flowcharting brethren seem to delight in creating, it is not hard to see how one might be inclined toward such an incorrect conclusion.

This is unfortunate.

There is no doubt that some aspects of what the instructional technologist does are rather difficult to learn. Unquestionably, some aspects of systematic instructional design are hard to put into practice. But that is true of many things worth doing.

Nonetheless, the basic idea of systematic design is simplicity itself. For when we talk about 'systematic instructional design', we are talking about sensible design, about 'thinking in the whole' rather than about 'thinking in isolated pieces'. To think like an instructional systems designer is to think like a composer rather than like a piccolo-player. I mean no disrespect to the piccolo-player; after all, where would the orchestra be without him? My point is that the piccolo-player's main concern is that of precise, pretty piccolo-playing, rather than of the integration of all the instruments of the orchestra to achieve a desired result.

If an instructor is truly to be a conductor of the educational orchestra, he must perform functions other than those performed by the instrumentalists themselves. If he is to consider himself a head man on the educational scene, his repertoire must include all the skills of that position, rather than just those that allow him to *be* one of the resources he is supposed to manage. He needs to be able to carry out those functions which will allow him to make more effective decisions for, and with, that primary reason for the existence of the entire educational enterprise – the student.

A first step toward development of the requisite skills is that of knowing just what they are, where they fit, and how they are used. This book is a good place to begin.

R. F. MAGER

Los Altos Hills 11 May, 1970

Contents

Introduction

1 Towards a technology of education and training

Learning Objectives

COGNITIVE OBJECTIVES

After carefully reading this chapter, you will be able to:

1. State why the concept of an educational technology has become necessary.

2. Distinguish between the two main definitions of educational technology.

3. Compare and contrast three broad assumptions about human nature, and relate these assumptions to three theories of organization.

4. Relate each of the three theories of organization to an appropriate theory of education and training.

5. State the characteristics of educational technology (3), and demonstrate its advantages over educational technology (1) and educational technology (2).

6. State what is meant by the systems approach to education and training.

7. State the characteristics of a theory of teaching, and indicate the usefulness of the concept.

AFFECTIVE OBJECTIVES

After reading this chapter, the author intends that you will:

1. Value the principle of a technology of education and training.

2. Incorporate the approach into your organization of teaching strategies, so that it becomes characteristic of your teaching style.

> Of the five vices, the vice of the mind is the worst. What is the vice of the mind? The vice of the mind is self-satisfaction.
>
> *Chuang-Tse*

Education and training have always tended to depend more upon contrivance than upon design, and for this reason art and cratfsmanship have been rightly emphasized in the teaching process. However, times have changed, and a more systematic approach is now necessary. In the past, ideas have always lived longer than people, but, today, people live longer than most ideas. As de Bono has pointed out (1969): 'technology has so speeded things up that ideas may have to be changed within a generation, instead of between generations. Yet our culture and education have always been concerned with establishing ideas, not with changing them.' We are living, in fact, in an age of instability or discontinuity (see Drucker, 1969), when skills based on mechanization are gradually being replaced by skills based on information and knowledge technology. In order to prepare themselves for this new role, education and training require a new conceptual framework against which decisions involving change and innovation can be made.

Associated with this problem of providing for change is the increasing concern that is being felt for effectiveness and efficiency in the learning process. Education and training now represent the largest single national expenditure, and many economists and politicians now believe that it is doubtful if society can any longer afford the high costs and low productivity associated with instruction. In the past, we have, to a very large extent, been concerned with teaching rather than with learning, with the means rather than with the ends of education. The last decade, however, has witnessed profound changes, and there has been an increasing concern with, and emphasis upon, the achievement of educational goals or objectives. To this end, teaching methods are now being more effectively exploited, so as to improve the overall quality of the learning experience.

The Nature of Educational and Training Technology

In the space of a very few years, there has emerged a true technology of education and training, which provides the necessary framework for planning and organizing learning resources, so as to realize specific learning objectives or performance levels. Argyris (1964) contends that the effectiveness of any organization depends upon its ability to accomplish three essential aims:

1. To achieve its goals.
2. To maintain itself internally.
3. To adapt to its environment.

If an organization fails to realize these aims, it is 'unhealthy', or steadily ineffective; if an organization realizes them, it is 'healthy,' and it is flexible, able to learn through experience, free to change, and free to respond to new circumstances. Educational technology is concerned with these very problems in an education or training context, and it is characterized by its disciplined and systematic approach to the organization of resources for learning. Although the development of educational technology cannot be entirely explained as the flowering of any purely educational or psychological theory, its antecedents are clearly discernible in the evolving principles of programmed learning. These are illustrated in Fig. 1.1.

THE TWO EDUCATIONAL TECHNOLOGIES

The term 'educational technology,' which also includes training technology, has generally come to have two very different meanings, depending on who is discussing the matter and the context of the debate. It is important, there-fore, to distinguish between these two meanings, each of which has entirely different associations and consequences. Lumsdaine (1964) has suggested that they can be most usefully distinguished as educational technology (1) and educational technology (2) in the following manner:

1. *Educational technology* (1). This is essentially a hardware approach, stressing the importance of teaching aids, and its origin lies in the application of physical science to the education and training system. This concept dominates most of the literature on the subject of educational technology. Closely related to this view is the widely held assumption that a technology of machines is intimately related to a technology of teaching, and progressive views are, accordingly, often associated with the possession of the latest projector or language laboratory. It is interesting to note, in this regard, that the teaching machine is the only mechanical aid to have been deliberately invented to fulfil an instructional requirement. All the other audiovisual aids commonly associated with education and training – television, projectors, tape-recorders, record-players, etc. – were invented and developed for markets other than the educational one. Fig. 1.2 illustrates some of the interrelationships that exist among the developments in hardware, and relates these to the development of an educational technology. In this way, the process of teaching has been gradually mechanized through the increasing use of teaching aids. These transmit, amplify, distribute, record, and repro-duce stimuli materials, with a consequent increase in teacher impact. At the same time, the teacher can deal with larger and larger groups of students, without decreasing the availability of properly qualified and experienced teachers. Thus, the aim of educational technology (1) has been to increase the impact that teaching makes, without necessarily substantially increasing the cost of each student taught. Indeed, since the educational and training system are able to deal with an increased number of students, the cost per pupil has sometimes even been reduced.

2. *Educational technology* (2). This concept is essentially a software approach,

1960	1963	1966	1970
Small steps	Task analysis	Task analysis	Systems analysis
Overt responses	Behavioural objectives	Behavioural objectives	Task analysis
Immediate feedback of results	Small steps	Subject analysis	Contrast analysis
Self-pacing	Logical sequencing	Flowcharts	Behavioural objectives
Validation	Active responding	Small steps	Structuring material (via analysis and synthesis)
	Immediate feedback	Active responding	Appropriate teaching strategy
	Self-pacing	Presentation as a communication problem	Controlled interaction via: digestible steps appropriate stimulus content relevant response modes reinforcement
	Validation	Validation	Presentation as a communication problem
			Appropriate instrumentation
			Validation and evaluation
			Installation and implementation

Fig. 1.1 Changing emphases of programmed learning

and refers to the application of learning principles to the direct and deliberate shaping of behaviour. Its origin lies in the application of behavioural science to the problems of learning and motivation; mechanization is seen purely as a problem of presentation. This view of educational technology is closely associated with the modern principles of programmed learning, and is characterized by task analysis, writing precise objectives, selection of appropriate learning strategies, reinforcement of correct responses, and constant evaluation. The converging streams of influence which have given rise to this position are illustrated in Fig. 1.3, where its close association with achievement testing, behavioural analysis, contiguity theory, and presentation modes is clearly discernible.

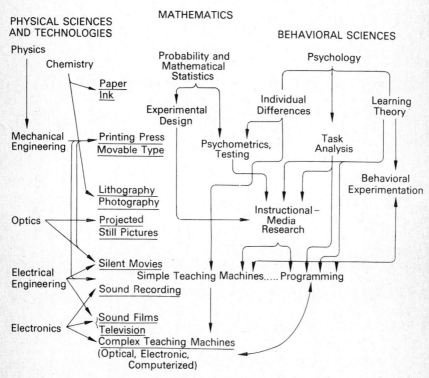

Fig. 1.2 Converging streams of influence affecting present concepts and practices in educational technology (1) (Reproduced with permission from Lumsdaine, A. A. (1964) Educational Technology, Programmed Learning and Instructional Science. In H. G. Richey, ed., *Theories of Learning and Instruction*. Chicago, Illinois: University of Chicago Press)

These two meanings of educational technology, the first concerned with teaching aids like teaching machines, and the second with learning aids like programmes, are obviously functionally related to each other. It is, therefore doubly unfortunate that these two meanings should have emerged, since they create unnecessary barriers and do little to further the concept.

If educational technology is to be useful to the practicing teacher, then it must be capable of reconciling these two views. Polarization of argument has often been characteristic of arguments dealing with change and innovation in education and training, and teachers have tended to think in dualistic terms like 'good versus evil', 'traditional versus progressive', 'teacher-dominated versus child-centred', 'hardware versus software', and 'teacher-teaching versus learner-learning'. A sequential, emerging, and transformational view of change and innovation has rarely been depicted, and patterns of change have not been available, therefore, to serve as a rationale for decision-making. For this reason, a new, more embracing view of educational technology is now necessary.

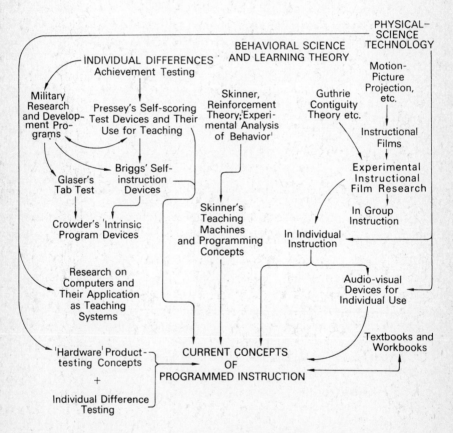

Fig. 1.3 Converging streams of influence affecting present concepts and practices in educational technology (2) (Reproduced with permission from Lumsdaine, A. A. (1964) Educational Technology, Programmed Learning and Instructional Science. In H. G. Richey, ed., *Theories of Learning and Instruction*. Chicago, Illinois: University of Chicago Press)

Theories of Organization and their Application to Learning

Traditionally, organization has been viewed as a means of arranging resources so as to accomplish a set of given objectives. This is a perfectly fair and reasonable way of looking at organization, but it is not the only way; indeed, this rather simple view may obscure the inner workings and internal purposes of organization. For example, a book, a lesson, a film, or a programme, are all designed to realize learning objectives of some kind or another, but this tells us very little about the way the material is internally arranged or structured, nor does it cast any light on the different behaviours of students using the materials.

An alternative, and probably more productive, way of looking at organization is to regard it 'as a mechanism having the ultimate purpose of offsetting those forces which undermine collaboration' (Scott, 1967). Underlying such a view is the idea that organization serves to achieve an objective by:

1. Coordinating resources and effort.
2. Dividing work and function among participants.
3. Using a hierarchy of authority and responsibility.

Scott points out that the ultimate objective of organization is to minimize conflict, as well as to lessen the importance of anything, or anyone, that tends to deviate from the planned course of action. In other words, organization increases stability by reducing any uncertainty about what is to be accomplished. It also increases the likelihood of being able to predict the actual outcome. Such a view of organization is already profoundly affecting company management, since stability and predictability are highly valued concepts in the industrial context. The philosophy is also meaningful and useful to a more rounded definition of educational technology.

ASSUMPTIONS ABOUT HUMAN NATURE

Some years ago, March and Simon (1958), working in the area of industrial management, pointed out that propositions about organization are, in fact, statements about human behaviour. Furthermore, imbedded in every such proposition is a set of assumptions about the nature of man. Three broad propositions are recognized by them:

1. *Classical theory of organization – task-centred.*
   'Propositions assuming that organization members . . . are primarily passive instruments, capable of performing work and accepting directions but not initiating action or exerting influence in any significant way.'
2. *Human relations theory of organization – relationship-centred.*
   'Propositions assuming members bring to their organization attitudes, values and goals; that they have to be motivated or induced to participate in the system of organization behaviour; that there is incomplete parallelism between their personal goals and organization goals; and

that actual or potential goal conflicts make power phenomena, attitudes, and morale centrally important in the explanation of organization behaviour.'

3. *Modern theory of organization – task- and relationship-centred.*
'Proposition assuming that organization members are decision-makers and problem-solvers, and that perception and thought processes are central to the explanation of behaviour in organizations.'

There is, of course, nothing contradictory about these three sets of propositions, human beings are all things. Although the three sets of assumptions were primarily written from the point of view of industrial management, they can be easily and usefully translated into educational terms.

LEARNING SYSTEMS

The classical theory of organization has been a popular one in education in the past, and vestiges of it are still discernible in the attitudes of some universities towards students, in the Victorian attitudes of some teachers towards pupils (particularly those with long hair), and in the attitudes of some companies towards apprentices. The student is typically regarded as a *given*, rather than as a *variable*, in the educational system; as a passive instrument to be manipulated and acted upon. Teachers associated with this classical approach see their role as that of custodians and benevolent autocrats, who attempt to realize *their* objectives by motivating, controlling, and modifying student behaviour through some variant of class-teaching based usually on talk and chalk. The approach is essentially task-centred. It is related to the teacher-dominated, doing things to, subject emphasis, class-teaching, limited resources, and teaching-aid practices, associated with stage 1 of McBeath's model of change illustrated in Fig. 1.4. In many ways, educational technology (1) is an application of presentday engineering principles to such a theoretical position, enabling the classical teacher to increase his overall effectiveness, as well as helping him to deal with larger and larger numbers of students. There is a marked tendency, in such an organization, to emphasize the importance of rote-learning, and to present materials so logically that they are immediately meaningful to the existing knowledge of the student. In other words, there is little 'discovery' or challenge.

The human relations theory of organization is characteristic of a great deal of education and training today. It represents a reaction to the classical tradition, and considers that, under traditional forms of educational and training organization, the intellectual potentialities of average and below average students are only partially realized. Accordingly, students are given the education and training best suited to their age, aptitude, and ability, so that they can fully realize their innate potentialities. The role of a teacher in such an organization is that of guide, adviser, counsellor, whose main responsibility is to avoid stifling students' initiative. Such an approach is essentially related to the permissive, doing things for, method emphasis, group-teaching, multiple resources, and learning-aid practices, associated with McBeath's stage 2. Educational technology (2) represents an application of presentday behavioural science principles to such a theoretical position, so as to ensure that learning materials are so carefully structured and designed that learning is enjoyable, rewarding, and successful. Rote-learning in such

STAGE 1	STAGE 2	STAGE 3
	Developments in Technology	
wheel	motor	jet propulsion
manpower	machine power	electronic controls
cottage industry	mechanization	automation
structures and functions	functions in structures	structures for functions
units	networks	constellations
explore	exploit	conserve
	Developments in Science	
certainties	confusion	probabilities
absolutes	relative absolutes	relatives
metaphor	towards models	functional models
linear	regular patterns	emerging patterns
closed system	open system	open systems
static	dynamic (in flux)	dynamic (evolving)
	Developments in Education	
Principles		
active mind	reactive mind	transactive mind
units (dualism)	unity (monism)	pluralism
autocratic	laissez-faire	democratic
Practices		
teacher-dominated	permissive	inquiry-centred
do things to	do things for	do things with
subject emphasis	method emphasis	discipline emphasis
product-oriented	process-oriented	performance-oriented
extrinsic manipulation	random reinforcement	meaningful involvement
standards grouping	age grouping	readiness grouping
class-teaching	group teaching	independent study
fixed stimulus	multiple stimuli	organized stimuli
limited access	random access	systematic access
limited resources	multiple resources	instructional systems
teaching aids	audiovisual techniques	instructional technology
Outcomes		
fixed response	varied response	response mastery
convergent thinking and rote memory	convergent thinking plus free expression	convergent and divergent thinking
competitive	cooperative	adventure
inner directed	other directed	self-actualizing

Fig. 1.4 A model depicting change as sequential, emergent, and transformational (Reproduced with permission from McBeath, R. J. (1969) Is Education Becoming? *AV Communication Review*, 17, 1, 36, 40)

an organization is minimal, and the importance of the meaningful learning of potentially meaningful tasks, through discovery, games, and project work, is duly emphasized. For a discussion of these two types of learning, the reader is referred to the writings of David Ausubel (1967).

The classical and the human relations views of organization represent two extremes. There is, however, another set of propositions concerning the nature of man that do not fit easily into either approach. These propositions, associated with modern organization theory, view human beings as natural decision-makers and problem-solvers. Furthermore, this viewpoint sees both the task-centred emphasis of the classical theory and the permissiveness of the human relations theory as reconcilable through the application of a systems approach to organization. The significant difference between this modern approach to organization and the two earlier ones is that it recognizes that all problems are likely to be different, and that there is unlikely to be a common solution or remedy. Accordingly, modern methods of analysis and synthesis, decision-making and rigorous empirical evaluation are all employed in problem-solving situations. Such a view destroys the essential polarity of the classical and human relations approaches, and introduces a continuum on which there is a third main alternative for a teacher to choose.

This modern approach to organization combines both the task and the human relations orientations of the other two theories. It is essentially student-centred, and sees education and training as both a social and technical system in which the needs of the task and the needs of the students have to be reconciled with the needs of the teacher and the needs of the organization (see Fig. 1.5). Such a view is related to the inquiry-centred, doing things with, discipline emphasis, independent study, instructional systems, and instructional technology practices of McBeath's stage 3. The form of educational technology, designated educational technology (3) (Davies, 1971), which stems from this approach to organization is distinctive and meaningful, incorporating as it does both educational technology (1) and educational technology (2) through the applications of a systems approach to education and training.

The New Educational Technology

The distinctive qualities of modern organization theory are: 'its conceptual-analytical base, its reliance on empirical research data, and, above all, its synthesizing, integrating nature' (Scott, 1967). These are all framed in an overall philosophy that believes that the only meaningful way of looking at organization is to study it as a system, and such a view is largely new to education and training. All too often, we have been accustomed to think of things as existing apart from what they actually do or accomplish. We tend to think of the blackboard, the language laboratory, the teaching machine, and the teacher as something quite separate from each other and from the system of which they are but a part. A more meaningful approach is to take a whole view, both task and human, of the learning system, and to determine how each of the many constituent parts interact with each other.

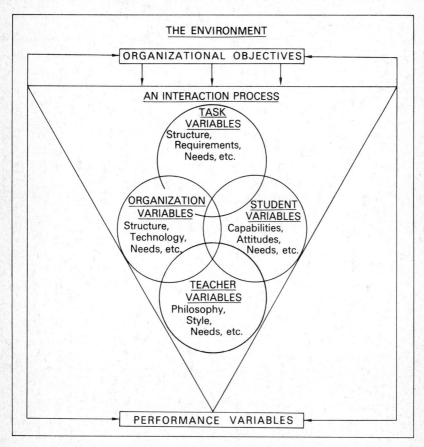

Fig. 1.5 Educational Technology (3)

THE SYSTEMS APPROACH

Isolated parts can rarely provide adequate information about a system, but a system can provide valuable information about the functions fulfilled by each of its components. Such an approach is nothing more than an application of the Gestalt concept that the whole is more than a simple summation of its constituent parts. Just as an atom, for instance, can only be described in terms of activity, so the resources of an educational environment can be described in terms of what they do and the roles they fulfill in realizing the system's objectives.

Systems analysis also has its own particular point of view. This involves asking a series of interrelated key questions not seriously considered by classical and human relation views of organization. These questions, which concern the operation of the *whole* system are:

1. How are the three objectives of a system (stability, growth, and inter-action) realized?
2. What are the strategic parts of the system?
3. What is the nature of their mutual interdependency?
4. What processes link these main parts?
5. How do these processes facilitate adjustment?
6. How are distortions or irregularities in the system recognized?
7. How can distortions and irregularities in the system be dealt with?

The reason such questions are asked is not only to discover principles or universals of organization, but also to help predict the likely effect that any change may have – both within the system itself, and within the environment in which the system operates. It is interesting to note in this regard, that the system concept as applied to education and training in the United Kingdom has tended to be misunderstood. Systems have been used, with little or no quantified data, for descriptive purposes – usually as a masterplan for research or investigation – rather than as a means of predicting the repercussions of change, innovation, or stagnation. Yet, probably, the most important argument for a systems concept of organization is that the environment within which the system exists is becoming increasingly unstable as a result of the rapid growth of technology and the changes in social and political mores (Schein, 1965).

A systems approach enables teachers and instructors, as well as research workers and administrators, to isolate and identify problems and select optimal strategies, and evaluate both their effectiveness and their effects on the working of the overall education or training system. Lange (1967), for instance, has shown how the introduction of progressive, but isolated, educational changes can cause inbalance in the overall system. He cites the case of programmed learning, and shows how the effects of its introduction can cause a linkage of change in a school or college organization – each link of change, of course, bringing its own concomitant problems and conflicts, not all of which may be welcome.

In the past, schools and colleges have tended to *adapt* rather than to *adopt* innovation, but this strategy is becoming less and less possible as the twin concepts of specific objectives and empirical evaluation become more and more characteristic of education and training practices. Change and innovation in education and training may well be unpopular with some teachers and administrators, but the systems approach undoubtedly intro-duces a new type of increased professionalism and expertise. The teacher is seen not only as a learning resource, but also as a manager of learning resources, able to balance and reconcile the conflicting task needs of the curriculum with the personal and group needs of his students.

Educational technology (3), combining both the hardware and the software approaches of the other two technologies, builds a bridge between educational theory and practice. As a result, there is beginning to emerge an associated general theory of teaching, a guide to pedagogy, so that we need no longer be overdependent upon a theory of learning. It is true, of course, that any adequate theory of behaviour should be able to encompass both teaching and learning, but only if teaching is regarded as 'the dependent variable' – or the condition not manipulated. Modern organization theory, and its associated system approach, regards teaching as an 'independent variable' – the condition to be manipulated – as a series of strategies at the behest of the teacher or instructor. This very simple, even obvious, change in approach makes it possible to deal with a whole class of phenomena up to now neglected by learning theorists, and also make possible a science *and* an art of teaching with a technology of its very own.

Bruner (1966) characterizes such a theory of teaching as one that sets forth rules concerning the most efficient way of achieving knowledge, skill, or attitudes, and he considers that these rules should be derived from a more general view of learning. A theory of learning is essentially *descriptive* in nature, in the sense that it tells what has happened after the event. On the other hand, a theory of teaching is *prescriptive* and *normative* in character, in that it can prescribe how to proceed and how a learning experience can be improved, and, at the same time, yield a yardstick for evaluating any particular method or technique. Such a theory of teaching will enable the teacher or instructor to:

1. Specify an optimal environment for learning.
2. Sequence and structure subject material so that it can be readily grasped by the learner.
3. Select an optimal teaching strategy, and explain why this strategy is likely to be more effective than another.
4. Distinguish between optional or enrichment types of audiovisual aid, and basic or essential audiovisual aids necessary to learning.

At the same time, it is to be hoped that a theory of teaching will suggest ways of stimulating and motivating students so that they are willing, eager, and able to learn. Such a theory will then lead directly to a theory of motivation, as well as to an educational theory of personality growth. In this way, the real aim and practices of education can be related to actual teaching practices in the classroom.

Conclusion

Education, as we have seen, is concerned with change, for we are living in an environment that is constantly creating problems of obsolescence. Unfortunately, past patterns of organization in education and training have tended to introduce a degree of rigidity and lack of flexibility that have made changes difficult to introduce or accept. Changes that have been introduced, like programmed learning and independent study, have tended to create new educational, social, status, and administrative problems, so that people have ultimately become disenchanted with them.

Modern organization theory and its systems concept, on the other hand, view change, innovation, and growth as the natural result of a concerted response to a new situation. Although debate and conflict may still be present, they are recognized as healthy organizational symptoms – not something to be suppressed, but faced. Teachers are seen as managers of learning resources, charged with the role of choosing or deciding between alternative teaching and learning strategies. Educational technology (3) provides the necessary conceptual framework for this new approach, and helps to ameliorate the problems stemming from the needs of an education or training system to survive, grow, and develop the capacity to adapt and to manage change.

Note on the Posttest

Now that you have read the first chapter, you will want to find out whether the learning objectives listed at the beginning of the text have in fact been successfully realized. For this reason, you should answer all the questions in posttest 1, each one of which is tied to a cognitive objective. Similar tests have been constructed for all the other chapters.

It is not possible, of course, to determine whether the affective or attitudinal objectives have been realized by questions of this type. However, if you incorporate the principles expounded in each chapter into your organization, so that they become characteristic of your teaching style, then it can be safely concluded that the affective objectives have indeed been accomplished.

Posttest 1

ANSWER ALL QUESTIONS

1. State why the concept of an educational technology has become necessary.

2. Distinguish between the two main definitions of educational technology as put forward by Lumsdaine.

3. Compare and contrast the three broad assumptions about human nature as put forward by March and Simon. Relate these three assumptions to three theories of organization.

4. Relate each of the three theories of organization to an appropriate theory of education and training.

5. State the characteristics of educational technology (3), and demonstrate its advantages over educational technology (1) and educational technology (2).

6. State what is meant by a systems approach to education and training.

7. State the characteristics of a theory of teaching, and indicate the usefulness of such a concept.

References and Reading List

ARGYRIS, C. (1964) *Integrating the Individual and the Organization.* New York: John Wiley.

AUSUBEL, D. P. (1967) A cognitive-structure theory of school learning. In L. Siegel, ed., *Instruction: Some Contemporary Viewpoints.* San Francisco: Chandler.

BRUNER, J. S. (1966) *Towards a Theory of Instruction.* Cambridge, Massachussetts: Harvard University Press.

CALLAHAN, R. E. (1962) *Education and the Cult of Efficiency.* Chicago, Illinois: University of Chicago Press.

DAVIES, I. K. (1971) Educational technology: The application of modern organization theory to education. In I. K. Davies and J. A. Hartley, eds., *Readings in Educational Technology.* London: Iliffe.

DE BONO, E. (1969) The Man who Thinks Sideways, In an interview with Pat Williams. *Observer Sunday Supplement,* 9 May 1969.

DRUCKER, P. F. (1969) *The Age of Discontinuity: Guidelines to Our Changing Society.* London: Heinemann.

ELY, D. P. (1970) Towards of Philosophy of Instructional Technology. *Journal of Educational Technology,* 1, 2, 81–94.

ETZIONI, A. (1964) *Modern Organizations.* Englewood Cliffs, New Jersey: Prentice-Hall.

GRIFFITHS, D. E., ed. (1964) *Behavioural Science and Educational Administration: The Sixty-third Yearbook of the National Society for the Study of Education.* Chicago, Illinois: University of Chicago Press.

HEINICH, R. (1968) Educational technology as technology. *Educational Technology,* 8, 1, 4.

HOYLE, E. (1965) Organizational analysis in the field of education. *Educational Research,* 7, 2, 97–114.

LANGE, P. C. (1967) Introduction: Issues and Problems. In P. C. Lange, ed., *Programmed Instruction: The Sixty-Sixth Yearbook of the National Society for the Study of Education.* Chicago, Illinois: University of Chicago Press.

LUMSDAINE, A. A. (1964) Educational technology, programmed learning and instructional science. In H. G. Richey, ed., *Theories of Learning and Instruction.* Chicago, Illinois: University of Chicago Press.

LUMSDAINE, A. A. (1964) Educational technology: Issues and problems. In P. C. Lange, ed., *Programmed Instruction: The Sixty-Sixth Yearbook of the National Society for the Study of Education.* Chicago, Illinois: National Society for the Study of Education.

MANN, A. P. and BRUNSTROM, C. K. (1969) *Aspects of Educational Technology III.* London: Pitman.

MARCH, J. G. and SIMON, H. A. (1958) *Organizations.* New York: John Wiley.

McBEATH, R. J. (1969) Is education becoming? *AV Communication Review*, 17, 1, 36–40.

MILES, M. B., ed., (1964) *Innovation in Education*. New York: Teachers College Press.

OWENS, R. G. (1970) *Organizational Behaviour in Schools*. Englewood Cliffs, New Jersey: Prentice-Hall.

SAETTLER, P. (1968) *A History of Instructional Technology*. New York: McGraw-Hill.

SAETTLER, P. (1969) Instructional Technology: Some concerns and desiderata. *AV Communication Review*, 17, 1, 357–67.

SCHEIN, E. H. (1965) *Organizational Psychology*. Englewood Cliffs, New Jersey: Prentice-Hall.

SCOTT, W. G. (1967) *Organization Theory: A Behavioural Analysis for Management*. Homewood, Illinois: Richard D. Irwin.

UNWIN, D. and LEEDHAM, J., eds. (1967) *Aspects of Educational Technology*. London: Methuen.

2 The teacher-manager

Learning Objectives

COGNITIVE OBJECTIVES

After carefully reading this chapter, you will be able to:

1. State five principles of learning.

2. Distinguish, in terms of a teacher's behaviour, between the two terms 'managing' and 'operating'.

3. List, and write short notes on, the four functions of a teacher-manager and training-manager.

4. Discuss the teacher's role as a decision-maker.

5. Identify and evaluate the three criteria available to teachers for selecting alternative strategies.

6. Show, by means of a diagram, the steps necessary in developing a learning system, and discuss these steps in terms of each of the four functions of a teacher-manager.

7. List the major effects that such an approach can have on the future of the education and training system.

AFFECTIVE OBJECTIVES

After reading this chapter, the author intends that you will:

1. Be aware of, and value, the concept of the teacher-manager.

2. Incorporate the concept into your value system so that it becomes characteristic of your teaching style.

> The manager works with a specific resource: man. And the human being is a unique resource requiring peculiar qualities in whoever attempts to work with it. For man, and man alone, cannot be 'worked'. *Peter F. Drucker*

Today, we live in a world of rapidly accelerating change brought about by the application of science and technology to almost every aspect of our everyday life. Paradoxically, however, this revolution has virtually bypassed education and training, despite vast and increasing investments in teaching systems. Indeed, the methods and techniques that some teachers and instructors use have changed little from the original Socratic model on which they were founded, while a great deal of the content of their courses has tended to become divorced from the realities and needs of everyday life and work.

However, after a long period of gradual and placid evolution, the conservative and traditional practices in the educational and training processes are gradually giving way. Progress, which has been so slow, is now accelerating to such an extent that an economy, built around the railroads in the last half of the last century and the automobile in the first half of the present century, is now being built around education and training in an effort to spearhead the constant war against unemployment, boredom, poverty, ignorance, and disease.

Learning and Teaching

Inevitably, education and training have become recognized as major problem areas, since the organizing and organization of men for learning demands something more than neat administrative solutions – plausible and convincing though these may be. Education and training systems are, in the final analysis, designed for learning, and they can only operate in an effective and efficient manner when human performance has been brought up to and maintained at a peak level of mastery. Viewed in this way, there are no such things as 'education and training objectives', there can only be objectives for learning.

The misunderstanding has partly arisen from the persistent and menacing confusion of learning with teaching, which have now become synonymous. We have tended to forget that the real essence of education is learner-learning and *not* teacher-teaching. Somehow, we have tended to create a mystical position for the teacher in the educational process, and have neglected the individual pupil's desire and capacity to create, discover, and learn for himself.

Every educational reformer from the time of Plato has fought against relegating the pupil to an inferior and subsidiary role. John Dewey (1916) stressed that, 'since learning is something that the pupil has to do himself and for himself, the initiative lies with the learner. The teacher is a guide and director, who steers the boat, but the energy that propels it must come from those who are learning.' Thus, students must be encouraged and stimulated to learn for themselves, and the real job of the teacher is to ensure that the students accept responsibility for their own learning by developing in them a taste and enthusiasm for it.

PRINCIPLES OF LEARNING

Although many teachers and psychologists would disagree as to the exact nature of the learning process, there are certain principles of learning upon which most educationalists would agree. Alvin C. Eurich (1962) of the Ford Foundation has summarized these as follows:

1. Whatever a student learns, he must learn for himself – no one can learn for him.
2. Each student learns at his own rate, and, for any age group, the variations in rates of learning are considerable.
3. A student learns more when each step is immediately strengthened or reinforced.
4. Full, rather than partial, mastery of each step makes total learning more meaningful.
5. When given responsibility for his own learning, the student is more highly motivated; he learns and retains more.

To a large extent, and for a great variety of reasons, teachers have been unable to fully implement these principles in their own classrooms; however, the application of science and technology to the educational process at last holds out the hope of realizing these principles in a new and dynamic way.

The very multiplicity of the problems that we encounter in our education and training programmes often tends to blind us to what we have yet to accomplish. Indeed, we have often sought answers to the wrong problems, and sometimes we have applied solutions without even bothering to determine whether a problem exists. As Father Brown once remarked in one of G. K. Chesterton's (1923) short detective stories, 'It isn't that they can't see the solution, it is that they can't see the problem.' Yet the problem is a very simple one, once it has been identified; it is the problem of effectiveness.

The cost of education still largely consists of the cost of paying teachers and of providing the buildings in which they teach, while a relatively small proportion is spent on support personnel, books, and equipment, and, until recently, an even smaller amount on research and development. At the beginning of the present century, both industry and education were comparable, from the point of view of the organization employed. They were both labour-intensive, and both tended to have most of their capital invested in expensive, long-lasting buildings. Indeed, 75 per cent of their capital was tied up in buildings, and only about 25 per cent invested in tools and equipment. Today, the industrial picture has changed, for the proportions have been exactly reversed; whereas the educational situation is almost completely unaltered, suggesting that educational techniques have tended to change little in the last 60 years.

The Teacher-Manager and Training Manager

Until now, the design of an educational course has ordinarily involved a combination of expert judgement and known principles of learning – with a seasoning of common sense. However, it may well be that the problem lies less in an acceptance of the learning principles involved than in putting them into effect in the actual learning situation. At the same time, the difficulty is intensified by the three problems of *who* ought to teach *what*, and to *whom*?

When we consider what qualities a good teacher should possess or what qualities make for a successful teacher, the answer is fraught with difficulty. Qualities such as sincerity, efficiency, courage, resolution, energy, tact, and personality all spring to mind: however, the list is seemingly endless, and, even after having compiled it, no one is really sure of how it can be used. A more useful approach is to consider what a teacher actually does; in other words, to adopt a functional rather than a qualities approach, and then to make sure that these functions are carried out in the most efficient, effective, and economical manner possible.

MANAGING AND OPERATING

Basically, there are but two kinds of activity in which a teacher or trainer can engage; they either *manage* learning resources or else they *operate* as a resource themselves. Bertrand Russell put this rather neatly when he said, 'Work is of two kinds: first, altering the position of matter at or near the earth's surface relative to other such matter; second, telling other people to do so. The first kind is unpleasant and ill paid; the second is pleasant and highly paid.' The moral should not be lost on teachers at the present time.'

When a teacher or instructor deliberately creates a learning environment in his classroom with a view to realizing predefined objectives, he is acting as a teacher-manager. When the same teacher or instructor physically teaches in that classroom, he then becomes one of his own resources, and takes on the role of a teacher-operator. He is saying, in effect, that he is the most appropriate resource available; more appropriate for realizing the learning objectives than any textbook, workbook, programme, film, tape, or record obtainable. On many occasions, this will probably be very true, but too often a teacher decides to engage in talk and chalk because he enjoys teaching: the decision to be a teacher-operator is taken on the basis of personal preference, rather than on the needs of the learning situation.

A recent study suggested that only about 43 per cent of a teacher's time was spent on classroom instruction, the rest of the time was spent on other socially necessary duties – some of which might be useful to both teacher and student, while others were mere wasteful, time-consuming chores, having little or nothing to do with the actual process of learning. In other words, a good deal of the teacher's time was spent in either performing work that others could do, or else doing work for other people. Industry, with its shortage of skilled manpower, is extremely suspicious of people who prefer to operate in this manner, yet it would appear that the teacher spends some 57 per cent of his time doing precisely this. Even the 43 per cent of time spent on teaching, contains a very high proportion of operating rather than managing activity. The danger lies not so much in the fact that teachers operate, we all have to do this at times, but in the fact that they may do more operating work than they should do or than the situation calls for.

TEACHING AND MANAGING

Since the time available and the capacities of teachers and training-managers must always be limited, it follows that they must concentrate, as far as possible, upon doing that work which stems from their unique organizational role as managers of resources for learning. Viewed in this way, it is possible to isolate and identify the four broad functions that characterize the work of a teacher-manager:

1. *Planning*. This is the work a teacher does to establish learning objectives.
2. *Organizing*. This is the work a teacher does to arrange and relate learning resources, so as to realize these objectives in the most effective, efficient, and economical way possible.
3. *Leading*. This is the work a teacher does to motivate, encourage, and inspire his students, so that they will readily realize learning objectives.
4. *Controlling*. This is the work a teacher does to determine whether his organizing and leading functions are successfully realizing the objectives which have been set. If the objectives are not being realized, then the teacher must reassess and regulate the situation – not change his objectives.

Although these four managerial functions are separate and disparate activities, they must be viewed as a cycle of related activities (See Fig. 2.1). Together, they define the specialized area of a teacher or instructor's profession-

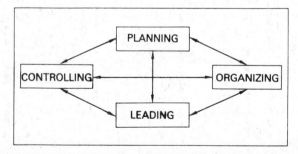

Fig. 2.1 The four interrelated functions of the teacher-manager and training-manager

23

al competence and expertise; together, they make up the education and training management process. However, there is another side to the manager's role, for the task of 'deciding' is just as important to the management process as the task of 'doing'.

The Teacher-Manager and Training Manager as a Decision-Maker

Today, as we have seen in the first chapter, we are living in the early phases of a revolution in education and training technology. One direct consequence of this is to be found in the increasing demands that are being made upon the decision-making responsibilities of teachers and instructors. A great deal of what teachers do, of course, has always involved making decisions, but as every manager knows there are decisions and decisions. In the past, many decisions made by teachers have tended to be made on a short-term basis, from moment to moment, or incident to incident – often as a matter of expediency. Today, this is no longer possible, and both short- and long-term decisions are becoming more and more necessary: before the lesson, during it, and even after the lesson has been terminated. These decisions are increasingly subtle and complex, and the variables involved are often shifting and ill-defined. All this demands an increasing degree of professionalism from teachers, as well as a framework within which decisions can be made.

In its simplest terms, decision-making involves determining precise and concrete goals or objectives, and then selecting, from among alternatives, a course of action that is most likely to lead to a successful outcome. This whole process is central to the manager's job, and the three terms, 'authority', 'responsibility', and 'accountability', are only meaningful within this management decision-making context. The teacher-manager has to *choose* what is to be done and who is to do it: when, where, and how. Indeed, the most cutting remark that can be made of a teacher is not that he has made mistakes and has been unsuccessful, but that he did not know where he was trying to go. No choice, of course, can really be judged in isolation. Virtually every decision a teacher or instructor makes must be geared within the framework of planning, organizing, leading, and controlling, although the character of the decision-making processes varies according to the function involved.

THE FUNCTIONS OF THE TEACHER-MANAGER

Planning is, without doubt, the key function of the teacher-manager, and his difficulty is to forecast requirements, define objectives, write a syllabus of instruction, determine the order in which the topics should be learned, allocate the time available, and budget the resources involved. In this way, he endeavours to bridge the gap between where his students are and where he wants them to go. Decisions of this kind call for a great amount of creative and imaginative thinking, and cover a wide range of activities that are almost completely unstructured in character. Indeed, despite the difficulties, skill, and professionalism involved in this type of decision-making, planning has become one of the more important preoccupations of teachers and instructors in the last decade.

Organizing involves the deliberate creation of a learning environment and the delegation of responsibilities, so as to realize the objectives of the education or training programme which the teacher-manager has planned. This organization, or arrangement of resources, is not at end in itself, but a means to an end, a tool to help achieve, not dictate, what has to be accomplished. The ultimate aim is to make it easier for students to work and learn together, and it is as well to remember that effective organizations can only be built on respect for the individual. Decisions concerned with organizing call for a deep understanding and concern for people, and necessitate balancing the social and the task requirements of the education and training programme.

Leading or directing is a highly personal function, and involves the teacher-manager's motivational style. His job is to guide, inspire, and supervise his students, so that they attain the agreed objectives. Although the concept is a very simple one, it involves work of extraordinary delicacy and complexity. Its ultimate aim is to so motivate and inspire students that they accept and exercise responsibility for their own learning. This leadership function provides for the inner needs of students, since well-led students do learn without plans and organization, but, backed by good plans and organization, well-led pupils become outstanding. The decisions associated with the leading function are of an unstructured variety, and call for a creative and imaginative approach to problems that are not directly quantifiable.

The controlling function is probably the most difficult one for the teacher-manager to exercise; its aim is 'to compel events to conform to plans' (Koontz and O'Donnell, 1968). Although planning always precedes controlling, plans are not self-achieving. Planning guides the teacher in his allocation of resources, while controlling enables him to monitor the progress that has been made. Deviations can then be corrected before the education and training programme gets out of hand. Decisions at this level should rely heavily on quantified comparisons against established and agreed standards of performance or mastery. To a very large extent, controlling involves making structured decisions, although the processes involved may be extremely complex in character, particularly when it involves taking corrective or remedial action.

DEVELOPING ALTERNATIVES FOR DECISION-MAKING

The most difficult and skilled part of management lies in developing alternative courses of action from which a manager can choose the optimal strategy for realizing his objectives. It would be very unusual to find that alternative strategies are lacking: indeed, if there appears to be only one course of action possible, it is highly probable that the problem has not been precisely enough defined. A manager's ability to develop alternatives is as important as his ability to make the right decisions, and, for the teacher-manager, both demand a degree of true craftsmanship. Koontz and O' Donnell (1968) put it quite well when they wrote: 'In choosing from among alternatives, the more an individual can recognize and solve for those factors that are limiting or critical to the attainment of a desired goal, the more effectively and efficiently he can select the most favourable alternative.' Once the alternative strategies have been selected, the teacher must decide which one is most likely to be optimal. To a very large extent, this is a matter of weighing expected results against desired objectives.

In selecting these alternatives, three bases can be used by the teacher for decision-making: experience, research, and analysis. Reliance on past experience probably plays a more important part than it really deserves in making decisions, for the past is certainly no infallible guide to the future. Good decisions can only be evaluated against future events, while experience belongs to the teacher's past. This does not mean to say that experience is to be discounted, only that it is but one guide to action.

Another criterion for selecting alternative courses of action is to be found in the findings of educational research and experimentation. Unfortunately, teachers seem to be little influenced by educational research, and seem to place little reliance upon it. Yet, Johnson (1966), surveying teacher's attitudes towards research, found that teachers who are most knowledgeable about research results, and those who did the most professional reading, placed significantly more value on the usefulness of research findings than those who were ignorant of them. This situation, however, is likely to change in the next decade, for the increased professionalism demanded of the teacher-manager makes it unlikely that apathy and indifference can long endure.

The final criterion for selecting alternative courses of action, particularly when important decisions are to be made, is to analyse or break down the problem into its constituent parts. Each of these can then be evaluated against the total education or training programme, rather than as isolated or unrelated problems. Unfortunately, few teachers have been trained in this 'quantitative common sense' or operations-research approach which involves the following five steps:
1. Analyse the overall system within which the problem is located.
2. Collect and evaluate the available data, and determine the relationship between these facts.
3. Isolate and identify the problem in the most detailed and precise form possible.
4. Select, from all the available alternatives, the strategy most likely to lead to a successful outcome.
5. Devise and employ measures most likely to evaluate the effectiveness of the course of action.
Figure 2.2 presents this operations-research system in rather more detail.

This analytical approach is probably the most profitable and meaningful one for a practicing teacher to adopt, aided by the conceptual framework provided by the four functions of the teacher-manager.

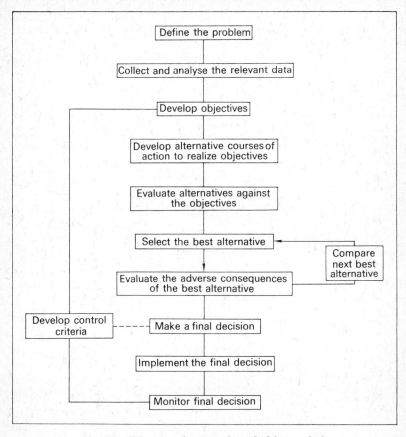

Fig. 2.2 The successive steps in a decision analysis

The Design of a Learning System

The philosophy of the teacher-manager introduces a further concept into education and training, which is of particular value in the design of a learning system. This is the concept of management by objectives, which is related to the simple idea that a manager cannot exercise his four functions unless he is able to determine whether his students are successfully realizing the learning objectives that have been set for them. Once the objectives have been defined and the learning resources organized, the main concern of the teacher or instructor is to manage in terms of the results that are obtained. If the objectives are being realized, well and good; if the objectives are not being

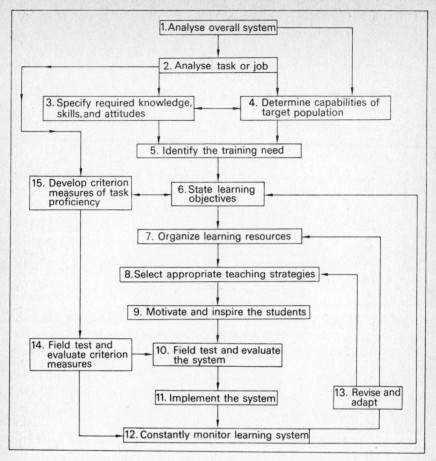

Fig. 2.3   The steps involved in developing a learning system

realized, the teacher must organize anew. Such an approach allows for the formulation of a single theory of teaching capable of providing what the US Senate Sub-committee on Economic Progress once described as, 'guiding principles for development and application of educational technology (which) would contribute immeasurably to healthy development of new systems and would help avoid waste of resources'. In these terms, a teacher would manage by exception rather than by convention.

STEPS IN DEVELOPING A LEARNING SYSTEM

In designing a course or programme for learning, a number of requirements must be taken into account. The teacher must consider not only the requirements of the task, but also the requirements of the students, the groups within which they work, and the organization of which they are a part. Although authors differ in the terms that they use to describe the processes involved in developing a learning system, most agree that it consists of a series of inter-related steps. These are summarized in Fig. 2.3, which should be closely compared and contrasted with the broadly similar operations-research approach shown in Fig. 2.2.

It will be seen from Fig. 2.3 that designing a learning system or programme involves an orderly sequence of 15 activities, the majority of which represent the basic framework of the course, while others – no less important – are concerned with validation of the system once it has been installed. The 15 activities can be summarized under the headings of:

1. *Planning.* This involves activities 1, 2, 3, 4, 5, 6, 14, and 15. All of these are concerned with defining the real nature of the problem that the learning system has to overcome.

2. *Organizing.* This involves activities 7 and 11, and deals with the way in which learning and teaching resources are arranged in accordance with the plans that have been agreed.

3. *Leading.* This involves activities 8 and 9, and concerns the way in which the teacher adds himself to the system so as to guide, help, and inspire his students.

4. *Controlling.* This involves activities 10, 12, and 13. All of these are concerned with evaluating the success of the learning system in realizing its objectives.

EFFECTS OF EMPLOYING SUCH AN APPROACH

The effects of employing such an approach can be very great indeed, for not only is the role of the teacher affected, but also the role of the student. Viewed in this way, the concept of a teacher-manager promises to:

1. Offer the possibility of developing a theory of teaching.

2. Change the teacher's function in the learning process.

3. Encourage the use of teacher-auxiliaries for the more routine and mundane operating duties.

4. Change the architectural basis of the school, from a teaching to a learning design.

5. Allow the use of more informal teaching methods.

6. Capitalize upon the advantages of allowing students to progress at their own individual rates of learning.

7. Change the nature of administrative and financial controls.

8. Encourage the development of working partnerships between educators and government, educators and industry, educators and society.

9. Encourage the development of more learning aids appropriate to the needs of the learning situation.

This does not mean that all these changes will be realized at once. But it does mean that the necessary conceptual framework is available for their develop-ment and standards of effectiveness introduced.

Conclusion

The concept of a teacher-manager, with the four functions of planning, organizing, controlling, and leading, offers a degree of renewed professionalism to a teacher and instructor. At the same time, it provides for the possibility of improving the overall effectiveness and quality of a student's learning experience. Three factors are particularly important in terms of this contribution: defining learning objectives, choosing appropriate teaching strategies, and assessing the success of the system in realizing its objectives.

This management approach towards learning and learning resources provides both a physiology and a pathology for education and training, for which learning prescriptions can be written. Just as medicine has moved its emphasis away from the treatment to the prevention of disease, so education and training can emphasize the prevention rather than the treatment of learning problems and failures. Such a technology is *not* an extension of past practices; it is a difference in kind. How quickly this will be realized, however, depends less on the money available, and more on teachers themselves. Success will be limited by imagination, rather than by courage; teachers must ensure that their thinking is contemporary with opportunity, and not limited by out of date patterns belonging to past education and training practices.

Posttest 2

ANSWER ALL QUESTIONS

1. State the five principles of learning as listed by Alvin C. Eurich.

2. Distinguish in terms of a teacher's behaviour, between the twin concepts of 'managing' and 'operating'.

3. List, and write short notes upon, the four functions of a teacher-manager.

4. Discuss the teacher's role as a decision-maker.

5. Identify and evaluate the three criteria available to teachers for selecting an optimal teaching strategy.

6. Show, by means of a diagram, the steps necessary in developing a learning system. Discuss these steps in terms of each of the four functions of a teacher-manager.

7. List the major effects that introduction of the concept of a teacher-manager can have on the future organization of education and training.

References and Reading List

ALLEN, L. A. (1964) *The Management Profession*. New York: McGraw-Hill.

BELLER, W. S. (1966) Educational technology: An emerging market for systems-orientated firms, *Technology Week*, 10 October 1966, 28–31.

BOWMAN, D. M. and FILLERUP, F. M. (1963) *Management: Organization and Planning*. New York: McGraw-Hill.

BROWN, J. W. and THORNTON, J. W. (1963) *New Media in Higher Education*. Washington DC.

BRUNER, J. S. (1965) *The Process of Education*. Cambridge, Massachusetts: Harvard University Press.

BRUNER, J. S. (1966) *Toward a Theory of Instruction*. Cambridge, Massachusetts: Harvard University Press.

CHESTERTON, G. K. (1923) The point of a pin. In *The Scandal of Father Brown*. London: Cassell.

DAVIES, I. K. (1965) Towards a technology of learning, *General Education Development*, USA EUR Pamphlet 626 – 5 –1, February 1965, 2–11.

DAVIES, I. K. (1966) Programmed learning and industrial training, *Communications in Industry*. London: Joint IEE/IERE Symposium, 12–14.

DAVIES, I. K. (1966) Training mechanical craftsmen. In symposium manual, *Programmed Learning for Industry*. Melton Mowbray: PERA, 1–17.

DAVIES, I. K. (1967) The Management of Learning, *Industrial Training International*, June 1967, 242–4.

DEWEY, J. (1916) *Democracy and Education*. New York: Macmillan.

EURICH, A. C. (1962) Technology in education, *New Society*, 13 December 1962, 11, 15–16.

FLYNN, J. M. (1970) The changing role of the teacher. *Educational Technology*, 10, 2, 3–6.

GOETZ, B. E. (1949) *Management Planning and Control*. New York: McGraw-Hill.

HANIKA, F. DE P. (1966) *New Thinking in Management*. London: Hutchinson.

JOHNSON, M. E. B. (1966) Teachers' attitudes to educational research, *Educational Research*, 9, 74–79.

KEPPEL, F. (1966) Technology serves your learning Program, *The Instructor*, June/July 1966, 39.

KOONTZ, H. and O'DONNELL, C. (1968) *Principles of Management: An Analysis of Managerial Functions*. New York: McGraw-Hill.

MACKENZIE, N. (1966) Education and the new technology, *Technical Education and Industrial Training*, 8 December 1966, 540–4.

MORRISON, A. and McINTYRE, D. (1969) *Teachers and Teaching*. London: Penguin.

OWENS, R. G. (1970) *Organizational Behaviour in Schools*. Englewood Cliffs, New Jersey: Prentice-Hall.

REDDIN, W. J. (1970) *Managerial Effectiveness*. New York: McGraw-Hill.

TAYLOR, G., ed. (1970) *The Teacher as Manager*. London: National Council for Educational Technology.

SECTION ONE
Planning

A manager does a certain kind of work that enables him to command the future and not be commanded by it.

Louis A. Allen

The planning function of the teacher-manager

Planning is the work a teacher does to establish learning objectives. When a teacher-manager plans, he attempts to:

1. Analyse the task.

2. Identify the training need.

3. Write the learning objectives.

In this way, the teacher-manager is able to forecast the learning requirements of the task, *before* he allocates the resources necessary to realize them.

3 Analysing the task

Learning Objectives

COGNITIVE OBJECTIVES

After carefully reading this chapter, you will be able to:

1. Distinguish between, and write short notes upon, the three different types of task analysis.

2. State the main sources of information for a task analysis.

3. Give an example, and draw a diagram, illustrating the relationship between the five behavioural levels or components of a task analysis.

4. Describe how the three types of task analysis are written.

5. Using the appropriate format, write a rule set for a cognitive task.

6. Using the appropriate format, carry out a job analysis, annotated with appropriate task levels, for a procedural task.

7. Using the appropriate format, carry out a skills analysis for a handwork job involving tools, or for single-purpose machine work.

8. State and recognize the circumstances when skills analysis is likely to be beneficial.

9. Summarize the uses of a task analysis.

AFFECTIVE OBJECTIVES

After reading this chapter, the author intends that you will:

1. Be aware of, and value, the importance of analysing the task before deciding whether or not training is necessary.

2. Incorporate the principle into your organization of professional strategies, so that it becomes characteristic of your managerial style.

> We may easily agree that the design of an educational sequence properly begins with a description of the behaviour it is intended to create. It is not as easy to agree how to render the description or what we shall include.
>
> *T. F. Gilbert*

One of the very first steps in developing an educational or training programme is to analyse the nature of the actual task involved. Some tasks, of course, are purely academic or intellectual in nature, others are primarily concerned with physical skills. However, regardless of the nature of the task, it is necessary to determine both the ingredients and the characteristics of the topic or job that the student has to learn. It is only when these precise characteristics are known that the training need can be established, and the learning objectives written. For this reason, great care must be exercised in carrying out the task analysis, for the ensuing document forms the basis of the learning prescription.

In some ways, the term 'task analysis' is an unfortunate one. It suggests that what is primarily involved is the breaking down of the task into its constituent parts. This, however, only describes part of the process, for it is also necessary to consider how these constituent parts are related and organized. Task analysis, therefore, is concerned with both analysis and synthesis. Its ultimate aims are to:

1. Describe the task which the student has to learn.
2. Isolate the required behaviours.
3. Identify the conditions under which the behaviours occur.
4. Determine a criterion of acceptable performance.

Without a proper task analysis, it is not possible to justify what you intend to teach, nor is it possible to decide on an optimal teaching strategy.

Types of Task Analysis

Three different types of task analysis are readily recognizable, each fulfilling entirely different needs:

1. *Topic analysis.* This involves a detailed analysis of intellectual tasks such as Ohm's law, latitude and longitude, solving simultaneous equations, and considering the character of Brutus in Shakespeare's *Julius Caesar*, etc.

2. *Job analysis.* This involves a detailed analysis of tasks involving physical or psychomotor skills. The technique concentrates on *what* is done when the task is carried out. Job analysis would involve such tasks as renewing the contact points in a car, setting up a lathe, fitting a film in a camera, etc.

3. *Skills analysis.* This involves the further analysis of psychomotor tasks, but this time concentrating on *how* the job is accomplished. Skills analysis

will need to be carried out, in addition to job analysis, when either the whole task or part of the task involves complex, intricate and subtle hand-eye coordinations. For instance, a full skills analysis would be necessary for such jobs as glassblowing and panel-beating; whereas renewing the contact points in a car would include a skills analysis, for instance, for that part of the job that involves using a feeler gauge.

There has been a tendency among many teachers and trainers to imagine that task analysis is only applicable to tasks involving psychomotor skills; furthermore, skills analysis and job analysis have often been regarded as competing rather than complementary techniques. Indeed, in the past, certain industrial organizations went so wholeheartedly for skills analysis that they created the impression that all training should be based upon it. This was a time-wasting and costly error of judgement. An essential component of the teacher's and trainer's role is to recognize the circumstances in which one strategy of analysis is likely to be more efficient than another.

SOURCES OF INFORMATION FOR TASK ANALYSIS

In carrying out a task analysis, whether it involves topic, job, or skills analysis, a number of sources of relevant information must be tapped, so as to ensure that a complete picture has been obtained. Obviously, the most important source of information must always be the 'master'; in other words, the man who can do the job at the required level of mastery. He must always be selected with great care, and steps must be taken to ensure that he is, indeed, proficient at the level which all students will be expected to attain. If the master's level of proficiency is too high, then the task analysis will set needlessly high levels of performance, with all the resultant dangers of over-training. If the master's level of proficiency is set too low, the resulting task analysis will be invalid, with a consequent danger of undertraining.

Once the master's behaviour has been analysed, his performance must be checked for accuracy and completeness. It is also important to check the

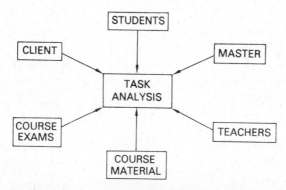

Fig. 3.1 Main sources of information for a task analysis

analysis under other operating environments and conditions, for these can sometimes affect the way that the task is accomplished. Other sources of information are indicated in Fig. 3.1 (see Davies, 1965). Teachers and instructors must be consulted, course materials and examination papers studied, students who are either learning or have just finished learning the task interviewed, and the person who initially sparked off the project questioned. All kinds of procedures can be used in consulting these sources, but the most common ones include observation, interviews, questionnaires, work diaries, film, closed circuit television, job checklists, and activity analysis. A detailed description of these techniques will be found in Gagne (1963).

Components of a Task Analysis

A task analysis is really an audit and inventory. In it, knowledge, skill, and attitudes are identified and isolated, with a view to ultimately synthesizing them into a hierarchical organization relevant to the writing of a learning prescription (see Gilbert, 1962). In carrying out such an analysis, the analyst or teacher must consider not only the physical components of the subject (use of tools, references, job aids, etc.), but also the mental components (procedures, decisions, abstractions, etc.).

The task analysis must isolate all those overt acts which characterize either the subject material or job mastery. One way of doing this is to think of a topic or job as a hierarchical organization of levels or components, each of which describe the job in successively greater detail. At the highest level is the topic or job itself. This consists of a number of duties; each duty contains a number of tasks, and each task consists of a number of task elements. Such an organization is schematically illustrated in Fig. 3.2. In topic analysis and job analysis, the task element is the smallest meaningful unit; in skills analysis, the task element is further broken down into 'acts'. An act is very similar to

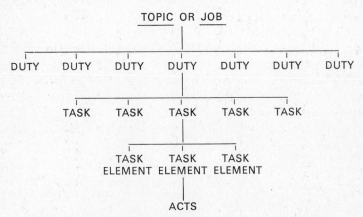

Fig. 3.2 The hierarchy of behavioural levels in a task analysis

a therblig in time and motion study, and consists of a basic movement that must be repeated if it is interrupted. Four acts or therbligs occur most frequently; reaching for an object, grasping it, moving it, and positioning it.

Let us take an example. In making a job analysis of a psychomotor skill, the job could be that of an engine mechanic. His job is made up of a number of duties, including tuning the carburettor, adjusting the tappets, changing the oil, and cleaning the sparking plugs. Each of these duties is made up of a number of separate tasks, all closely related to each other in sequence. For example, the duty of changing the engine oil includes the tasks of jacking-up the car, placing an oil container underneath the sump, taking out the sump drain plug, allowing the oil to drain away, etc. Finally, each task includes a number of task elements. Jacking-up the car, for instance, involves acquiring the right kind of jack, positioning it underneath the jacking-up points, and manipulating the jack so that it raises the car to the required level.

Even in more specifically cognitive or intellectual skills, a similar classification can be employed. The job or topic of solving mathematical problems by using logarithm tables, could include the duty of multiplying two numbers together. This duty would consist of the following tasks: finding the characteristics and mantissae of the two numbers, adding the logarithms together, antilogging the sum, fixing the decimal point, and connecting the answer to the appropriate number of significant figures. Finally, the task elements involved in finding the mantissae, for example, would consist of locating the first two significant figures of each number in the lefthand column of the logarithm tables, locating the third figure of each number in the appropriate middle columns headed $0-9$, and locating the fourth figure in the add column headed $1-9$ on the righthand side of the page.

Writing a Topic Analysis

Although there are a number of different ways of making a topic analysis (see Evans, Glaser, and Homme, 1962; Glaser, 1963; Mechner, 1965), few of them are structurally detailed enough as to make them practicable for our purpose. One of the most useful methods of topic analysis is based on the well-known matrix technique of programme writing (Thomas, Davies, Openshaw, and Bird, 1963). This involves identifying the topic, breaking down the topic into its constituent parts, and arranging these parts, in a hierarchical form, on an analysis sheet.

In order to make a topic analysis, the teacher – who in this case is the master – will need to collect together all the relevant subject material and ensure that it is technically accurate and up to date. It would be old-fashioned, for instance, to cite the use of fishplates between lengths of railway line as a precaution against the effects of expansion. Science and technology have now become popular, and scientific facts and applications, which were previously the preserve of the enlightened, are now everyday knowledge. This means that the teacher can no longer rely on the standard textbooks and reference books, but must look elsewhere for the latest findings and applications. Many teachers may well feel that this step is unnecessary because of their level of scholarship or their considerable teaching experience, but no step highlights deficiencies in knowledge more than topic analysis.

Once the subject material has been collected, the next step is to refine and limit the topic that the student is required to learn, and to ensure that it is as self-contained as possible. For instance, the topic of the theory of conservation of energy, involves duties such as Ohm's law and Joule's law. Often these topics and duties will be laid down in the syllabus, or prescribed in some other way, but usually in only the vaguest of terms. In any case, syllabuses are only an indication of content, and do not attempt to prescribe the order in which topics should be taught. Many teachers fall into the trap of slavishly following the order given in a syllabus to the detriment of their student's learning. One of the most important duties of the teacher is to reconcile the dictates of the syllabus, on the one hand, with the educational and learning needs of their students on the other.

IDENTIFYING TASK ELEMENTS OR RULES

Once the duty has been carefully delimited, it must be broken down into its *smallest* constituent parts. These, as we have seen, are called task elements, but in topic analysis they are more usually referred to as 'rules'. The identification of rules is probably the most skilled part of the whole process of topic analysis, and it demands that the teacher or analyst is – in every sense of the term – a subject matter expert. Although the teacher-analyst will be aided in his task by his experience, there is a considerable risk that the rules that he identifies will be too wide. It is also essential to ensure that the rules are carefully written and sequenced. Although the task of rule-writing will be initially somewhat lengthy and laborious, experience and practice soon speed up the process.

In order to identify the rules, the teacher-analyst should ask himself five critical questions:

1. What does he expect the student to *do* to demonstrate that he has learnt the topic?
2. What questions does he expect the student to answer?
3. What tasks, procedures, and techniques does he expect him to perform, and at what level does he expect them to be executed?
4. What discriminations does he expect the student to make, and in what terms does he expect these discriminations to be made?
5. What total changes in behaviour does he expect, and in what form does he expect to observe and measure them?

Such a definition of what the student is intended to *do* as a result of the planned learning experience, can best be referred to as the anticipated or *criterion* behaviour.

Writing rules is a way of life, a habit soon acquired by practice. In essence, a rule is a statement of generality, a definition, a fact, or an item of information. For instance, each of the following statements constitutes a rule:

1. Metals expand when heated.
2. A sonnet has fourteen lines.
3. A contract is an agreement enforceable by law.
4. Latitude is angular distance north and south of the Equator.

Each rule should be complete in itself, a complete fact or idea. They form the raw materials or building blocks, which – related and interrelated together – will make up first the duty and then the topic.

Rules should be written in such a way that:
1. They contain only *one* fact or idea.
2. They are written at the same level of generality as all preceding rules.
3. They take the form of simple, declarative (kernel) sentences.
4. They avoid negative forms, qualifications, and conjunctions.
5. They possess only *one* active verb.
6. They are critical and essential to the task.

Generally speaking, they will rarely contain more than a dozen words; indeed, the shorter and simpler the rule, the better it will be.

It must be borne in mind that the objective is not to write as many rules as possible, but only to write those that are intellectually necessary to the task. Every step must be taken to avoid the common mistake of attempting to teach too much in too short a time. Accordingly, the rules must be carefully sifted; each fact should be considered in relation to the task, and material outside the chosen parameters should be rejected. In this way, rules can be gradually revised and refined until only the absolutely essential ones remain.

ARRANGING THE RULES INTO A LOGICAL SEQUENCE

As the rules are written, of course, they will be arranged into some type of natural sequence. Steps must now be taken to ensure that this sequence is a completely logical one from the point of view of the subject material. Each rule should lead naturally to the next, so that – in effect – they set up and completely describe the duty. This sequence is likely to be based upon the teacher's own subject expertise, upon his teaching experience, upon intuition, and upon his own learning experience.

The following, traditional rules of sequence will often prove helpful in arranging the rules:

1. Proceed from the known to the unknown.
2. Proceed from the simple to the complex.
3. Proceed from the concrete to the abstract.
4. Proceed from observation to reasoning.
5. Proceed from a whole view to a more detailed view to a whole view.

In accomplishing this, it will often be found useful to so write and arrange the rules that they appear to complement each other. A word, topic, or concept introduced in one rule, is built-on or expanded upon in the next. In this way, the rules are chained or dovetailed together, and new teaching points are not suddenly, but gradually, introduced into the sequence.

An example of a rule-set for Ohm's law is shown in Fig. 3.3. In this particular case, the rule-set is written for students preparing for the City and

---

TOPIC: Theory of Conservation of Energy
DUTY: Ohm's Law

A. *Task: Concept of electrical charge*

Rule 1. An electric charge is produced by friction.
„ 2. The electron is the basic unit of charge.
„ 3. The electron is an impractical unit of charge.
„ 4. The coulomb is the practical unit of charge.
„ 5. Current is a flow of charge.

B. *Task: Concept of electrical current*

*Rule 5. Current is a flow of charge.
„ 6. Current is measured in coulombs per second.
„ 7. One coulomb per second is called an ampere.
„ 8. When current flows work is done.
„ 9. Energy is used when work is done.
„ 10. Energy must be supplied for current to flow.

C. *Task: Concept of electromotive force*

*Rule 10. Energy must be supplied for current to flow.
„ 11. Electromotive force is a measure of the rate at which energy is supplied.
„ 12. Energy is measured in joules.
„ 13. Electromotive force is the rate of supply of energy per unit current.
„ 14. The unit of electromotive force is the volt.

D. *Task: Concept of resistance*

Rule 15. Current meets resistance in flowing through a load.
„ 16. The resistance depends upon the nature of the load.
„ 17. Materials offering little resistance are termed conductors.
„ 18. Materials offering very great resistance are termed insulators.
„ 19. In overcoming resistance work is done.

E. *Task: Concept of potential difference*

Rule 20. The energy used in moving a charge is proportional to the size of the charge.
„ 21. The rate at which energy is used is proportional to the rate at which charge flows.
„ 22. The rate at which energy is used is proportional to the current.
„ 23. Potential difference is the rate at which energy is used per unit of current.
„ 24. The unit of potential difference must be the volt.
„ 25. Potential difference is proportional to current.

F. *Task: Principle of Ohm's law*

*Rule 25. Potential difference is proportional to current.
„ 26. Potential difference equals current multiplied by a constant.
„ 27. The constant is resistance.
„ 28. Resistance equals potential difference divided by current.
„ 29. The unit of resistance is the ohm.

* Rules which overlap two related concepts.

Fig. 3.3 A topic analysis: Ohm's law and its five constituent concepts (Concept A + Concept B + Concept C + Concept D + Concept E = the principle of Ohm's law)

Guilds of London Institute examination in Engineering Science (Course no. 49). Paragraph 6 of the associated syllabus reads, 'The simple electric circuit, electromotive force, potential difference, resistance, the ampere, the volt, the ohm and the coulomb. Common conducting and insulating materials. Ohm's Law.'

The organization adopted by Fig. 3.3 follows the following form:

1. *Topic*. Theory of conservation of energy.
2. *Duty*. Ohm's law.
3. *Tasks*. Concepts of electric charge, electrical current, electromotive force, resistance, and potential difference. The principle of Ohm's law.
4. *Task elements*. Rules 1 to 29.

It will be seen that while the syllabus has been covered, the sequencing has not been strictly followed. Furthermore, the rules or task elements naturally cluster into a series of interrelated tasks so that:

$$\text{Concept A} + \text{Concept B} + \text{Concept C} + \text{Concept D} + \text{Concept E}$$
$$= \text{Principle of Ohm's law}$$

In this way, a series of 29 rules has been organized into a related and interrelated sequence of concepts, setting up and establishing the principle of Ohm's Law.

Writing a Job Analysis

In a topic analysis, the teacher or instructor is the master, but in a job analysis the master* is the tradesman doing the job at the required level of mastery. For this reason, a job analysis takes place at the workplace, not in the library or study. The task analyst observes what the tradesman does, how he does it, what he does it with, what he does it to, and, finally, why he does it. This enables the characteristics of the job to be identified and isolated, so that meaningful predictions can be made about the training requirements of the task.

Every job is but a small part of a much larger system, and, furthermore, is affected by that larger system. Thus, the first step in carrying out a job analysis is to describe, analyse, and review the relevant operational system within which the job is performed. In this analysis, every effort must be made to study the management system in so far as it affects the job, both from the point of view of the task itself and from the point of view of the interpersonal relationships that are involved. Work, in other words, is viewed within the framework of a sociotechnical system (see Trist *et al.*, 1963), and in this way it is possible to ask what *combination* of technology, initial worker characteristics, and organizational structures are most likely to result in an effective and efficient work organization. Such an approach ensures that the job is not viewed in isolation, and that solutions other than training are explored.

---

* In work study and work measurement, the term 'experienced worker standard' (EWS) is usually employed to refer to the master. EWS is equivalent to the 100 performance of the British Standard Scale.

After having carried out this general systems analysis, the analyst will have defined the major parameters of the job. Once these have been determined, he is ready to begin making his analysis of an actual job within the system. The first step is to identify and isolate a particular task, and to interview the tradesman so as to determine the objectives that he wishes to realize. It is important that the job should then be done at the usual workplace, and, during this run-through, the analyst should make no attempt to make any record. The aim of this initial phase is to gain an overview of the task, which can serve as a conceptual framework for the actual analysis. Questions involving the working strategy can then be discussed, and particular difficulties highlighted.

IDENTIFICATION OF CUES OR SIGNALS

In analysing any job, the identification of cues that signal a required course of action is particularly important. The cue may be a light, a needle on a dial, the pitch of gear whine, the smell of hot and inadequate lubricant supply. On the other hand, the cue may be a partially complete table, a particular mathematical symbol, or even a rebuke from the supervisor. However, while there can be an endless list of cues, they can be broadly classified into one of four types – depending upon the type of information that they carry.

The following types of cue are readily recognizable:

1. *Cues which carry two state or go-no-go information.* Here the cue is a simple one, and is presented in an unambiguous form, e.g., the warning lights on a dashboard of a car, a particular temperature, a flat car tyre, etc.

2. *Cues which carry digital information.* Here the cue is *one* of a discrete number of states, e.g., the position of a gear lever, tabular information, a predetermined film rinsing time, etc.

3. *Cues which carry continuous or scalor information.* Here the cue constantly signals any theoretically infinite number of states, e.g., an instrument reading, a micrometer reading, etc.

4. *Cues which carry vector information.* Here the cues have both magnitude and direction, e.g., an ammeter with charge and discharge positions, a turn and slip indicator, metal shaping, etc.

In some jobs, only one type of cue may be involved; in others, all types of cue are present, e.g., in the cockpit of a VC 10 aircraft. Each cue, with information as to its type, must be recognized and entered on the task analysis record sheet, since it may well determine the course of action that is taken by the master.

IDENTIFYING TASK ELEMENTS

Once the cues have been recognized, it is a fairly straightforward matter to identify the resulting behaviour. This is best done by asking, 'What does the master *do*?' And then get the master to carry out the job at a speed dictated by the analyst. As each of the task elements is performed, a short description of it should be entered on the analysis sheet – together with an occasional note on any special difficulties, tips or hints, or operating standards. An example of such an analysis is shown in Fig. 3.4. It will be seen that the job analysis is so comprehensive and detailed that it could be used as an actual aid to performing the job.

Just as particular care has to be taken in writing the rules for a topic analysis, so the task elements of a job analysis must be precisely recorded. Task elements, as we have seen, form the basic raw material of the job. They should be written in such a way that:

1. They contain only *one* action or movement.
2. They are written at the same level of generality as all the preceeding task elements.

LEVEL	TASK ELEMENT	NOTES
5	Remove the ignition key	Safety requirement
5	Release bonnet catch	
5	Raise the bonnet	
4	Remove the distributor cap	
4	Remove the rotor arm	
4	Remove the nut holding the nylon insulating washer in position	
4	Lift the nylon insulating washer from its locating stud and set aside for reuse	
4	Slip the LT leads off the locating stud	
4	Remove and discard the movable contact	
4	Remove the screw(s) retaining the fixed contact and set aside	Either 1 or 2 screws
4	Remove and discard the fixed contact	
4	Place the new fixed contact in position	
4	Relocate the fixed contact retaining screws, but do not tighten	
4	Place the new movable contact in position	
4	Replace the LT leads over the locating stud	
4	Replace the nylon insulating washer over the locating stud	
4	Replace the retaining nut over the nylon insulating washer and tighten	
4	Insert vehicle starting handle	See footnote for vehicles having no starting handle
3	Turn the engine until the heel of the movable contact comes on to one of the lobes of the distributor drive	
3	Select feeler gauge of correct thickness	Details in manual
4	Insert gauge between spring of movable contact and fixed contact	
4	Close the fixed contact on to the gauge	
4	Tighten down the screw(s) holding the fixed contact, etc., etc.	
	(*NB*. This example is incomplete)	

Fig. 3.4 A job analysis: renewing the contact points in a motor car (Reproduced with the permission of Wing Commander C. A. Thomas)

3. They take the form of a simple, declarative (kernel) sentence.
4. They avoid negatives, qualifications, and conjunctions.
5. They possess only *one* active verb.
6. They are critical and essential to the task.

The cardinal principle in writing task elements is that they should be expressed in such specific detail that a student, who knows only the names, location, and identity of the components, can perform the task – but without the speed and accuracy of the master.

CLASSIFICATION OF TASK ELEMENTS

In order to determine the actual conceptual nature of the work involved, each task element should be categorized. Such a classification scheme has been devised by Davies and Thomas (1967), and used successfully on a large-scale task analysis of a complete RAF trade. In this scheme, each task element is graded on a five-point scale, the details of which are shown in Fig. 3.5.

It will be seen that from the taxonomy of task levels that:

1. *Level 5 is defined as a signal task.* Task elements that are categorized as

LEVEL	DEFINITION	DESCRIPTION	EXAMPLE
5	A signal task element	A simple action – the need for the action is obvious and there is immediate feedback as to success of action.	Switching on lights at nightfall.
4	A procedural task element	An action forming part of a routine or subroutine. The actions have to be carried out in a fixed order.	The changing of a wheel on a motor car would follow a prescribed pattern.
3	A simple discriminatory task element	An action in which essential differences or similarities have to be recognized; the discriminations will be simple and straightforward.	The reconnection of ignition leads to sparking plugs.
2	A complex discriminatory task element	An action, similar to 3, but involving finer and/or multiple discriminations.	The same example as in 3, but where the lengths and curvature of the leads cannot be used as cues for discrimination. The firing order would have to be determined and reference made to the distributor.
1	A diagnostic or problem-solving task element	An action concerned with the detection, isolation, identification or correction of faults.	The use of an electronic test set on a faulty vehicle and subsequent interpretation of of results would include the type of task element.

Fig. 3.5   **A taxonomy of task elements or levels for use in a job analysis**

level 5 involve simple actions that are carried out in response to a cue or prompt. In every case, there will be clear indication that an action is required, and there will also be immediate feedback as to whether the action has been successfully accomplished.

2. *Level 4 is defined as a procedural task.* Task elements that are categorized as level 4 form part of a series of associated elements, which have to be carried out in a fixed sequence as a routine or subroutine. Most routine servicing and functional checks are procedural in character. While there may be some latitude in the sequencing of subroutines, once a particular sub-routine has started, the order of the task elements is fixed and predetermined. It is true, of course, that the first task element in a procedure could be classified as level 5, but the convention is to categorize every task element in the routine or subroutine as level 4.

3. *Levels 3 and 2 are defined as discriminatory tasks.* Both these levels involve the recognition of essential differences or revealing contrasts. In some cases, the discriminations are easily made but are, nevertheless, critical (level 3); in other cases, the discriminations are more difficult and subtle, and can involve multiple discriminations of a fine order (level 2).

4. *Level 1 is defined as a diagnostic or problem-solving task.* Task elements that are categorized as level 1 involve diagnostic or problem-solving strategies and cover three related activities:

(a) The detection of faults from observable symptoms.
(b) The isolation and identification of the sources of the fault.
(c) The correction of faults.

Further study of Fig. 3.4 will demonstrate the application of these levels to the task of renewing the contact points in a car. It will be seen that, of the completed sequence, 13 per cent of the task elements involve level 5, 78 per cent involve level 4, and only 9 per cent level 3. The task is, thus, basically a signal and procedural one. Such a system of classification, enables the analyst to pinpoint those areas where skills analysis might be most profitable. In this particular example it would be at level 3.

CHECKING THE JOB ANALYSIS

When the analysis of a particular job has been completed, the analyst should check it out. This should be done first with the tradesman himself, in case certain task elements have been omitted, and then with the tradesman's supervisor, so as to ensure that the actions and standards are acceptable. Once the job analysis is agreed, it should be repeated under as wide a range of operating conditions and environments as possible. This, in fact, is a very rapid procedure, since the analyst simply watches the job being done, compares the actions with those on his analysis sheet, and records any deviations.

In this way, differences in carrying out a job can be isolated and identified. These must then be critically studied so as to determine whether they are due to:

1. Operating under different working conditions.
2. Variations in the nature of the task itself.
3. Differences in skill levels or attitudes to the job.
4. Employing more or less effective methods of working.
5. Simple variations in style.

The analysis sheets can then be amended or annotated accordingly, and the differences agreed.

Writing a Skills Analysis

Skills analysis is clearly distinguishable from topic and job analysis, in the sense that it is concerned with *how* a job is done, in addition to *what* is done. In other words, skills analysis builds on the basis laid down by job analysis, and adds to it an analysis of the knowledge and skills used by an experienced, as distinct from an inexperienced, worker. Every job has a 'knowing' and a 'doing' side, and the important thing is to identify these two aspects of the task. For instance, in a job analysis it is often enough to state that the tradesman 'replaces the rotor arm', whereas, in a skills analysis, it would be necessary to add:

1. How he identifies the rotor arm and the shaft.
2. Which fingers of which hand are employed.
3. How he positions the rotor arm to locate the keyway.
4. How he ensures that the rotor arm is well seated.
5. Any special precautions that should be taken, etc.

Job analysis and skills analysis are not mutually exclusive in character; skills analysis is supplementary to job analysis.

Initially, the late Dr A. H. Seymour called the technique of skills analysis 'process analysis', although in America the term 'analytical method' (AM) is still preferred. The Department of Employment and Productivity *Glossary of Training Terms* (1967) defines skills analysis as: 'The identification and recording of the psycho-physiological characteristics of skilled performance, and the determination of the effector*, receptor† and decision-making functions involved.' In other words, skills analysis is concerned with studying both the overt and the covert manifestations of skill, and – in so doing – has redeemed the tendency to concentrate only on the observable manifestations of a worker's behaviour. It is, therefore, a depth analysis of skilled performance, and its application has dramatically reduced training time and costs by at least 50 per cent (Ramsden, 1966). The excellent book by W. D. Seymour (1968) is particularly recommended as a simple, but authoritative, guide to the technique.

---

* Effector processes involve those senses which are concerned with actual motor movements, e.g., fingers, hands, legs, muscles, etc.
† Receptor processes involve those senses which are concerned with incoming sensations, e.g., sight, touch, hearing, taste, and smell.

Skill has been defined by Mace (1950) as 'an ability to produce consistently an intended effect with accuracy, speed and economy of action'. In order to gain an adequate view of such behaviour, it is necessary to consider:

1. What actions does the experienced worker perform at each stage of the task?
2. What information does he obtain via his five senses at each of these stages?
3. How does he use this information to determine and control those bodily movements that are necessary to skilled performance?

The answers to these three questions supply the raw material of skills analysis. By using this information, it is argued, it is possible to bring unskilled personnel up to the master's or experienced worker's standard (EWS) of quality and output in the shortest possible time, since one can concentrate on the critical interactions between manual, sensory, and mental work processes.

ANALYSING THE SKILL

Crossman and Seymour (1957) have developed a comprehensive method of analysing perceptual activities. Each activity, they argue, is first, planned, then, initiated, next, controlled, then, terminated, and, finally, checked. These five phases extend to effector, receptor, and mental (decision-making) processes, and enable the tradesman to organize the information coming to his senses more effectively. In this way, the acquisition of such a tempora: sequence allows him to make decisions more effectively and quickly, and sc become more efficient and skilled at the job. Analysing a skill necessitates the recognition and isolation of these successive stages in the perceptua processes, and the identification of the relative importance of each to each of the senses in particular jobs. For instance, an experienced typist will spenc less time than a trainee visually checking that she is using the right finger, since she will know by the feel and rhythm that she is making the correct movements.

Some jobs, like assembly work, are mainly concerned with manual skills, but a large proportion of industrial work involves jobs in which knowledge is as important, or more important, as the manual skills involved. This knowledge will include information about the factory and workplace, information about the job itself and the processes involved, as well as quality information about fault finding and fault diagnosis. In order to obtain this information about the knowledge requirements of the job, it is necessary to talk to the master at considerable length, and try to get him to say why he carries out particular actions and how he knows when the actions are necessary. All this involves striking up a close personal relationship, so as to obtain and record the shopfloor job lore in the skills analysis. Merely watching a workman doing the job will reveal little of the complex decision-making processes involved.

The first step in carrying out the skills analysis is to identify and record every detail of every act or body movement that the master makes in doing the job. This will include such details as which parts of the body are involved and over what distances, as well as identifying which senses are used in order to accomplish each of the actions. Each piece of information must be seen within the five stage activity framework of planning, initiating, controlling, terminating, and checking, and particular care should be taken to identify and isolate the cues which begin and terminate each cycle or subroutine.

All this information must be included on a chart similar to that shown in Fig. 3.6, dealing with the removal of stems from tobacco leaves. This chart, which follows the traditional format for a skills analysis, records the effector and receptor processes involved in the task. Details of any special coordinations of movements or senses, judgements or decisions, safety requirements, and sources of outside information about the task are added to the chart in the column headed 'comments'.

CIRCUMSTANCES CALLING FOR A SKILLS ANALYSIS

It has been pointed out by Wellens (1968) that there is a tendency to consider that 'all training of operators and other manual workers should, without exception, be based on skills analysis. This is quite wrong.' In the majority of work situations, a job analysis is sufficient, particularly when it is remembered that making a full skills analysis may involve many months of highly skilled work. The real difficulty lies in deciding when a skills analysis may be profitably carried out.

Generally speaking, the following circumstances, while not exhaustive, may be used as indicators of situations calling for skills analysis:
1. Tasks that call for operations involving complex, subtle hand, finger, and/or eye coordinations.
2. Tasks that call for unusual movements, postures, or rhythms not found in everyday life, e.g., movements concerned with the hand-operated safety guards on power presses.
3. Tasks that call for abnormal use of the senses, e.g., inspection of hand-sewing needles requires highly developed discrimination in the senses of touch.
4. Tasks that call for a great deal of covert information–processing and decision-making which might be overlooked in a conventional job analysis.
On some occasions, a complete skills analysis of the task may be necessary. Whenever possible, however, skills analysis should be confined to those subroutines where the special circumstances listed above are found to occur. In this way, the expense and time involved in making a skills analysis can be reserved for those occasions when benefits are likely to be greatest. It is interesting to note, in this regard, that many so-called skills analyses are often no more than job analyses set down in the skills analysis format. Only in particular critical areas does the analysis become a skills analysis in the *real* sense of the term.

ITEM	LEFT HAND	RIGHT HAND	VISION	OTHER SENSES	COMMENTS
1. Select leaf			Eyes to pile of leaf, determine leaf for selection and point of grasp.		
		Grasp leaf with T, 1 and 2, move with leaf until nose is visible.			
			Determine position on nose approximately 1″ from top of leaf		
	Grasp selected point with T and 1 on either outer sides of leaf touching stem with tips of both T and 1				
2. Remove stem	Hold leaf stationary while stem is being drawn out to 6″, rotate hand once in clockwise direction while RH is wrapping leaf around back of hand during the continued drawing out of the stem process. When leaf has passed around heel of hand, and RH starts to draw leaf up back of hand, release hold of nose with T and 1 and lightly hold leaf in hand with 3 and 4 by holding leaf against palm.	Release hold on leaf and regrasp stem immediately below lefthand T and 1, with fingernails of T and 1 RH. Break stem and commence to draw stem out from leaf, to about 6″. Pass hand holding stem behind LH and continue to draw stem leaving the leaf lightly resting against the back of the LH.			During removal of stem hold leaf in LH at right-angles to body; draw stem with RH towards body until about 6″ of stem has been parted from the leaf.
	Grasp leaf lightly as close to stem as possible with T and 1st and 2nd T. Controlling hold by applying sufficient pressure on stem against 1st knuckles of 1 and 2 to enable end of stem to be removed cleanly.	Bring stem between T and 1 LH to cross over 1 and 2 at 1st knuckle joint of LH.	Control passage of stem between fingers of LH.		
				Kinaesthetic (LH). Sufficient control to hold leaf while end of stem is being removed without holding up normal movement or allowing 'flags' to remain on removed stem.	
Place leaf on band	Rotate hand once in anti-clockwise direction to unwrap leaf from hand. Reposition T, 1 and 2 on nose of leaf holding leaf on left hand side at nose T on front face of leaf, 1 and 2 on back.	Put aside clean stem in stem bag to RH side.			
		Grasp nose with T on front and 1st and 2nd at back on RH side of leaf at nose. Tear along stem by moving RH across in front of stationary LH quickly, holding nose of leaf firmly during tearing. Hold RH side of leaf lightly between 3 amd 4 and palm and grasp nose of LH side of leaf with T on top and 1 and 2 on underside of leaf.	Control RH grasp		
				Kinaesthetic (LH). Tension critical to spread leaf fully without tearing.	

3.6 A skills analysis: **wrapper stemming (GTW) for spun pipe tobacco** (Reproduced with permission from Seymour, W. D. (1966) *Skills Analysis Training*. London: Pitman).

Conclusion

Topic, job, and skills analysis all entail a great deal of time and effort, and may seem to involve going into much unnecessary detail. However, it must be stressed that analysis is essential if intelligent decisions are to be made of the training need and the necessary teaching strategies. As Mager (1967) has pointed out: 'With the task steps identified in this detail, we can better avoid the teaching trap of including more theory than is necessary or desirable, and keep the course performance-orientated. Without this detail, we might add hours or days of unnecessary theory.' The important thing is not to make a more detailed analysis than the situation requires. However, job analysis highlights the individual task elements, which warrant further detailed study by skills analysis.

Once the decision is made as to whether training is necessary, the task analysis becomes a very important source of information. It constitutes a detailed course syllabus, while the analysis can also be conveniently transformed – with very little effort – into a lesson plan that covers not only what the student must learn, but also how it can be accomplished. Finally, the task analysis can be used to decide problems of sequencing, as well as which task elements form a complete learning sequence or subroutine. If a formal education or training programme is unnecessary, the analysis can be re-written in the form of a job aid, such as a check list, algorithm, or decision table. It can also form the raw material for a textbook, technical manual, workbook, or précis.

The technique of writing a task analysis can also be profitably employed as a learning strategy. Students, themselves, can make a task analysis of the topic, job, or skill that they are required to learn and master. In so doing, they will acquire a useful analytical skill, 'discover' the components of the task for themselves, and acquire a useful and permanent record of the knowledge and skills required in the form of a job aid.

Posttest 3

ANSWER ALL QUESTIONS

1. Distinguish between, and write short notes on, the three different types of task analysis.

2. State the main sources of information for a task analysis.

3. Give an example and draw a diagram depicting the relationship between the five behavioural levels or components recognized in task analysis.

4. Describe how the three types of task analysis are written.

5. Using the appropriate format, carry out a short task analysis for:
    (a) A cognitive task for classroom presentation.
    (b) A job involving a procedural task.
    (c) An analysis of the skills involved in a handwork job involving tools *OR* single purpose machine work.

6. State the circumstances when a full analysis of skill is likely to be beneficial.

7. Summarize the uses of a task analysis.

References and Reading List

CROSSMAN, E. R. F. W. and SEYMOUR, W. D. (1957) *The nature and acquisition of industrial skills.* London: DSIR.

DAVIES, I. K. (1965) A design for programmed learning, *Journal of Programmed Learning*, 2, 2, 71–3.

DAVIES, I. K. (1965) The analytic and synthetic stages of program writing, *Journal of Programmed Learning*, 2, 2, 76–87.

DAVIES, I. K. and THOMAS, C. A. (1967) *Task Analysis of RAF Photographers: Planning Paper.* Brampton, Huntingdon: HQ RAF Training Command.

DEPARTMENT OF EMPLOYMENT AND PRODUCTIVITY (1967) *Glossary of Training Terms.* London: HMSO.

EVANS, J. L., GLASER, R., and HOMME, L. E. (1962) The ruleg system for the construction of programmed verbal learning sequences, *Journal of Educational Research*, 55, 513–18.

GAGNE, R. M., ed. (1963) *Psychological Principles in System Development.* New York: Holt, Rinehart and Winston.

GANE. C. P. and Woolfenden, P. J. (1968) Algorithms and the analysis of skilled behaviour, *Industrial Training International*, 3, 7, 312–17.

GILBERT, T. F. (1962) Mathetics: the technology of education, *Journal of Mathetics*, 1, 1, 7–73.

GLASER, R. (1963) Research and Development issued in programmed instruction. In R. T. Filep, ed., *Perspectives in Programming.* New York:

MACE, C. A. (1950) The analysis of human skills. *Occupational Psychology*, 24, 3, 125.

MAGER, R. F. and BEACH, K. M. (1967) *Developing vocational instruction.* Palo Alto, California: Fearon.

MECHING, W. H., SMITH, R. G., RUPE, J. C., and COX, J. A. (1963) *A Handbook for Programmers of Automated Instruction.* Washington DC: HUMRRO.

MECHNER, F. (1965) Analysis and specification of behaviour for training. In R. Glaser, ed., *Teaching Machines and Programmed Learning II: Data and Directions.* Washington DC: National Education Association.

RAMSDEN, J. (1966) Skills analysis training, *Industrial Training International*, 1, 3, 116–23.

SEYMOUR, W. D. (1954) *Industrial Training for Manual Operations.* London: Pitman.

SEYMOUR, W. D. (1966) *Industrial Skills.* London: Pitman.

SEYMOUR, W. D. (1968) *Skills Analysis Training.* London: Pitman.

SEYMOUR, W. D. and WELLENS, J. (1967) An interview: Skills analysis training, *Industrial Training International*, 2, 2, 57–64.

SMITH, R. G. (1964) *The Development of Training Objectives*. Washington DC. HUMRRO Research Report No. 11.

THOMAS, C. A. (1968) The application of task analysis in specifying training requirements, *Industrial Training International*, 3, 3, 128–31.

THOMAS, C. A. and DAVIES, I. K. (1967) *Training Requirements for RAF Photographers: First Phase Report*. Brampton, Huntingdon: HQ RAF Training Command Research Report No. 235.

THOMAS, C. A., DAVIES, I. K., OPENSHAW, D., and BIRD, J. (1963) *Programmed Learning in Perspective*. New York: Educational Methods Inc.

TRIST, E. L. *et al.* (1963) *Organizational Choice*. London, Tavistock Plans.

WELLENS, J. (1968) Editor's note, *Industrial Training International*, 3, 3, 131.

4 Identifying a training need

Learning Objectives

COGNITIVE OBJECTIVES

After carefully reading this chapter, you will be able to:

1. Distinguish between the costs that arise from too little training and the costs that arise from too much training.

2. Distinguish between acquiring a basic repertoire of behaviours and enlarging this repertoire by restructuring it into new patterns of behaviour.

3. Recognize and distinguish between accomplishment and acquirement, in terms of performance deficiency.

4. Recognize, distinguish between, and write short notes on, deficiencies of knowledge and deficiencies of execution.

5. Using the Birkbeck model of occupational psychology, compare and contrast the alternative strategies available for overcoming performance deficiency.

6. List the conditions under which off-the-job training is likely to be optimal.

7. State the three goals of training.

8. Distinguish between realm and domain theory, and state the pedagogical importance of each.

9. State how the training need can be isolated and identified.

10. Isolate and identify a training need, given a task analysis and associated documents listing relevant personal details of the target population.

AFFECTIVE OBJECTIVES

After reading the chapter, the author intends that you will:

1. Value the principle of identifying the training need.

2. Incorporate the principle into your organization of managerial strategies, so that it becomes characteristic of your managerial style.

'Say, Bill,' said the production manager to the company training officer, 'engineers these days just don't seem to be creative.'
'Well, we can help you, Harry,' replied Bill. 'Do you want our one day lecture presentation, our two day seminar, or a two week workshop in Scotland.'

Once the task analysis has been completed, but before the learning objectives are written, it is necessary to isolate and identify those parts of the task that require formal training. Whenever a problem involving a deficiency in knowledge, skill, or attitude exists, it is all too easy to fall into the trap of thinking that some form of formal training programme is necessary. It is almost as if every problem can be solved by a course of training. Very often, we fail to consider all the possible alternatives, and thereby fail to choose the approach which is most likely to be optimal. It is often better to decide what we must *not* teach or need not teach, in order to determine what we *must* teach.

This is not meant in any way to decry the importance of formal training programmes. The intention is to highlight the fact that good teachers and instructors are in short supply, their time is necessarily limited, formal training is expensive, and training may be the wrong solution to the problem anyway. In adopting this questioning approach towards identifying the *real* training need, there is the danger that, unless great care is exercised, very high costs can be involved by teaching too little, as well as by teaching too much. The problem is to keep these two opposing strategies in balance, for while the costs of too little training are fairly obvious, the costs associated with too much training are more subtle and insidious.

Generally speaking, the costs of too little training and too much training can be summarized under the following headings:

1. *Costs of too little training arise from:*
   (a) The necessity for additional training on-the-job.
   (b) The slowing down of production, and the underutilization of machines.
   (c) An increase in the proportion of work rejected on inspection for not meeting the laid down standards.
   (d) An increase in the wastage of materials.
   (e) Increased demands on supervisors' time.
   (f) An increased possibility of damage to equipment.
   (g) An increased possibility of danger to personnel.
   (h) Job dissatisfaction, because the worker is inadequately prepared for the job he is called upon to do.
2. *Costs of too much training arise from:*
   (a) More courses are organized than are strictly necessary.
   (b) Courses tend to be longer than they need be.
   (c) More instructors, accommodation, and equipment are employed than the job actually demands.

(d) Students, who might possibly be perfectly competent when it comes to doing the job, fail the training course because of a syllabus that sets too high standards. This often occurs when the training tends to be theoretical rather than practical in nature.

(e) Irrelevant criteria may be used to select students for training, and so the available labour market becomes unnecessarily reduced in size.

(f) Job dissatisfaction, because training prepares the worker for a higher calibre job than the one he is actually going to do.

In other words, an overstatement of a training need results in excessive costs, since men and resources are taken away from productive work. An understatement of a training need results in personnel working inefficiently. The tendency, however, is to overtrain rather than to undertrain; to under-estimate rather than to overestimate student capabilities.

Performance Deficiency

The teaching of adults and of children is different in a number of very important respects. Most of these differences are fairly obvious, but there is one key difference that is often overlooked. In teaching children, a teacher has two main aims:

1. To teach the children to acquire a basic repertoire of behaviours (knowledge, skills, and attitudes).

2. Whenever possible, to enlarge this basic repertoire by rearranging or restructuring it into new patterns of behaviour.

Teaching adults, on the other hand, ordinarily involves more rearranging of behaviours and less teaching of new behaviours, since most adults will have already acquired their basic repertoire for most tasks. This point is a very important one, and has often been overlooked in programmed learning. Since most acts of mastery will exist in the repertoire of behaviours in an adult, learning for adults will usually involve rearranging this repertoire so that 'acts will occur in a different sequence and on different occasions than they do in the initial repertoire' (Gilbert, 1962). Indeed, this phenomena is the whole basis of reinforcement theory, for if a behaviour is to be strengthened or reinforced by its consequences, the response must already be present in the repertoire in order to produce its consequences.

Many adults, for instance, do not know the colour code for resistors. But is this really true? Most adults already associate colour and number in one way or another. Green and five are already associated (we talk about five green fingers), black and zero (black is associated with nothingness), brown and one (one brown penny), etc. So there are two strategies available to a teacher:

1. He can work on the assumption that students who do not know the colour code for resistors really *do not know it*. In these circumstances, he will have to start from scratch, and teach the colour-number associations

as if they did not already exist. There will have to be a great deal of rote-learning, of constant repetition and rehearsal, as well as continuous testing. All this will take a very long time, and the lesson will tend to be uninteresting – if not boring.

2. Or he can work on the assumption that students who do not apparently know the colour code, really *do know it*. In these circumstances, he will make use of the associations already in their repertoire. Teaching is now a very much simpler and more interesting affair, and will consume considerably less time than the alternative strategy.

John Dewey's definition of education as 'the reconstruction of experience' is a restatement of the optimal strategy.

Thus, 'the first rule for limiting instructional objectives is to remove from the list of potential objectives any skills in which students are *not* already deficient' (Gilbert, 1967). This rule can be stated as:

$$PD = M - I$$

where PD stands for performance deficiency, M stands for the complete set of behaviours necessary to do the job (these are obtained by the task analysis), and I stands for all the behaviours necessary to do the job that the student already possesses. An approach such as this seeks to highlight the usefulness of what a student already knows, and thus limits the training need to those areas in which he is deficient.

ACCOMPLISHMENT AND ACQUIREMENT

In considering this phenomena of 'performance deficiency,' Gilbert (1967) stresses the essential difference – often overlooked by teachers and instructors – between *accomplishment* and *acquirement*. Achievement has two main aspects:

1. *Acquirement*. This refers to what a person has already learned, in other words his basic repertoire of behaviours.

2. *Accomplishment*. This refers to the value of this basic repertoire.

A student's level of acquirement, in terms of the knowledge, skills, or attitudes that he already possesses, may be very high indeed, but this knowledge is of little value if his level of accomplishment is low.

A child, for instance, may be able to carry out successfully, but separately, every action involved in tying shoelaces, but still be unable to tie them because he does not know the correct sequence of actions. Thus, a small deficiency in acquirement (correct sequencing) can make a very large difference in accomplishment (tying shoelaces). As Gilbert has pointed out (1964):

You say that you know nothing about bank tellering, but this is not true. If you examine all the operations a bank teller uses to balance his books, you will find that you have already acquired most of them. Nevertheless, the few operations you have not acquired prevent you from accomplishing the objectives of the bank teller's job. In terms of what the teller and you know about his job, there is very little difference between you; in terms of the value of what you know, you are worlds apart.

Once the essential difference between acquirement and accomplishment is appreciated, it will be seen that the concept of performance deficiency involves acquirement *not* accomplishment. Accomplishment is important when we are concerned with selection, promotion, or transfer to another department.

As a corollary to this discussion of accomplishment and acquirement, it is as well to remember that individual differences among students will often be small compared with the communalities that will exist among them. However, the *effects* of these differences may be very large indeed, although

---

Foremen in a chemical plant were charged with looking after a boiler, which produced steam essential to one of the processes. As the water was taken from the local river it contained natural impurities which tended to change in concentration; accordingly, various adjustments to the doping plant were made by the foremen in order to compensate for this variation. Since the job was badly carried out, the company felt that the foremen's attitudes towards the problem were poor, and the consultants were asked to prepare a four to six weeks' course on water chemistry. However, when the consultants examined the problem in the field, they found that there was a wide gap between the management's conception of the job and what actually happened in the plant.

Each shift foreman took water samples, and sent them to the lab for analysis. The lab then sent a report to the doping plant of the total dissolved solids, sulphite, sulphate, phosphate, oxygen and acidity, together with a statement of the limits. The foreman was then supposed to apply his knowledge of water chemistry, and calculate how much chemical to add, which control on the doping plant to operate and by how much. However, it was found that the men actually worked according to a series of rules of thumb. Further, the doping chemicals were all white in colour and were kept in identical, but differently labelled, storage drums. As they were weighed out and added to the plant in the open air, the pressure for haste – particularly during bad weather – made mistakes likely. It was obvious that the foremen were not making incorrect decisions because of any poor attitude towards the job; the rules for making the decisions were just too complicated for them, and their ability to carry out the decisions correctly were handicapped by a poor working environment. The whole situation was then further confounded by the fact that if any foreman did do the job correctly he never knew, since the next sampling of the water impurities and the analyst's report went to the foreman on the next shift. This foreman, in his turn, could not tell whether the impurities were there because his colleague had made a mistake, or whether the composition of the river water had changed slightly since the last doping.

Attitude was obviously not the real problem. The rules were extremely complicated, and if they were going to be understood a postgraduate course in water chemistry was necessary. Since all foremen had the same difficulties, selection was unlikely to help solve the problem. Yet mistakes result in boiler corrosion, and a new boiler costs something in the region of £50,000. Two recommendations were, therefore, made and accepted. First, the environment was improved by erecting a shed over the chemical mixing area as protection from the rain, the chemicals were made up in differently coloured and shaped one-pound bags to make their identification easier even in the dark and to save weighing. Lastly, the job itself was improved by developing job aids – set out in eight charts – on which the foremen were given three hours instruction. In this way, 100 foremen were trained at a cost, not counting the consultant's fee, of £20 per head.

Fig. 4.1 A case study illustrating deficiencies of knowledge and execution, and the strategies used to overcome them (Summarized with permission from Gane, C. P. (1968) Training for Results, *Management Today*, November 1968, 119–26)

a small change in acquirement would probably result in doubling or even tripling the effectiveness and, therefore, the value of the student's performance.

CLASSES OF PERFORMANCE DEFICIENCY

Once a performance deficiency has been recognized, it is necessary to diagnose its character before deciding upon what course of action is most likely to overcome it. Generally speaking, performance deficiencies can be classified (Gilbert, 1967) under one of two headings:

1. Deficiencies of knowledge.
2. Deficiencies of execution.

Gilbert suggests that answering 'Yes' to the question, 'Could this person perform correctly if his life depended on it?' will nearly always isolate and identify a deficiency of execution.

In describing deficiencies of performance, however, it is important that they are not exaggerated (as many managers are tempted to do), nor should they be underestimated. Fig. 4.1, based on a report by Gane (1968), illustrates this point, and shows that by altering the working environment and by supplying job aids the need for training can be systematically reduced. In this case, management were willing to finance a four to six week course on boiler water chemistry, whereas the application of task analysis and performance deficiency analysis suggested that the same objectives could be achieved by a three hour course on using job aids. This case study also underlines the point that any deficiencies in performance must be stated in terms that are capable of observation and measurement in order that a meaningful estimate can be made of their importance and value.

STRATEGIES FOR OVERCOMING PERFORMANCE DEFICIENCIES

Some years ago, Rodger and Cavanagh (1962) put forward a comprehensive, and operationally useful, framework of the field of occupational psychology. This is shown in Fig. 4.2. It will be seen that the model can also serve as a

---

Fitting the man to the job:
Through:
1. Vocational guidance.
2. Personnel selection.
3. Occupational training and development.

Fitting the job to the man:
Through:
1. The development of methods of work.
2. Equipment design.
3. Arrangement of working conditions and rewards.

Fig 4.2 The Birkbeck model of occupational psychology (Reproduced with permission from Rodger, A. and Cavanagh, P. (1962) Training Occupational Psychologists, *Occupational Psychology*, 32, 2, 83–8)

framework for deciding which strategies can be used for overcoming performance deficiencies, since we can do one of two things:

1. Fit the man to the job.
2. Fit the job to the man.

No one strategy is more important than the other when it comes to diagnosing a particular problem, both need to be taken into account. All too often, however, we have tended to use one strategy to the exclusion of the other. In trying to fit men to the job, we have overemphasized the importance of training and selection, and neglected the alternative strategy of either changing the job or changing the demands that the job makes on the man. The decision as to which approach is likely to be the most effective largely depends upon the nature of the task and the type of performance deficiency it is necessary to combat.

Deficiencies of knowledge are probably best overcome by formal education and training programmes, by guidance, and by the use of such job aids as checklists, functional flow diagrams, logical trees, and algorithms. In such circumstances, man must be fitted to his job either by training or by giving him the information he needs in the form of job aids. Deficiencies of execution, however, are rarely overcome to any extent by formal training and education programmes. Their solution involves fitting the job to the man, and this means management changes in the working conditions, in the organization, in the information systems, in the methods of working, and in the form of motivation employed. Often, of course, both approaches are necessary, and what, at first sight, appears to be a problem of training is really a problem that involves training, selection, and methods of work.

An example of this type of analysis is to be found in the study carried out by Wing Commander C. A. Thomas and I. K. Davies (1967) into the training needs of Royal Air Force photographers. In order to tackle this problem, the investigators used the type of task analysis for physical skills described in the last chapter, together with the associated task level annotations. As a result of the task analysis, it was found that 45 jobs were carried out by RAF photographers, and, when these jobs were analysed, it was found that they could be classified under one of the following headings:

1. *The Air Role*
   (a) Work in air-camera sections.
   (b) Work in photographic processing units.
2. *The Ground Role*
   (a) Work in illustrative photography.
   (b) Work in lithography.

An analysis of the task levels entered on the 45 task analysis sheets (see Fig. 4.3) shows that:

1. Approximately 90 per cent of all the task elements involved level 5 (signal tasks) and level 4 (procedural tasks).
2. Approximately 10 per cent of all the task elements involved level 3

(simple discriminatory tasks), level 2 (complex discriminatory tasks), and level 1 (diagnostic tasks).

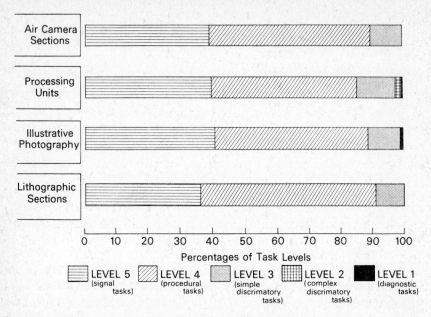

Fig. 4.3 RAF study to determine the training needs of photographers – analysis of task levels

In other words, 90 per cent of all the work done, regardless of role, consisted of procedural routines of varying lengths. The formal training requirements for such work are minimal, and most of the training is better carried out on the job with the help of close supervision, guidance, and job aids. It is only that area of the work which involves levels 1, 2, and 3 that formal training is likely to have any real benefits, and even here task analysis shows that training must concentrate on teaching the necessary discriminations and diagnostic procedures. Of course, the problem was not quite so simple as it is presented here, since task levels 1, 2, and 3 did not characterize particular jobs. Instead, they formed sequences between or within different procedures. The recognition, however, that jobs were largely procedural enabled the investigators to see through the problem to the actual performance requirements of the task.

The Goals of Formal Training

Once the training need has been established, it is necessary to consider how the need can best be met. Two general strategies are available: training on the job, and training off the job. The decision as to which strategy is likely to be optimal can only be made on the basis of a feasibility study, but, wherever doubt exists, on the job training is to be preferred. Generally speaking, off the job training, however, will be necessary whenever:

1. The job is complex, particularly if the complexity arises because of demands for information processing and decision-making.
2. The job is dangerous, or if equipment can be damaged by incompetent handling.
3. There is constant change calling for rapid regrouping of knowledge and skills.
4. The job forms part of a new operational system still under development.
5. Men have to be prepared for jobs that do not already exist.
6. There are motivational or attitudinal problems that cannot be tackled in the formal work environment.

In other words, training on the job is best reserved for work which is simple and safe, is relatively stable and undergoes little change or innovation, and experiences no time or cost pressure to bring people up to a level of minimum proficiency.

In practice, it is not so difficult to decide, on the basis of a feasibility study, which strategy is likely to be the most effective, but all too often the wrong decisions are still made. This usually occurs because managers are not clearly aware of the three board aims or goals of training, whether it be formal (on the job) training or informal (off the job) training. These goals have been summarized by Crawford (1963) as:

1. To increase proficiency of performance.
2. To decrease costs and learning time.
3. To decrease the requirements for particular levels of intelligence, aptitude, and ability.

In other words, training should only be carried out when it is believed that the same results, in terms of on the job performance, cannot be obtained so efficiently, effectively, and economically by any other strategy. While the majority of training programmes successfully realize these goals, far too many fail to do so. The surprising feature of this situation, however, is that little or no attempt is made to analyse the results of training in terms of these three very simple and obvious criteria.

Something of the real nature of the problem can be illustrated by the data shown in Fig. 4.4. Baldwin et al. (1957) carried out a study with US Army radar technicians, showing that, if a base line of 100 is used as the average performance of training school graduates, there was a performance deficiency of some 40 points between personnel finishing a course and the minimum level of satisfactory work proficiency. In order to correct this deficiency over six months' work experience was necessary. Training, in other words, was failing to prepare the men for the work that they were called upon to perform, even though the minimum level of job proficiency was known to the system managers. In terms of the goals suggested by Crawford, training was failing on the first two counts.

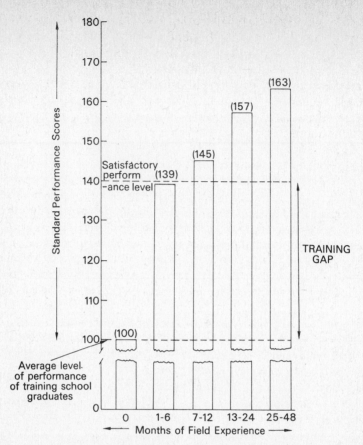

Fig. 4.4 Average proficiency in test performance for US Army radar technicians according to the number of months of field experience (Reproduced with permission from Baldwin, R. D. *et al.* (1957) The AAFCS M33 Mechanic Proficiency Test – Part 1: Comparison of Mechanics with and without Full Experience; Part 2: Development of Cross Validation, Washington DC, *HUMRO Technical Report*, 3, 8, May 1957)

Fleishman (1953) has described how an internationally known engineering company decided to train foremen in leadership principles and techniques by running a two week formal course at their training centre. The initial results of the course were quite encouraging, but a follow-up of the long-term effects of the course proved rather disconcerting. Fleishman found the following:
1.   Foremen who worked for considerate managers tended to become *more* considerate themselves as a result of the training programme.
2.   Foremen who worked for less considerate managers tended to become *less* considerate after training.
In other words, the formal training programme was only effective in those departments of the organization which favoured the objectives of the course, in the other departments training had a contrary effect.

Similarly disconcerting results have been reported by Sykes (1962), who investigated the effects of supervisory training in changing supervisors' attitudes to, and expectations of, management in a medium-sized contracting firm. As a result of attending the course, the men became so dissatisfied with management, that within twelve months almost half of the supervisors either left the company or began actively to look for jobs elsewhere. The moral is a simple one, having identified a training need you must ensure that the type of training you give realizes your objectives.

What Theory Should Be Taught?

One of the most difficult decisions that teachers and instructors have to make in organizing a course of formal training concerns the teaching of theory. Almost everyone agrees that the theoretical side of a subject forms an important part of most educational and training programmes. The difficulty lies in deciding how much theory is necessary. If too much is included, we can so burden the students and subject material that it is difficult to overcome the performance deficiency. If we decide not to teach any theory at all, student learning can lack the background and conceptual framework necessary to a true understanding of the subject.

Generally speaking, there is a tendency to teach too much theory, and a good deal of the theory that is taught is the wrong theory anyway. For instance, Knight (1961) has demonstrated that unskilled personnel with no experience can identify and locate faults – given a course of approximately seven days on fault-finding on a superhet radio receiver – more expertly than personnel trained in a conventional manner by means of a course containing a complete exposition on radio theory and superhet receivers.

In order to limit and identify the theory necessary to a true understanding of the task, it is important to distinguish between two different types of theory (see Gilbert, 1962):

1. *Realm theories*. These are theories that have to be learnt because they are essential to the subject matter. For instance, in teaching physics, it is necessary for students to learn Charles' law and Boyle's law in order to appreciate the relationship between pressure, volume, and temperature in gasses.

2. *Domain theories*. These are theories that are pedagogically useful to learning. For instance, centrifugal force is a theoretical construction that enables dynamic problems to be restated in terms of static problems. Domain theories normally take the form of such useful teaching devices as analogies, mnemonics, and models or paradigms.

Realm theories, although important from a subject point of view, are not necessarily helpful to learning. Domain theories are helpful to learning, but are not necessarily essential to the subject matter – in fact, they can often be forgotten once the topic has been mastered.

The teacher's problem is to balance these two types of theory, always making certain that domain theories are available when needed. Fortunately, on many occasions, one theory can serve both functions. The principle of the conservation of energy, which is essential to the subject of energy flow, is also pedagogically useful, since it can help to establish meaningful relationships between such diverse topics as Ohm's law and Joule's law. Indeed, one of the great criticisms of the traditional teaching of physics has been the tendency to break down the subject into separate topics (like heat, light, sound, magnetism, and electricity) in the belief that students would be confused with too many facts or concepts at one time. As Michels (1958) has pointed out, this 'method of teaching belies the very nature of the subject, for the chief thing that distinguishes the physical sciences from other intellectual activities is the existence of a central theory, based on a very few simple laws and principles, which applies to all phenomena.' Such fundamental principles as the conservation of energy, the conservation of matter and the conservation of momentum are excellent examples of theories, that serve both realm and domain functions.

Unfortunately, while there is an excess of realm theories, there is a dearth of domain theories; for this reason there is a tendency for some teachers either to use bad or even harmful domain theories, or not to use them at all. The basic rule of thumb in deciding what theory should be taught is fortunately a simple one:
1. Teach as *little* realm theory as is possible, consistent with the task that has to be accomplished.
2. Teach as *much* domain theory as is pedagogically necessary.
3. Whenever possible, ensure that domain and realm theory are one and the same.
The difference between good teaching and bad teaching, between new mathematics and physics and old mathematics and physics, can be partly characterized in these terms.

Conclusion

In the past, there has been a tendency – particulary in industry and commerce – to believe that education and training schemes are the most appropriate way of ensuring that performance is brought up to required standards of proficiency. But, as we have seen, there is more than one way of overcoming performance deficiencies, and training is not necessarily the best or only strategy – a point that courses on instructional technology tend to ignore, with resulting financial penalties to the company or organization.

One of the more successful ways of deciding what training is necessary, is to decide what training is *not* necessary. This involves determining the actual character of any performance deficiency, so that alternative strategies, such as organizational change, can be considered. What is left when all the alternative strategies to training have been examined, can be rewritten in the form of learning objectives in preparation for an education or training programme.

Posttest 4

ANSWER ALL QUESTIONS

1. Distinguish between the costs that arise from too little training, and the costs that arise from too much training.

2. Distinguish between *acquiring* a basic repertoire of behaviour and *enlarging* a repertoire of behaviour by restructuring it into new patterns of behaviour.

3. Distinguish between 'accomplishment' and 'acquirement' in terms of performance deficiency.

4. Distinguish between, and write short notes on, 'deficiencies of knowledge' and 'deficiencies of execution'.

5. Using the Birkbeck model of occupational psychology, compare and contrast the alternative strategies available for overcoming performance deficiency.

6. List the conditions under which off the job training is likely to be optimal.

7. State the three goals of training as summarized by Crawford.

8. Distinguish between realm theory and domain theory, and state the pedagogical importance of each.

9. State how the training need can be isolated and identified.

10. Using a task analysis, and associated documents listing the relevant personal details of the target population, isolate and identify the training need in a real-life situation.

References and Reading List

BALDWIN, R. D., MAGER, R. F., VINEBERG, R., and WHIPPLE, J. E. (1957) *The AAFCS M–33 Mechanic Proficiency Test: Part 1 and Part 2*. Washington DC: Human Resources Research Office. Technical Report No. 38, May 1957.

CRAWFORD, M. P. (1963) Concepts of training. In R. M. Gagne, ed., *Psychological Principles in System Development*. New York: Holt, Rinehart and Winston.

FLEISHMAN, E. A. (1953) Leadership climate, human relations training and supervisory behaviour, *Personnel Psychology*, 6, 205–22.

GAGNE, R. M., ed. (1963) *Psychological Principles in Systems Development*. New York: Holt, Rinehart and Winston.

GANE, C. P. (1968) Training for results, *Management Today*, November 1968. 117–26.

GEIS, G. L. (1970) Premature instruction. *Educational Technology*, 10, 4, 24–30.

GILBERT, T. F. (1962) Mathetics: the technology of education, *Journal of Mathetics*, 1, 1, 7–73 and 1, 2, 7–56.

GILBERT, T. F. (1964) A dialogue between teaching and testing. In G. D. Ofiesh and W. C. Mierhenry, eds., *Trends in Programmed Instruction*. Washington, DC: Department of Audiovisual Instruction.

GILBERT, T. F. (1967) Praxeonomy: a systematic approach to identifying training needs, *Management of Personnel Quarterly*, 6, 3, 20–33.

GLASER, R., ed. (1965) *Training Research and Education*. New York: John Wiley.

KNIGHT, M. A. G. (1961) *An Experimental Training Course in Fault Diagnosis*. Research Report No. 202. Brampton, Huntingdon: HQ RAF Training Command.

MICHELS, W. C. (1958) The teaching of elementary physics, *Scientific American*, April 1958, 3–9.

RODGER, A. and CAVANAGH, P. (1962) Training occupational psychologists, *Occupational Psychology*, 36, 1–2, 82–8.

SYKES, A. J. M. (1962) The effect of a supervisory training course on changing supervisors' perceptions and expectations of the role of management, *Human Relations*, 15, 227–43.

THOMAS, C. A. and DAVIES, I. K. (1967) *Training Requirements for RAF Photographers: First Phase Report*. Brampton, Huntingdon: HQ RAF Training Command.

5 Writing objectives

Learning Objectives

COGNITIVE OBJECTIVES

After carefully reading this chapter, you will be able to:

1. Distinguish between an aim and an objective.

2. State four reasons for specifying objectives.

3. Recognize, and discriminate between, cognitive, affective and psychomotor objectives.

4. List four ways in which Bloom's taxonomy can be useful to the teacher or instructor.

5. State what words should be avoided and what words should used when writing clear objectives.

6. List, and write short notes upon, the three types of information essential to a clear objective.

7. Write a clear objective using either the Mager or the Miller system.

AFFECTIVE OBJECTIVES

After reading this chapter, the author intends that you will:

1. Be aware of, and value, the importance of clear objectives to the learning process.

2. Incorporate into your teaching behaviour either the Miller or Mager system of writing objectives.

> Objectives are not only the goals towards which the curriculum is
> shaped and toward which instruction is guided, but they are also
> the goals that provide the detailed specification for the construction
> and use of evaluative techniques. *Benjamin S. Bloom.*

There is probably no single procedure in education and industrial training
that is more important than writing learning objectives, or what Gilbert
(1962) has more accurately described as 'prescribing the mastery response.'
Yet, while interest and investment in education and training grow rapidly,
and various authorities in management and cost effectiveness increasingly
stress the importance of defining objectives, statements and specifications
of so-called 'educational' and 'training' objectives tend to be more spoken
and written about than practised.

Historically, the process of precisely defining learning objectives is not
new, but the present movement has four main roots : programmed learning
(Mager, 1962), military instructional design (Miller, 1962), school examinations and the measurement of achievement (Bloom, 1956), and changing
emphases in management philosophy (Drucker, 1954). Other influences,
from operations research and economics, have introduced the associated
concept of utility. In terms of actual impact on educational and training
practices, however, Mager and Bloom have undoubtedly been the most
influential. For this reason, the reader is strongly advised to refer to what
they have written, and to consider their advice in terms of Dewey's dictum
that 'any aim is of value in so far as it assists observation, choice and planning
from moment to moment and from hour to hour'.

Learning Aims and Objectives

In its very broadest sense, a learning objective is a statement of proposed
change. This change, desired and valued by teachers and trainers, is expected
to occur in the thoughts, actions and feelings of the students in their charge
as a result of some educational or training experience. No experience, of
course, can be judged as good or bad in its own right. The only test of
quality lies in whether or not the experience has been successful or unsuccessful in bringing about the desired change in the learner's behaviour.

When people talk of change in this context, they usually use the word
'aim,' and more occasionally 'objective'. The two words, though, are at
different levels of abstraction, and are not interchangeable:

1. *An aim or goal is a general statement of intent.* As such it has very little
precision or direction. It is not especially helpful to the classroom teacher,
and it does not assist him to decide which teaching strategy should be used
or what form any evaluation should take. A typical example of an aim is
that every child should acquire the following:

(*a*) A flexible mind and ability to think straight.

(*b*) An acquaintance with the nature of heat, light, and sound.

(*c*) A practical capacity for measuring the properties of matter.

(*d*) An awareness of the uses of physics in the world beyond the class-room.

(*c*) A glimpse of the power of physics gained by generalization and abstraction.

2. *An objective is very much more specific and precise.* It provides both the teacher and the student with a very great deal of concrete help and direction. Indeed, it has been argued that an objective will give both teachers and students 'some direction with regard to both the subject *content* and the mental *processes* which the student is expected to develop' (Bloom, 1963). A typical example of an objective is that the student will, without reference materials and using his own words, complete the following tasks without error in a period not greater than thirty minutes:

1. State the historical evidence to prove what living in a country where people have equal rights is like.

2. List the evidence for the proposition that 'policies pursued in the past have not been consistent with the idea of a government of equal rights'.

3. Write down three arguments *for* and three arguments *against* the proposition that 'certain policies pursued in the past are undesirable'.

REASONS FOR SPECIFYING OBJECTIVES

Students today have very different objectives to students of a generation ago. The nature of education and training has also changed, and the tendency today is towards a more direct and straightforward emphasis on learning – in the sense that the appropriateness and effectiveness of teaching is being more and more questioned. For this reason, writing precise behavioural objectives, capable of observation and measurement, is becoming increasingly important. Writing such objectives:

1. Limits the task, and removes all ambiguity and difficulties of inter-pretation.

2. Ensures that measurement is possible, so that the quality and the effectiveness of the learning experience can be determined.

3. Enables both teachers and students to distinguish between different varieties or classes of behaviour, and so helps them to decide which learning strategy is likely to be optimal.

4. Provides a complete but terse summary of the course, which can serve as a conceptual scaffold or 'advance organizer' for learning. Ausubel (1967), among many others, believes that such advance organizers are of great importance, and statements of behaviourable objectives, of course, are ideally suited to perform this function.

Objectives are needed in every area where performance and results directly and vitally affect the overall nature of education and training. Little skill is necessary for translating educational objectives into a final criterion test or examination, although – as we shall see later in this book – considerably greater skill and professional expertise are required to relate teaching strategies to learning objectives.

Bloom's Taxonomy of Learning Objectives

If you examine a great number of learning objectives or even examination questions, you will find that they can be broadly classified under one of three main headings or domains:

1. Cognitive objectives.
2. Affective objectives.
3. Psychomotor objectives.

Cognitive objectives are concerned with information and knowledge; as such, realizing cognitive objectives is the basic activity of most educational and training programmes. Affective objectives, on the other hand, emphasize attitudes and values, feelings and emotions; accordingly, they are the proper concern of education. Psychomotor objectives involve muscular and motor skills, or manipulation of material or objects, or some activity which requires neuromuscular coordination. Realizing psychomotor objectives is, of course, the primary concern of a good deal of industrial-vocational training.

Bloom and his colleagues at the University of Chicago have produced a most important classification or taxonomy of both cognitive objectives (Bloom, 1956) and affective objectives (Krathwohl, Bloom, and Masia, 1964). Unfortunately, they have produced no comparable scheme for the psychomotor area, although a tentative classification has been made by Simpson (1969). The taxonomy arranges objectives in the cognitive and affective domains into six major classes; these are shown in Fig. 5.1. A useful way of looking at the two domains is that in the cognitive domain a teacher is interested in what the student will *do*, whereas in the affective domain, the teacher is additionally concerned with what he *does to it* or *with it*.

COGNITIVE DOMAIN		AFFECTIVE DOMAIN
6	Evaluation	Organization and characterization
4, 5	Analysis and synthesis	Conceptualization
3	Application	Valuing
2	Comprehension	Responding
1	Knowledge	Receiving

Fig 5.1 Bloom's cognitive and affective domains

An old educational axiom states that 'growth occurs from within,' and this inner growth is demonstrated in the two taxonomies by the way in which they are internally related and interrelated. The objectives in one class, for example, 'application' make use and build on the behaviours implicit in the preceding objectives, in this case, 'knowledge' and 'comprehension'. Similarly, there is a great deal of correspondence between the classes in each domain; this is particularly noticeable between 'knowledge' and 'receiving' (level 1), and also 'analysis and synthesis' and 'conceptualization' (levels 4 and 5). A more detailed illustration of these relationships will be obtained by studying Fig. 5.2.

Both cognitive and affective objectives are of great practical use to the teacher and instructor not only in planning, but also in exercising his organizational and controlling functions. The taxonomies, shown in Figs. 5.3 and 5.4, serve as a complete conceptual framework, on which can be positioned any learning objective or related test question. Such a scaffold or ideational map enables the teacher to:

1. Select his range of objectives and test questions.
2. Relate and interrelate his objectives and associated test questions to other objectives and questions in both cognitive and affective domains.

COGNITIVE OBJECTIVES	AFFECTIVE OBJECTIVES
1. The lowest level in this taxonomy begins with the student's recall and recognition of KNOWLEDGE.	1. The lowest level begins with the student merely RECEIVING stimuli and passively attending to it. It extends to his more actively attending to it,
2. It extends through his COMPREHENSION of the knowledge,	2. then his RESPONDING to stimuli on request, willingly responding and taking satisfaction in responding,
3. To his skill in the APPLICATION of the knowledge that he comprehends.	3. to his VALUING the phenomena or activity so that he voluntarily responds and seeks out further ways to take part in what is going on.
4. The next levels progress from his ability to make an ANALYSIS of the situations involving the knowledge, to his skill in the SYNTHESIS of it into new organizations.	4. The next stage is his CONCEPTUALIZATION of each of the values to which he is responding by identifying characteristics or forming judgements.
5. The highest level lies in his skill in EVALUATION, so that he can judge the value of the knowledge in realizing specific objectives.	5. The highest level in the taxonomy is the student's ORGANIZATION of the values into a system which is a CHARACTERIZATION of himself.

Fig. 5.2 **The relationship between the cognitive and affective domains** (Reproduced with permission from Krathwold, D. R., Bloom, B.S., and Masia, B. B. (1964) *Taxonomy of Educational Objectives, Handbook II: Affective Domain.* New York: McKay)

3. Ensure a proper balance and weighting is given to objectives and questions.

4. Determine that higher-order objectives are being realized, since it is only at these higher levels that the educational value of what is being accomplished is beyond dispute.

Inevitably, lower-order cognitive objectives tend to be mundane in character, and are unlikely to be particularly exciting; yet most teachers *hope* that their students will develop a continuing and growing interest in the material they have learnt. Many courses, however, which start off with an interest in developing positive attitudes in their students, often have their affective objectives and higher-order cognitive objectives diluted, or even eroded away, as the course loses its initial freshness and sparkle.

The vast majority of the questions in GCE O level examinations tend to be concerned with knowledge and comprehension, a few questions in GCE A level examinations test application and analysis, and it is a very good

DIRECTION	CATEGORY
LOW LEVEL	1. *Knowledge.* (Remembering facts, terms, and principles in the form that they were learned.) (a) Knowledge of specifics. (i) Knowledge of terminology. (ii) Knowledge of specific facts. (b) Knowledge of ways and means of dealing with specifics. (i) Knowledge of conventions. (ii) Knowledge of trends and sequences. (iii) Knowledge of classifications and categories. (iv) Knowledge of criteria. (v) Knowledge of methology. (c) Knowledge of universals and abstractions in a field. (i) Knowledge of principles and generalizations. (ii) Knowledge of theories and structures. 2. *Comprehension.* (Understanding material studied without necessarily relating it to other material.) (a) Translation. (b) Interpretation. (c) Extrapolation. 3. *Application.* (Using generalizations or other abstractions appropriately in concrete situations.)
MEDIUM LEVEL	4. *Analysis.* (Breakdown of material into constituent parts.) (a) Analysis of elements. (b) Analysis of relationships (c) Analysis of organizational principles. 5. *Synthesis.* (Combining elements into a new structure.) (a) Production of a unique communication. (b) Production of a plan or proposed set of operations. (c) Derivation of a set of abstract relations. 6. *Evaluation.* (Judging the value of material for a specified purpose.) (a) Judgements in terms of internal evidence.
HIGH LEVEL	(b) Judgements in terms of external criteria.

Fig. 5.3 Condensed version of the taxonomy of educational objectives in the cognitive domain (Reproduced with permission from Bloom, B. S. (1956): *Taxonomy of Educational Objectives, Handbook I: Cognitive Domain.* New York: McKay)

DIRECTION	CATEGORY

LOW LEVEL
 	
HIGH LEVEL
	1. *Receiving.* (Paying attention.)
	  (a) Awareness.
	  (b) Willingness to receive.
	  (c) Controlled or selected attention.
	2. *Responding.* (Committed and actively attending.)
	  (a) Acquiescence in responding.
	  (b) Willingness to respond.
	  (c) Satisfaction in response.
	3. *Valuing.* (Concepts are seen to have worth.)
	  (a) Acceptance of a value.
	  (b) Preference for a value.
	  (c) Commitment (conviction).
	4. *Organization.* (Construction of a system of values.)
	  (a) Conceptualization of a value.
	  (b) Organization of a value system.
	5. *Characterization of a value complex.* (Acceptance of value system.)
	  (a) Generalized set.
	  (b) Characterization.

Fig. 5.4 Condensed version of the taxonomy of educational objectives in the affective domain (Reproduced with permission from Krathwold, D. R., Bloom, B. S., and Masia, B. B. (1964) *Taxonomy of Educational Objectives, Handbook II: Affective Domain.* New York: McKay)

university final examination that really concentrates on synthesis and evaluation. Once teachers and instructors, however, are appreciative of the value of using such a taxonomy when they plan their objectives and examinations, perhaps the overall quality of the work accomplished in the classroom and the examination room will improve. Since each class of objectives builds on all preceding classes, standards can be raised to a more desirable level by teaching and testing a student's ability to evaluate – because this also involves teaching and testing all the other classes of objectives.

The Characteristics of a Clear Objective

Once the character and the identity of an objective have been determined by task analysis and the use of Bloom's taxonomy, it is important that it should be written in a clear and precise fashion. There should be no room for any doubt about what an objective means or implies. Mager (1962) underlines this point when he writes that, 'An objective is an *intent* communicated by a statement describing a proposed change in the learner – a statement of what the learner is to be like when he has successfully completed a learning experience. It is a description of a pattern of behaviour (performance) we want the learner to be able to demonstrate.' In other words, an objective is a statement of performance and responsibility; a goal which it is fully intended to reach.

Teachers and instructors, of course, have always stressed the importance of stating aims, indeed every lesson plan begins with such a definition.

Unfortunately, the majority of such aims are formulated at such a high level of abstraction as to be almost completely useless. Statements such as 'to learn to appreciate good music,' 'to understand the principles of electronics,' 'to know how to use a slide rule' are so generalized, and require so many complex changes in the individual, that they have little or no utility when it comes to organizing learning experiences and evaluating procedures. Statements such as these are only useful for defining broad general responsibilities, and even then many aims which seem worth while turn out to be meaningless when subjected to the kind of analysis that we are making.

A great deal of the difficulty associated with such broad statements is a semantic one. What is meant or implied by the verb 'to understand,' and how will we determine whether a student 'understands'. What do we mean by 'the principles of electronics,' how many 'principles' are there, will we allow a student full marks if he states all the principles in one textbook, but omits those in another. Discussions such as these take on real meaning when it comes to planning a lesson, and become an embarrassment when evaluation becomes necessary.

If an objective is to communicate, ambiguity and vagueness must be avoided. Some words commonly used in writing objectives are vague and open to many interpretations; others are more precise and tell you what to expect. A list of such words is shown in Fig. 5.5. In order to ensure that communication does indeed take place, it is advisable to formulate the objective in terms that the learning experience is expected to produce. In other words, objectives should be stated in *action* terms. After all, if you consider that something is worth teaching, then time spent on writing a clear, comprehensive objective can only be worthwhile.

In selecting action verbs, it is necessary to ensure that the word selected is directly related to the objective that it is hoped to realize. If a student is asked to *précis* a statement, then the cognitive objective most likely to be involved, according to the Bloom taxonomy, is 'synthesize': similarly, if a student is asked to *relate* a list of phenomena, then the likely affective

WORDS OPEN TO MANY INTERPRETATIONS	WORDS OPEN TO FEWER INTERPRETATIONS
to know	to write
to understand	to recite
to *really understand*	to identify
to appreciate	to differentiate
to *fully appreciate*	to solve
to grasp the significance of	to construct
to enjoy	to list
to believe	to compare
to have faith in	to contrast

Fig. 5.5 Words commonly used in stating learning objectives (Reproduced with permission from Mager, R. F. (1962) *Preparing Objectives for Programmed Instruction*. San Francisco, California: Fearon)

objective is 'value'. Figures 5.6 and 5.7 indicate the relationship between action verbs and different domains and classes of objectives. The two classifications can either be used in writing objectives or in framing the appropriate test questions.

Once the problem of language is appreciated, only one further difficulty remains. In order to be useful, an objective – unlike an aim – should contain three types of information:
1. A statement of the performance or behaviour required.
2. A statement of the conditions under which mastery will be observed.
3. A description of the standards to be reached.
If any of these ingredients are missing, then interpretation difficulties are likely to be experienced, even though the missing information can sometimes be derived from context. In industrial training, a fourth type of information is often included, describing any precautions or safety procedures that might be necessary because of inherent dangers in the situation.

STATING THE BEHAVIOUR REQUIRED

In describing the behaviour that is required of a student when he demonstrates his mastery of the subject or the skill, it is important to identify, in very clear terms, exactly what he will do. This involves saying how he will recognize the cue or situation which will cause him to commence the action or behaviour, as well as how he will recognize that the action has been successfully accomplished. At the same time, he will need to know:
1. What has to be done.
2. What it has to be done to.
3. What he has to do it with.
In other words, the description should be written in such a way that a wide range of unskilled people, knowing the correct terminology and given unlimited time, could teach themselves, if they were unfortunate enough to be without the help and guidance of a teacher.

DEFINING THE CONDITIONS UNDER WHICH MASTERY WILL BE OBSERVED

A teacher or instructor usually has a very clear idea of the kind of conditions he wishes to impose on a student when he tests or examines him. Generally speaking, these conditions are dictated by the job itself and come from the task analysis; sometimes they are conditions that the teacher imposes on the task to make it more difficult or challenging, although this practice is not recommended. In any case, a student needs to be put in the picture. Despite this very obvious point, some teachers and examiners still ask students, who have been taught to use a slide rule, to describe in an essay how they would use a slide rule to help solve a given problem. There is, of course, a world of difference between using a slide rule and describing how you would use one; the behaviours involved are quite different, even if the student has the necessary narrative skills to write a clear description of a complex act.

CLASS	ASSOCIATED ACTION VERBS		
Receiving	listen attend prefer	accept receive perceive	be aware favour select
Responding	state answer complete	select list write	record develop derive
Value	accept recognize participate	increase develop attain	indicate decide influence
Organization	organize judge relate	find determine correlate	associate form select
Characterization	revise change face	accept judge develop	demonstrate identify decide

Fig. 5.6   Affective objectives and associated action verbs

CLASS	ASSOCIATED ACTION VERBS		
Knowledge	define state list name	write recall recognize label	underline select reproduce measure
Comprehension	identify justify select indicate	illustrate represent name formulate	explain judge contrast classify
Application	predict select assess explain	choose find show demonstrate	construct compute use perform
Analysis	analyse identify conclude differentiate	select separate compare contrast	justify resolve break down criticize
Synthesis	combine restate summarize précis	argue discuss organize derive	select relate generalize conclude
Evaluation	judge evaluate determine recognize	support defend attack criticize	identify avoid select choose

Fig. 5.7   Cognitive objectives and associated action verbs

Similarly, geography teachers who insist on their students bringing atlases to class, always seem to test without them. Students, who have been successfully solving simultaneous equations, sometimes find that in the end of course or term examination they are given either more difficult equations to solve or problems which require them to recognize a situation involving the use of a simultaneous equation. In far too few instances, have students had an opportunity to practise their skills under these wide ranges of conditions.

When we write objectives, therefore, we must state the range of conditions under which the student's mastery will be tested. This does not mean that every possible condition has to be included, but it does mean that any situation which could affect the student's performance must be clearly communicated to him. These will include conditions that:

1. *Restrict or broaden what the student has to do.* This might include information such as whether the student might be required to solve problems up to and including three decimal places, and whether he can or cannot use log tables, or whether only one particular proof will be accepted, etc.

2. *Restrict the task to limited or unlimited environmental conditions.* This might include such limitations as expecting the student to locate and identify a fault on a piece of equipment *in situ* without removing it to a workshop where better facilities would be available. It could also involve such considerations as to whether or not he could use reference materials and job aids, limited or unlimited tools and/or equipment.

DESCRIBING THE STANDARDS TO BE REACHED

Few teachers or instructors seem to have any real difficulty in deciding whether or not a student has reached an adequate level of performance, although they do appear to have some difficulty in stating what that level is or even implies. For this reason, a clear objective will always include a statement of the standards of accuracy expected of the student, as well as the speed with which he is expected to accomplish the task. Three pieces of information are important when it comes to defining or laying down standards of accuracy:

1. The percentage or number of problems the student must answer correctly.
2. The percentage of correct answers he must obtain.
3. The tolerances within which he must work.

Once these have been included in the objective, the student will know exactly what is expected of him.

Two Methods of Writing Objectives

There are many ways of writing objectives, but two schemes have been found to be especially helpful. One was developed by Dr Robert F. Mager (1962), whose main interests have been in the cognitive and affective areas; the other was developed by Dr Robert B. Miller (1962), whose main interests have been in the area of psychomotor skills. Although the two schemes have different backgrounds and histories, both were published in the same year, and both have many features in common.

MAGER-TYPE OBJECTIVES

Mager (1962) considers that a clear objective should be written in the following manner:

1. 'First, identify the terminal behaviour by name; we can specify the kind of behaviour which will be accepted as evidence that the learner has achieved the objective.

2. 'Second, try to further define the desired behaviour by describing the important conditions under which the behaviour will be expected to occur.

3. 'Third, specify the criteria of acceptable performance by describing how well the learner must perform to be considered acceptable.'

Although the three statements are not always necessary, it is a very good rule of thumb for beginners that they follow the layout exactly.

A typical Mager-type objective in the case of students learning network analysis would be:

The student will:

1. Construct a simple network containing up to ten events, from

2. a narrative describing the activities,

3. without error or job aids, and within a period of time not exceeding thirty minutes.

A set of objectives for a 7 hour training session with 24 adult students on the value of sensitivity training in education and industrial training is illustrated in Fig. 5.8.

COGNITIVE OBJECTIVES

By the end of the day, participants will be able to:
1. Describe what happens in a T group.
2. State the objectives of a T group.
3. List the advantages and disadvantages of the T group strategy in changing attitudes.
4. State the situations in which the T group method is likely to be an optimal learning strategy.
5. State what aspects of the T group method can be employed in conventional teaching.
6. State the nature and importance of feedback.
7. Recognize feedback when it is given.

AFFECTIVE OBJECTIVES

1. Be aware, by experience, of the nature of a T group.
2. Respond to the feelings of a T group situation.
3. Develop a sense of the value of the T group strategy in education and training.

Fig. 5.8 Learning objectives for a seven hour training session for 24 adult students. (The aim of the course was 'to introduce them to, and get them to value, the T group method as an educational and training strategy.)

Miller (1962) tackles the problem of writing objectives more from the point of view of skills analysis, and for him a clear objective should be preferably written in the following manner:

1. An indicator on which the activity-relevant indication appears.
2. The indication or cue which calls for a response.
3. The control object to be activated.
4. The activation or manipulation to be made.
5. The indication of response adequacy or feedback.

The level of detail used in writing such descriptions is about the same as would be used for writing a set of technical instructions useful to a novice. Indeed, Miller has pointed out that a clear objective written in the above manner could be used as a procedural manual for doing the job.

A typical Miller-type objective would be:

1. Given a car radiator.
2. Told to fill it with an appropriate quantity of antifreeze for a British winter, the student will:
3. Test the contents with a hydrometer,
4. Calculate the amount of antifreeze required for temperatures not below $-10°C$, using an appropriate antifreeze calculating chart.
5. To an accuracy of within $\frac{1}{8}$ of a pint.

A comparison of the Miller and the Mager formats will show that they bear a marked resemblance; indeed, Mager sometimes prefers to follow the format now associated with Miller. However, the layout and the greater detail of the Miller-type objective does have a number of advantages for objectives in the psychomotor domain.

Conclusion

Stating objectives in performance terms, indicating the range of conditions under which performance is expected, and then defining acceptable levels of student performance, are important steps in educational methodology. Neither teacher nor student are left in any doubt as to what is expected of them recalling Whitehead's (1959) insistence that education should turn out people who *know* something well and can do something well. Such an approach enables us to: organize and explain the learning phenomena in a small number of precise statements; test these statements against actual experience; predict behaviour; appraise the soundness of decisions while they are still being made; and help teachers and students to analyse their experience and so improve their performance. In this way, teachers and students are able to view evaluation as an integral part of the total learning system, rather than as an irrelevant chore to be accomplished as quickly as possible and then forgotten.

However, it would be foolish to imagine that by simply defining one's objectives there will necessarily be an overall improvement in the quality of education and training. Clearly defined objectives derived from a bad syllabus will undoubtedly improve the overall quality of teaching; they will also result in teaching material which should not be taught at all. For this reason, task analysis and the writing of learning objectives must be considered as complementary rather than competing activities.

Posttest 5

ANSWER ALL QUESTIONS

1. Distinguish between an 'aim' and an 'objective'.

2. State four reasons for specifying objectives.

3. State the difference between 'cognitive', 'affective', and 'psychomotor' objectives.

4. List four ways in which Bloom's taxonomy can be useful to a teacher or instructor.

5. State, with examples, what kinds of words should be avoided, and what kinds of words should be used when writing clear behavioural objectives.

6. List, and write short notes upon, the three types of information essential to a clear, behavioural objective.

7. Write a clear, behavioural objective, using either the Mager or the Miller system, for a subject with which you are acquainted.

References

AUSUBEL, D. P. (1967) A cognitive-structure theory of school learning. In L. Siegel, ed. *Instruction: Some Contemporary Viewpoints*. San Francisco, California: Chandler.

BLOOM, B. S. (1956) *Taxonomy of Educational Objectives, Handbook 1: Cognitive Domain*. New York: McKay.

BLOOM, B. S. (1963) Testing cognitive ability and achievement. In N. L. Gage, *Handbook of Research on Teaching*. Chicago, Illinois: Rand McNally.

DRUCKER, P. (1954) *Practice of Management*. New York: Harper.

GAGNE, R. M. (1962) Military training and principles of learning, *American Psychologist*, 17, 2, 83–91.

GILBERT, T. F. (1962) Mathetics: the technology of education, *Journal of Mathetics*, 1, 1, 7–73.

KRATHWOHL, D. R., BLOOM, B. S., and MASIA B. B. (1964) *Taxonomy of Educational Objectives, Handbook II: Affective Domain*. New York: McKay.

MAGER, R. F. (1962) Preparing objectives for programmed instruction. San Francisco, California: Fearon.

MAGER, R. F. and BEACH, K. M. (1967) *Developing Vocational Instruction*. San Francisco, California: Fearon.

MILLER, R. B. (1962) Task description and analysis. In R. M. Gagne, ed., *Psychological Principles in System Development*. New York: Holt, Rinehart and Winston, 353–80.

SIMPSON, E. J. (1969) *Psychomotor Domain: a Tentative Classification*. Urbana, Illinois: University of Illinois (unpublished paper).

SMITH, R. G. (1964) *The Development of Training Objectives*. Washington, DC: The George Washington University, Human Resources Research Office.

WHITEHEAD, A. N. (1959) *The Aims of Education*. New York: Macmillan.

SECTION TWO
Organizing

People in a group undertaking will always find work to do. The important requirement is that they perform work that will contribute to objectives, and not the work they happen to want to do.

Louis A. Allen

The organizing function of the teacher-manager

Organizing is the work a teacher does to arrange and relate learning resources, so as to realize agreed learning objectives in the most effective, efficient, and economical way possible.

When a teacher-manager organizes, he attempts to:

1. Select an appropriate teaching tactic.

2. Select appropriate audiovisual learning aids.

3. Select an appropriate class size.

4. Select an appropriate strategy for communicating complex rules, procedures, and instructions.

In this way, the teacher-manager is able to create the optimal learning environment for realizing the objectives of the education or training programme which he has planned. This organization of learning resources is not an end in itself, but a tool to aid not dictate what has to be accomplished.

6 Selecting an appropriate teaching tactic

Learning Objectives

COGNITIVE OBJECTIVES

After carefully reading this chapter, you will be able to:

1. Distinguish between teaching strategies and teaching tactics.

2. List the five classes of learning structure, and draw their characteristic matrix patterns.

3. Distinguish between the five learning structures in terms of their prerequisites.

4. State the appropriate teaching tactic for each learning structure.

5. Distinguish between the five learning structures, in terms of the importance of practice and their resistance to forgetting.

6. Relate different classes of learning objective to appropriate classes of learning structure.

7. Explain why transfer of training can occur in some situations and not in others.

AFFECTIVE OBJECTIVES

After reading this chapter, the author intends that you will:

1. Be aware of, and value, the importance of relating teaching tactics to the structure of the task.

2. Incorporate this principle into your organization of managerial strategies, so that it becomes characteristic of your teaching style.

> Any idea or problem or body of knowledge can be presented in a
> form simple enough so that any particular learner can understand
> it in a recognizable form.
>
> *Jerome S. Bruner*

The purpose of teaching is to bring about a desired change in the learner's
behaviour. In other words, teaching should make a student different, in
terms of what he can do or accomplish. This change is normally brought
about by the teacher or instructor employing a teaching strategy so as to
accomplish his objectives. Indeed, all too often there has been a tendency to
view the problem of instruction as simply one of deriving *one* overall teaching
method, leavened occasionally, if there is time, with audiovisual aids, in
order to increase the impressiveness of the presentation.

Unfortunately, teaching is not quite that simple, and different tasks call for
different methods and techniques. Their selection, moreover, is not merely a
matter for the whim of the teacher. It is also dependent on the nature of the
task (as revealed by the task analysis), the nature of the learning objectives
that are to be realized, and the ability, aptitude, preknowledge, and age of
the students. While educational technology is not yet able to do more than to
suggest the difference between a successful learning experience and an unsuccessful one, research is now sufficiently well advanced to generate a set of
principles that suggest optimal teaching methods and techniques.

TEACHING STRATEGIES AND TECHNIQUES

The task analysis and the learning objectives constitute a prescription for
learning; they prescribe, in effect, what has to be accomplished. In order to
bring these changes about, teachers have two ways or methods of proceed-
ing:

1. *Teaching strategies*. These involved broad methods of instruction, and
they will be considered in a later chapter. There is, for instance, a lecture
strategy, a tutorial strategy, a lesson strategy, a case study strategy, etc.
Regardless of the variety available to the teacher, they can be regarded as a
broad way of operating or manoeuvring.

2. *Teaching tactics*. These involve more detailed aspects of instruction than
strategies; indeed, the same tactic can occur in every teaching strategy. For
instance, a teacher may decide to use a lecture strategy to teach Ohm's law.
In order to do this he will need, as we have seen in chapter 3, to teach his
students:

(a) Twenty-nine rules.

(b) Five concepts.

(c) One principle.

Each one of these three requirements will necessitate a different teaching
tactic, although all three tactics will be imbedded in the same teaching

strategy. If instead of a lecture the teacher decides to use a seminar strategy, the tactics will still be broadly similar.

This distinction between teaching strategies and teaching tactics is an important one; indeed, the difference between good teaching and indifferent teaching may be more a function of tactics than it is of teaching strategies or teacher personality. Furthermore, there is reason to believe that students who have an appreciation of teaching tactics can successfully employ them themselves, so as to improve the overall quality of their own learning experience.

The Importance of Structure

Tasks vary in a number of important ways, and one of the purposes of task analysis is to expose their component parts and reveal their basic ordering. These structural characteristics are of great importance to both teaching and learning, for they can be used as criteria with which the optimal teaching tactic can be chosen. Structure, in fact, is a primary factor in most, if not all, human learning, and teachers and instructors have a clear responsibility to ensure that students realize their objectives by capitalizing on the structural characteristics of the task. Indeed, the essence of good teaching, and the basis of modern curricula reform, is to present the learner with a useful organization, rather than to teach the subject as a collection of isolated facts, ideas, and techniques.

Once the importance of the underlying structure of the task is appreciated, teaching and learning are greatly simplified for the subject can be presented as an organized body of knowledge. This structural approach has considerable advantages:

1. *It enables a teacher to:*
   (a) Select appropriate teaching tactics, depending on the classes of structure involved in the task.
   (b) Demonstrate the relationship between different classes of learning objective and different classes of structure.
   (c) Increase his student's depth of understanding by using the innate structure of the task as a vehicle for presenting facts and incorporating additional facts into the students' repertoire.
   (d) Present the information in such a way that it is more likely to be remembered.
2. *It enables a student to:*
   (a) Select appropriate learning tactics, depending on the classes of structure involved in the task.
   (b) Perceive the relationship between different classes of learning objective and different classes of structure.
   (c) Increase his depth of understanding by using the innate structure of the task as a vehicle for learning facts and incorporating additional facts into his repertoire.

(d)   Remember the information once it has been learnt.

Such a structural approach to learning and teaching has particular merit. As Bruner (1965; 1966) has pointed out, it confers the ability to simplify the presentation of information, generate new propositions, and increase the actual manipulability of the material involved. It must be remembered, however, that the optimal structure of a body of knowledge is not absolute but relative, and must be constantly related to the needs of the student and the objectives to be realized.

Types of Learning Structure

Every task, by very definition, must possess a unique structure or organization. However, five basic classes of learning structure are recognizable as being useful and meaningful to the teacher and learner:

1.   Signal structures.
2.   Chain structures.
3.   Multiple-discrimination structures.
4.   Concept structures.
5.   Principle structures.

These five learning structures are defined in Fig. 6.1, where examples of each are also given. Some authors, like Gilbert (1962) and Mechner (1965), recognize only three of these structures (chains, multiple-discriminations, and concepts), arguing that signals are, in fact, simple chains and that principles are a special case of concepts. Others, like Gagne (1965a), who has written probably the most detailed and authoritative account of learning structures, recognize eight 'conditions'. Not all of these, however, are structural in form.

RECOGNIZING LEARNING STRUCTURES

A detailed examination of the task analysis will reveal both the number and the character of the learning structures involved in the task. In looking at the rules, task elements, or acts, answering the following questions will often help a teacher or instructor to isolate and identify the classes of learning structure involved:

1.   What major patterns or clusters of task elements are discernible?
2.   Where does each pattern begin and where does each pattern end?
3.   How are the patterns alike and how are the patterns different?
4.   What name, title, or keyword can be given to each pattern, so as best to describe or summarize its contents?

An examination of the Ohm's law rule set, shown in Fig. 3.3, page 42, where each of the structures is identified and named, will help the reader to practise the skill involved in recognizing learning structures.

LEARNING STRUCTURE	DEFINITION	EXAMPLES	PREREQUISITES
Signal	A signal involves a specific response to a specific stimulus.	Learning definitions in science. Warning light in a car dashboard.	—
Chain	A chain involves a fixed sequence of verbal or motor responses.	Carrying out cockpit checks in a VC 10. Setting up a lathe or tying a shoelace.	Each of the links or signals making up the chain must already have been acquired by the student.
Multiple-discrimination	A multiple-discrimination involves distinguishing one category of phenomena from another.	Distinguishing between latitude and longitude. Distinguishing between different waveforms on an oscilloscope.	Each of the chains or signals making up the set to be discriminated between must already have been acquired by the student.
Concept	A concept involves making a generalization about a whole class of related phenomena.	Classifying or making generalizations about objects or events, e.g., resistence, evil, loyalty.	Each of the chains or signals making up the class or set to be generalized about must already have been acquired by the student.
Principle	A principle involves a chain of concepts.	Fundamental truths or laws, e.g., Joule's law, theory of conservation of energy.	Each of the concepts making up the principle must already have been acquired by the student.

Figure 6.1 Classes of Learning Structure: Definitions, Examples, and Prerequisites.

Perhaps one of the best ways of appreciating what is meant by signals, chains, multiple-discriminations, concepts, and principles is to be able to visualize them. One way of doing this is to employ the well-known technique of matrix analysis developed by Thomas, Davies, Openshaw, and Bird (1963). This involves determining whether any significant relationships exist between the rules in the rule set, and recording the nature of these relationships on a matrix. In order to do this, rule numbers are written in serial order along the diagonal line of squares on a sheet of graph paper, beginning at the top left-hand corner and finishing at the bottom righthand corner of the matrix. For reference purposes this diagonal is referred to as the 'definition line'.

Each rule is then compared with every other rule, in order to determine whether any relationship exists between them. For instance, rule 1 is compared with rule 2; rule 1 with rule 3; rule 1 with rule 4, and so on, to the end of the rule set. If a relationship is found to exist between two rules, this is recorded on the matrix by shading the appropriate cell according to a predetermined key. A relationship, for instance, between rule 1 and rule 2 is shown in the top diagram of Fig. 6.2. Since the relationship that exists between rule 1 and rule 2 must obviously also exist between rule 2 and rule 1, it is plotted twice on the matrix – once above the definition line and once below it.

In deciding whether there is a relationship between two rules, it is important to realize that the relationship must be an *immediate* one. We are not interested in relationships through other rules. Furthermore, the aim is not to record as many relationships as possible, but only those that are intellectually necessary for the task. This means that the number and the character of the relationships recorded on the matrix can, and will, vary depending on the nature of the learning objectives that have been set.

Broadly speaking, two relationships are of interest, and these will be shaded differently on the matrix. These are:
1. *Relationships of association*. A relationship of association exists when two rules have some element or identity in common. For example:
   Rule 1. Copper expands when heated.
   Rule 2. Iron expands when heated.
Both these rules are related by association, since they set up the idea that 'metals expand when heated'.
2. *Relationships of discrimination*. A relationship of discrimination exists when two rules have an important difference or point of revealing contrast. In any relationship of discrimination, there must always be, by very definition, a relationship of association, but it is the dissimilarity that forms the essential teaching or learning point. For example:
   Rule 1. Metals expand when heated.
   Rule 2. Metals contract when cooled.
Both these rules are associated, since both rules are concerned with the effect

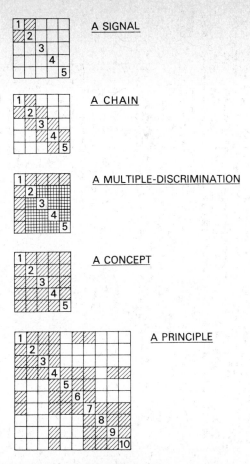

Fig. 6.2 Characteristic matrix patterns

of heat on metals. However, the essential learning point is the contrast or discrimination between the two statements.

Generally speaking, there will be many more relationships of association than relationships of discrimination. Although both are important, discriminations play a very critical role in the learning process. Indeed, emphasizing the discriminations involved in the task can often shorten the amount of time necessary to learn it. For instance, the colour code for resistors can be written as a programme for individual learning. If the task is taught as a series of signals, something like one hundred frames are necessary; if the task is presented as a series of discriminations, the same task can be accomplished in four frames!

As the presence or absence of relationships are established, so they should be entered on the matrix. Figure 6.2 shows the idealized, but characteristic, matrix patterns for each of the five classes of learning structure.

1. *Signals.* These involve a single relationship of association between two rules. In other words, rule 1 is related to rule 2, and rule 2 is related to rule 1. Each rule, therefore, is a signal or stimulus for the other.

2. *Chains.* These involve a string of relationships of association between a number of neighbouring rules. In other words, rule 1 is related to rule 2, rule 2 is related to rule 3, rule 3 is related to rule 4, and so on, to the end of the chain. Rule 1, however, is *not* related to rules 3, 4, or 5, and neither is rule 2 related to rules 4 or 5.

3. *Multiple-discriminations.* These involve a solid block of relationships, in the sense that every rule is related to every other rule in the block. However:

    (a)   The first rule is related to every other rule by association.

    (b)   All other rules are related to each other by discrimination.

The first line of associations is necessary in order to tie all the discriminations into one block.

4. *Concepts.* These involve a solid block of relationships similar to that for multiple-discriminations. However, in this case, *all* the relationships are associative in character.

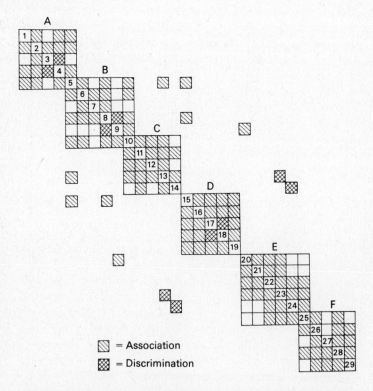

Fig. 6.3   **Matrix for Ohm's law (Concept A + Concept B + Concept C + Concept D + Concept E = Principle F of Ohm's law.**

5. *Principles.* These involve two or more concept blocks, which are joined or related by:

(a) Overlapping concept blocks. For instance, in the Ohm's law rule set, concept A overlaps concept B, in the sense that they have rule 5 in common. Or,

(b) Outrider relationships. For instance, concept B is related to concept C, for rule 5 is related by association to rule 13.

In practice, of course, learning structures are not so clearly discernible as in Fig. 6.2, but they are, nevertheless, easily recognizable. The more loose and amorphous they become, however, the more difficult they will be to learn and remember. Figure 6.3 illustrates the matrix patterns for the Ohm's law rule set.

Structure and Tactics

Each of the five classes of learning structure will vary in terms of their prerequisites and properties, and each of them will require a different teaching and learning tactic. Fig. 6.4 summarizes the relationships between structures and tactics; it also indicates the relative amounts of practice necessary for their acquisition, as well as the resistance of each structure to forgetting. Each structure will now be studied in turn, so that the hierarchical nature of the classification can be appreciated.

SIGNAL LEARNING

Signal learning, or 'stimulus response learning' as it is sometimes called, represents the most elementary and basic class of learning structure. It is acquired as a result of conditioning, and involves the student making a specific response to a specific stimulus, e.g.:

Question   What is the value of π?
Answer $3\frac{1}{7}$

Learning definitions in science, or a new vocabulary in a foreign language, are common examples of signal learning.

Teaching or learning signals involves a relatively simple tactic, providing the student is willing to put in the necessary amount of time and effort. Basically, the teaching-learning tactic involves:

1. *Establishing contiguity.* The student must be given the necessary stimulus and caused to respond immediately – initially by reading off the response or by having the response prompted. This will establish the necessary contiguity (or close proximity) between the stimulus and response.

2. *Constant practice and rehearsal.* The signal must be constantly practised and rehearsed, so as to establish the necessary link or bond between stimulus and response. As the practice continues, prompts and cues should be gradually withdrawn or 'vanished', so that the student is left to stand more and more on his own feet.

STRUCTURE	TEACHING TACTIC	RESISTANCE TO FORGETTING	EFFECT OF PRACTICE*
Signal	1. Give student the stimulus and cause him to respond. 2. Reinforce him for correct responses (ignore incorrect ones). 3. Gradually shape his responses towards mastery via a series of successive approximations. 4. Continuously practise responses.	Marked resistance	Very important
Chain	1. Give student a bird's eye view of the chain. 2. Establish chain by beginning at the beginning and work forwards, or begin with the last act and work backwards. Chain can also be established by rote. 3. Practise chain to smooth out the rough spots.	Motor chains: marked resistance. Verbal chains: little resistance.	Important
Multiple-discriminations	1. Make all stimuli and responses as distinctive as possible. Mediation can help. 2. Present all conditions (signals or chains) to be discriminated between at once. 3. Force student to discover discrimination. Begin with easiest discrimination, and move to more subtle ones. 4. Rehearse discriminations to overcome interference.	Little resistance.	Little importance.
Concept	1. Make all stimuli and responses as distinctive as possible. 2. Present all conditions (signals or chains) to be generalized about at once. 3. Force student to generalize or classify the conditions. 4. Cause student to discriminate between the concepts with which it might be confused.	Marked resistance.	Little importance.
Principle	1. Give student a bird's eye view of the principle. 2. Establish chain by beginning at the beginning and work forwards, or begin with last concept and work backwards. Lead him to make a verbal statement of the principle. 3. Practise chain to smooth out rough spots.	Marked resistance.	Important.

* Assume learning under ideal conditions with all prerequisites fulfilled.

Fig. 6.4 Classes of learning structure: teaching tactics

3. *Reinforcing the correct responses.* Students should be rewarded or reinforced for correct responses; incorrect responses should be ignored. Wherever possible, situations likely to cause error should be avoided, since repetition and rehearsal of error can lead to learning the wrong signals.

Constant rehearsal and practice of signals can be very boring to the learner, and teachers, therefore, have a particular responsibility to make the task as satisfying and reinforcing as possible. They should also explain why the signals need to be acquired; if the task can be shown to have face validity, then the student is more likely to invest the required effort.

One particularly important characteristic of signal learning is its great resistance to forgetting. Although there is inevitably some loss of knowledge after an interval of time, signals are surprisingly resistant to extinction, providing some form of reinforcement is still occasionally given (Ferster and Skinner, 1957).

CHAIN LEARNING

The chaining of behaviour is a particularly common class of learning. Sometimes the chain will consist of a sequence of verbal actions, like reciting a poem; on other occasions, the chain will consist of a sequence of motor actions, like riding a bicycle. However, regardless of the variety of chain involved, the structure is still basically the same. A chain, in essence, consists of a rigid sequence of two or more previously learned signals, which must be carried out in a predetermined order. Before the chain can be learnt, however, each of the constituent signals must already be known to the student. If this essential prerequisite is not fulfilled, learning difficulties are likely to ensue.

Teaching or learning chains involve establishing contiguity between the successive links. This can be accomplished by using one of three tactics:

1. *Progressive-chaining.* The chain can be acquired progressively, starting with the first signal, then the second, and so on, to the end of the chain.

2. *Rote learning.* The chain can be learnt by rote, using worked examples or mnemonics as examples.

3. *Retrogressive chaining.* The chain can be acquired backwards, starting with the last act and then moving retrogressively through the sequence to the beginning of the chain.

It is difficult, at the present time, to indicate which of the three tactics is most effective, for the experimental evidence is too conflicting. However, there is a suggestion that retrogressive chaining is faster and more effective for learning complex chains (Lewis, Horabin, and Gane, 1967).

The retrogressive tactic has a reinforcement advantage over the other two methods. The end product of the chain, at every stage of the learning process, is the final act of mastery. Furthermore, each act is self-completing, so that revision and consolidation problems are kept to a minimum, while the novelty of working backwards can be a very powerful motivating force.

Regardless of whether a retrogressive or a progressive tactic is employed, the student should not be expected to perform at mastery level immediately he starts to learn the chain. Instead, his behaviour should be gradually shaped towards mastery via a series of successive approximations. For instance, a child's behaviour is gradually shaped by his parents when they teach him to ride a bicycle. At first, they support him, then, he is taught to ride the bicycle with outriders, and, gradually, these are adjusted until they give less and less support as his confidence and skill increase.

Practice and repetition are always a problem when it comes to learning and remembering a chain. Theoretically, practice should be unnecessary, for, if all the prerequisites for the chain have been fulfilled, the chain should form itself on the very first occasion. Unfortunately, this rarely happens, and so some repetition and practice are necessary, if only to iron out the rough spots in the chain. Forgetting can be something of a problem with chains; while motor chains seem to be retained fairly easily over long periods of times, verbal chains are easily forgotten, if interference takes place or the chain is broken.

MULTIPLE-DISCRIMINATION LEARNING

Acquiring multiple-discriminations is a matter of some considerable importance in education and training, and it is surprising, therefore, that so many learners should be left to discover them for themselves. A multiple-discrimination involves distinguishing one category of phenomena from another, and typical examples involve distinguishing between latitude and longitude, morse code signals, and different waveforms displayed on an oscilloscope. However, before multiple-discriminations can be learnt, each of the signals or chains making up the set to be discriminated between must already be in the student's repertoire of behaviour.

The natural tendency is to teach each of the conditions (signals or chains) involved in the multiple-discrimination separately. For example, latitude is taught step by step, and then longitude. Inevitably, this results in waste of time and effort, and, even more seriously, it will often result in the student being unable to make the necessary discrimination.

Teaching or learning multiple-discriminations involves a straightforward tactic:

1. *Distinctive conditions.* One of the main difficulties with multiple-discriminations is that stimuli and their associated responses can often become confused. Acquiring one association can interfere with the acquisition of the remainder. Accordingly, both stimuli and responses must be made as distinctive as possible. One way of doing this is to use mediators or linking prompts between each stimulus and response. In the case of the resistor colour code, brown and one can be made more distinctive by using the mediation of 'one brown *penny*'.

2. *Simultaneous presentation.* All the conditions should be presented

together, in the same moment of time. This forces the necessary discriminations to occur, beginning with the easiest, and gradually moving to more and more subtle instances.

As with signals and chains, correct discriminations must be confirmed, and, as far as possible, teachers must ensure that errors are made as unlikely as the circumstances permit.

Practice appears to play a different and more limited part in learning multiple-discriminations, than it does in signal or chain learning. It does not appear to strengthen discriminations once they have been acquired, although it can be used to widen the range of the discriminations involved in the task. It is of some interest to note, however, that it does not appear to matter whether the multiple-discriminations were easy or difficult to learn; once they have been acquired, they are remembered about equally well (Underwood, 1953). Unfortunately, multiple-discriminations appear to be highly subject to forgetting, although spaced practice can help to prevent extinction from occurring.

CONCEPT LEARNING

Concept learning involves the student making a generalization about a whole class of phenomena that may differ from each other in outward appearance. For instance, oranges, lemons, limes, and grapefruit are outwardly different in appearance, but the common response 'citrus fruit' identifies the concept. In making responses that classify or generalize phenomena, the student has to respond to the stimuli in abstracted properties like colour, shape, number, position, size, etc. A student deals with concepts when he is concerned about such generalizations as evil, magnetism, leadership, and morale.

Concepts, of course, can be acquired by trial and error, as can any of the other classes of learning structure. However, this is not a particularly effective tactic, unless the teacher's aim is to set up conditions for discovery learning – with unlimited time available for its accomplishment. Otherwise, the first step is to ensure that the prerequisites for concept formation have been fulfilled; in other words, the student must have already acquired the conditions (signals and chains) making up the class of phenomena that is to be generalized about. It is also necessary to define limits to the variability that will be tolerated, before a condition will be classified as *outside* the concept or generalization.

Learning concepts is not necessarily a verbal matter, although making it one can often make learning relatively easier. The tactic for teaching or learning a concept involves two processes, for the student must:
1. *Generalize within the class*. The student should be presented with a set of related, but different, stimuli, to each of which he makes the same response. For example, shown triangles, squares, circles, and rectangles, the student could be expected to respond 'geometrical figures'.
2. *Discriminate between classes*. Once the generalization has been acquired,

the student must learn to discriminate between the concept and all other concepts with which it is likely to become confused. The concept of electromotive force is often confused with the concept of potential difference. So, once both concepts have been acquired, the student must learn to discriminate between them, i.e., between the two concepts, and between instances of the two concepts. In other words, acquiring a concept involves learning how to make the same classifying response to all conditions falling within the class, but different classifying responses to all conditions falling outside the class. Once the concept has been acquired, students should be required to identify more and more subtle instances of the generalization until the learning objectives have been achieved.

Recent research (Davies, 1967) has demonstrated that repetition, rehearsal, and practice contribute little or nothing to either the acquisition of a concept or its retention. For this reason, they should be kept to an absolute minimum. If a concept has not been acquired as a result of one teaching procedure, repetition of that procedure is unlikely to help. The teacher or instructor is advised to change his approach, and to tackle the problem from another direction. Repeating the procedure will only waste time, energy, and student goodwill.

PRINCIPLE LEARNING

Principles, in simple terms, consist of a chain of two or more concepts. An example of a very elementary principle is the simple proposition that 'metals expand when heated'. Here the three concepts of 'metal', 'heat', and 'expand' are chained together in a precise and predetermined way. However, the chain linking each concept is rather different to the chain we studied earlier:
1. In a principle, the chain actually represents the *relationship* between the concepts.
2. In a chain-learning structure, the chain represents the bonds or links between each of the acts.
Insight, in very limited terms, can be regarded as a matter of suddenly acquiring a knowledge of the relationships between a group of concepts.

Obviously, the primary prerequisite to the learning of a principle is the existence of the necessary concepts in the student's repertoire. Once these are present, the tactic for learning a principle involves:
1. *Recalling the concepts.* The learner should be required to recall the concepts making up the principle, and, if necessary, these should be made as distinctive as possible.
2. *Chaining the concepts.* Once the concepts have been recalled they should be chained together (retrogressively or progressively) in the same way as signals are chained together. Verbal statements or cues can be used to help the student if necessary.
Once the principle has been acquired, it is often a good idea to get the student to state the principle in his own words, and to require him to give examples

of the principle at work. Great care needs to be taken to ensure that conceptual chains, rather than verbal chains, have been acquired. We all know the driver who can recite the Highway Code, but who never seems to be able to put its principles into practice.

Few principles are learnt in isolation, for organized knowledge, in effect, represents a whole hierarchy of principles defining each topic. Some principles like 'metals expand when heated' are relatively simple and elementary, others like the second law of thermodynamics are much more complex. However, the learning tactic involved is broadly the same. Repetition and practice have not been shown to be important conditions for learning principles, other than for smoothing out some of the rough spots. For this reason, practice should be kept to the very minimum, so as to prevent boredom and frustation from setting in. Learning principles can be a very exciting affair, and the tactics that teachers and instructors employ should make the acquisition of principles as rewarding a learning experience as possible. Fortunately, once principles have been learnt they show a marked resistance to forgetting.

Tactics for Teaching Ohm's Law

Let us take an actual teaching example. We have seen that Ohm's law is a principle made up of a chain of five concepts. In order to teach this topic, the following tactics could be employed:

1. *Establish the signals.* Students must learn the 29 rules as a set of signals. An appropriate tactic would be to ask a series of questions (e.g., How is an electric charge produced? What is the basic unit of charge? etc.). The student can either discover the answers for himself from books, etc., or he can have been previously supplied with the rule set. The important point is to rehearse and practise the rules until they have been completely learnt.

2. *Establish the concepts.* Once the signals have been acquired, the student can begin learning the concepts. These should be presented one by one, if possible in some non-verbal form. The student should then be required to make a generalization about the rules making up the concept set, and relate this generalization to the broad view he has been given. Finally, he should be required to discriminate between the concepts with which it might become confused, e.g., between potential difference and electromotive force.

3. *Establish the principle.* When all the concepts have been acquired, they must be chained together so as to establish the principle. This can be done by presenting the concepts retrogressively, and getting the student to derive the principle for himself. Finally, he should give examples of the principle.

Since only a verbal knowledge of Ohm's law will have been gained, it is essential that the student should finally verify the relationships between current, resistance, and potential difference in the laboratory for himself.

It does not matter whether the teacher aims to use a lecture or a lesson strategy to teach the principle of Ohm's law, the tactics should broadly follow the sequence set out above. Indeed, the users of a programmed book, a conventional textbook, or even a film, would be well advised to establish the signals, to establish the concepts, and, then, to establish the principle.

Learning Structures and Learning Objectives

Although learning structures are clearly discernible in the task analysis, they can also be identified from the wording of the learning objectives. Every objective, by very definition, must be specific in terms of its actual content, but the form of the objective will reveal the class of learning structure involved. For instance, action verbs, like 'state', suggest a signal or verbal chain while 'distinguish between' implies that a multiple-discrimination is required. Figure 6.5 relates the five classes of learning structure to five classes of learning objective.

TRANSFER OF TRAINING

In education and training, there has always been the hope that students would transfer or apply what they have learnt in one situation to more novel situations with which they are unfamiliar. Research on this problem of transfer of training, however, has not yielded any clear-cut results; indeed, many of the findings have been contradictory.

An examination of Fig. 6.5 suggests a possible explanation. It will be seen that objectives can be allocated to one of two categories:

1. *Specific objectives.* These objectives are particularly precise, and involve the production of specific responses to specific stimuli. Indeed, the objectives

	LEARNING STRUCTURE	ASSOCIATED LEARNING OBJECTIVE
TRANSFER PRECLUDED	*Signal*	Given a specific stimulus, the learner will make, as directed, one of the following responses: 1. A copy of that stimulus. 2. A specific response which identifies that stimulus.
	Chain	Given a specific stimulus, the learner will make a pre-determined sequence of responses.
	Multiple-discrimination	Given two or more potentially confusable stimuli, the learner will make an equal number of responses which distinguish between the stimuli.
TRANSFER INCLUDED	*Concept*	Given two or more different stimuli, the learner will make a response which identifies the class and distinguishes it from other classes.
	Principle	Given two or more stimuli classifiable as concepts, with instructions to produce the principle, the learner will perform the required combination.

Fig. 6.5 Learning structure and associated learning objectives

actually preclude the possibility of transfer taking place. Objectives falling into this category involve signals, chains, and multiple-discriminations.

2. *General objectives.* These objectives are more broadly stated, and are concerned with the ability to classify and generalize. Indeed, they actively encourage the possibility of transfer. Objectives falling into this category involve concepts and principles.

In other words, the simpler classes of learning structure are the antithesis of transfer, while the two higher and more complex classes actually require transfer to take place for their successful accomplishment.

Conclusion

There has been a natural tendency in the past to believe that all learning is basically the same (see Thorndike, 1931). Accordingly, the teacher's task was seen to be a relatively simple one, and involved finding one, overall, successful teaching strategy. The foregoing discussion, however, has attempted to establish the principle that different classes of learning require different learning tactics, as well as different kinds of strategies. Once this is appreciated, the problem of selecting an optimal teaching and learning tactic can be made against the basic criterion of the learning structure or objective to be realized.

Such a view looks upon teaching from a new direction. The teacher is seen as a manager of learning tactics and strategies, tasked with restructuring the student's cognitive behaviour. In the past, the importance of cognitive restructuring has been generally underestimated, partly because of a tendency to focus undue attention on such situational factors as question-technique, blackboard work and class activity. The present approach, which emphasizes the structural properties of the task, offers something of a model against which important decisions can be made.

Posttest 6

ANSWER ALL QUESTIONS

1. Distinguish between 'teaching strategies' and 'teaching tactics'.

2. List the five classes of learning structure, and draw their characteristic matrix patterns.

3. Distinguish between the five learning structures in terms of their prerequisites.

4. State the appropriate teaching tactic for each learning structure.

5. Distinguish between the five learning structures in terms of:
   (a) the importance of practice, and
   (b) their resistance to forgetting.

6. Relate the different classes of learning objective to appropriate classes of learning structure.

7. Explain why transfer of training can occur in some situations and not in others.

References and Reading List

BELBIN, R. M. (1965) *Training Methods*. Paris: OECD.

BRUNER, J. S. (1965) *The Process of Education*. Cambridge, Massachusetts: Harvard University Press.

BRUNER, J. S. (1966) *Toward A Theory of Instruction*. Cambridge, Massachusetts: Harvard University Press.

BRUNER, J. S., GOODNOW, J. J., and AUSTIN, G. A. (1956) *A Study of Thinking*. New York: John Wiley.

DAVIES, I. K. (1965) The analytical and synthetic stages of program writing, *Programmed Learning: the Journal of the Association for Programmed Learning and Educational Technology*, 2, 2, 76–87.

DAVIES, I. K. (1967) *Mathetics: an experimental study of the relationship between ability and practice in the acquisition of basic concepts in science*. Research Branch Report No. 224. Brampton, Huntingdon: HQ RAF Technical Training Command.

DAVIES, I. K. (1969) Structure and strategy – instructional decision-making, *Royal Air Force Education Bulletin*, 6, 48–56.

FERSTER, C. B. and SKINNER, B. F. (1957) *Schedules of Reinforcement*. New York: Appleton-Century-Crofts.

GAGNE, R. M. (1963) Learning and proficiency in mathematics, *Mathematics Teacher*, 1, 144–53.

GAGNE, R. M. (1965a) *The Conditions of Learning*. New York: Holt, Rinehart and Winston.

GAGNE, R. M. (1965b) The analysis of instructional objectives for the design of instruction. In R. Glaser, ed., *Teaching Machines and Programmed Learning, II*. Washington, DC : National Education Association, 21–65.

GAGNE, R. M. and Bassler, O. C. (1963) Study of Retention of Some topics in Elementary Non-Metric Geometry, *Journal of Educational Psychology*, 54, 123–31.

GARNER, W. R. (1962) *Uncertainty and Structure as Psychological Concepts*. New York: John Wiley.

GILBERT, T. F. (1962) Mathetics: The Technology of Education, *The Journal of Mathetics*, 1, 1, 7–73; 1, 2, 7–56.

GOODNOW, J. J. (1955) Determinants of Choice Distribution in Two Choice Situations, *American Journal of Psychology*, 68, 106–16.

HARTLEY, J. and WOODS, P. M. (1968) Learning poetry backwards, *Journal of the National Society for Programmed Instruction*, 7, 10, 9–15.

HILGARD, E. R. and Bower, O. (1968) *Theories of Learning*. New York: Appleton-Century-Crofts.

LEAVITT, H. J. and SCHOLSBERG, H. (1944) The retention of verbal and motor skills, *Journal of Experimental Psychology*, 3, 404–17.

LEWIS, B. N., HORABIN, I. S., and GANE, C. P. (1967) *Case Studies in the Use of Algorithms*. Oxford: Pergamon.

MECHNER, F. (1965) Science education and behavioural technology. In R. Glaser, ed., *Teaching Machines and Programmed Learning. II.* Washington, DC: National Education Association, 441–507.

SHRIVER, E. L. (1960) *Determining Training Requirements for Electronic System Maintenance.* Alexandria, Virginia: HUMRRO Technical Report.

THOMAS, C. A., DAVIES, I. K., OPENSHAW, D., and BIRD, J. (1963) *Programmed Learning in Perspective: A Guide to Program Writing.* Chicago, Illinois: Educational Methods Inc.

THORNDIKE, E. L. (1931) *Human Learning.* New York: Appleton-Century-Croft.

UNDERWOOD, B. J. (1953) Studies of distributed practice. *Journal of experimental psychology*, 45, 133–259.

7 Selecting appropriate audiovisual learning aids

Learning Objectives

COGNITIVE OBJECTIVES

After carefully reading this chapter, you will be able to:

1. Distinguish between realism and task theories.

2. Distinguish between optional and essential AV materials.

3. List the properties of AV materials.

4. Distinguish between criterion and mediating media, in terms of both learning and teaching processes.

5. List the three broad generalizations that can be drawn from a review of the whole field of AV research.

6. Write short notes on the research findings dealing with: audio aids; simple visual aids; 3D aids; films and television; simulators and language laboratories; visits and field excursions.

7. State the two criteria against which AV materials can be selected.

8. Draw a table, or use words, to state the conditions under which the use of varying types of AV aids are likely to be optimal.

9. Select appropriate AV materials so as to enable a student to achieve mastery.

AFFECTIVE OBJECTIVES

After reading this chapter, the author intends that you will:

1. Be aware of, and value, the importance of selecting AV learning aids in terms of the objectives to be realized and the structural characteristics of the task.

2. Incorporate this principle into your organization of managerial styles, so that it becomes characteristic of your teaching style.

> Throughout the ages the problem has always been how to get communication out of information. *Peter F. Drucker.*

Teachers are faced with such a burgeoning mass of audiovisual materials that it is often difficult to select those items that are most likely to help them in their task. However, once the learning objectives and the subject matter structures have been carefully isolated and identified, teachers are in a much better position to select those AV materials that are most likely to help their students reach the required levels of mastery. Audiovisual aids are, after all, aids to learning, and unless they actively help promote behavioural change their utilization, to say the very least, is questionable. Readers who wish to study the actual creation and use of educational media are referred to two beautifully presented texts: one by James Brown and his colleagues (1969) and the other by Ed. Minor and Harvey Frye (1970)

REALISM AND TASK THEORIES

In the past, discussions on audiovisual aids have tended to be dominated by what Dwyer (1967) calls 'realism theories'. This approach carries the basic assumption that complete learning can only come from employing those AV materials that approximate most closely to reality. In other words, in selecting aids, real objects are preferable to pictures, pictures are preferable to detailed drawings, and detailed drawings are preferable to simple line drawings or sketches. The more qualities AV materials share with reality, the easier learning will be (Miller *et al.*, 1957). Accordingly, there has been a tendency for teachers to fill all the available communication channels with as much information as it is possible to insert into the media, whilst still maintaining clarity of presentation.

Research, as we shall see, questions this underlying assumption. It suggests that a more powerful learning approach is to relate the qualities of the audiovisual materials to the demands of the task. As Bruner and his colleagues (1956), and more lately as Travers and his associates (1964), have pointed out, realism is no guarantee that useful information will be perceived, learned and remembered. This means that in some situations a simple line drawing may be infinitely more preferable to the real object or a field excursion. The underlying assumptions of such a task theory are that reality may be too demanding, and that the best criterion for selecting appropriate AV materials is the task itself.

OPTIONAL AND ESSENTIAL AV MEDIA

At this point, it is important to distinguish between two broad categories of audiovisual materials or media, both of which require different types of decision from the teacher or instructor:

1. *Optional or enrichment media.* These can be selected by a teacher as a

matter of personal whim – providing there is sufficient time and finance available.

2. *Necessary or obligatory media.* These should be used by teachers so as to help them realize the learning objectives of the task. Time and finance ought to be made available for them.

This chapter is not concerned with optional or enrichment materials; these are matters for individual teachers to decide as a matter of personal preference. Decisions involving necessary or obligatory media, on the other hand, are more critical, and require a considerable amount of professional experience and expertise. In order to realize the full potentialities of such materials, however, it is necessary to consider the properties possessed by audiovisual materials themselves.

The Purposes and Use of AV Media

It is unfortunate that audiovisual materials are so often referred to as 'teaching aids'. As we have seen, the only real justification for their use is that they actively help students to realize their learning objectives. On some occasions, however, so called 'aids' can actually become hindrances, if not barriers, to learning, for they can get between a student and his objectives. This is a problem of planning and organization, of course, but the real issue is that audiovisual materials should only be employed when effective use can be made of their distinctive properties.

PROPERTIES OF AV MATERIALS

A useful rule of thumb to apply when decisions have to be made is to ask the question, 'How will this aid be *used* so as to capitalize on its distinctive attributes?' Generally speaking, audiovisual materials have five properties:
1. The ability to help promote perception.
2. The ability to help promote understanding.
3. The ability to help promote transfer of training.
4. The ability to provide reinforcement or knowledge of results.
5. The ability to help retention.

Not all media, of course, possess these properties to the same extent. Nevertheless, these are the attributes that a teacher must capitalize upon, otherwise the materials will lose their *raison d'être* in the learning process.

CRITERION AND MEDIATING MEDIA

While all audiovisual aids are, by very definition, aids to learning, they can accomplish this in a number of ways. From the point of view of classroom utilization, however, AV materials can best be classified into two broad classes on the basis of function, (see Gropper, 1966):

1. *Criterion media.* These consist of audiovisual aids, like pictures, maps, and real objects, which a student will be required to describe, reconstruct,

interpret, or identify, in order to demonstrate that he has achieved mastery. In other words, these media are part of the criterion, and they will be shown as such in the statement of learning objectives: e.g. 'The student will draw a diagram to illustrate the relationship between . . . .'

2. *Mediating media.* These consist of audiovisual aids, which are *not* part of the criterion situation. In other words, students will not be required to describe, reconstruct, interpret, or identify them. Their sole function is to help students to gain an insight into, or a knowledge of, some phenomena or event. Once learning has taken place, the aid should be forgotten or 'vanished' as quickly as possible. Graphs are a case in point. Students are unlikely to be expected to describe a graph illustrating the decline in a country's economic position, but they could be expected to describe the actual decline. The graph, in such a situation, is a means to an end.

This distinction between criterion and mediating media is an important one. While criterion media facilitate learning by enabling a student to *practise* a skill, mediating media help him to *acquire* that skill. This means that the two media must be presented and used differently. Mediating media, for instance, must be gradually removed or vanished as learning takes place, so that the student is left with fewer and fewer props or supports. Criterion media, on the other hand, must be constantly practised and rehearsed so that they are not forgotten. How all this can best be accomplished is suggested by reviewing the research literature.

A Review of the Research Literature

Audiovisual aids have probably one of the largest collections of research literature in the whole field of education and training. Unfortunately, the data are complex, often they are highly specific to particular situations, and sometimes the findings seem to be conflicting and contradictory. Individual studies are rarely meaningful by themselves, and it is often more pertinent to review the whole literature and try to perceive overall trends in the data and findings. The generalizations that result can then be used as a basis for making decisions, and these must be, by their very nature, rather more significant than decisions based solely on personal bias or unevaluated value judgements.

In reviewing the field of audiovisual aids, three broad generalizations can be drawn:

1. Students do learn from AV materials.

2. The amount they learn depends upon the appropriateness of the AV aid to the learning objectives and the structural properties of the task.

3. Learning from AV aids can be directly and appreciably enhanced by teachers in the following ways.

    (a) Introducing the materials and stating the objectives to be realized by them.

(b)   Obtaining student participation, particularly with more able students. (There is a faint suggestion in the literature that low IQ students retain significantly more if they learn without actively responding to AV aids like films and television).

(c)   Employing attention calling devices like arrows and pointers; questions and discussion; assignments and projects.

(d)   Repeating student exposure to the materials.

These findings are particularly important for they mean that audiovisual materials are worth using, and that they are also worth using well. Furthermore, since the amount actually learnt depends on the learning objectives involved and the structural properties of the task, these two factors, as we shall see, would seem to provide a useful criterion against which media decisions can be made by the teacher manager.

AUDIO-AIDS

Radios, record-players, and tape-recorders are rapidly becoming as commonplace in the classroom as they are in everyday life. They are inexpensive to buy, easy to use, and – except for radios – remarkably flexible. Tape-recorders have the additional advantage that recordings can be made by teachers without any special skills or equipment; they can also be purchased from commercial sources. The advent of the casette tape-recorder is likely to have a profound effect on classroom practice. Indeed, a number of children's schools already have vast libraries of teacher produced five-minute lecturettes for use in project work and individual assignments.

Sound presentations, however, which rely on only one of the five senses, do have a number of drawbacks from the learning point of view. As long ago as 1894, Munsterberg observed that presentations involving only the sense of hearing were inferior to presentations involving both sight and sound. Some years ago, Day and Beach (1950) reviewed 50 years of research literature, comparing visual and auditory presentations, and also concluded that combined sensory presentations led to greater comprehension than either auditory or visual presentations by themselves. A more recent study by Hinz (1969) reemphasized the relative inefficiency of the auditory approach, and concluded that the visual mode also had a stronger transfer effect. The research literature also contains a suggestion that less able students may experience more learning difficulties from sound presentations than their more able colleagues, but this finding still needs to be confirmed.

It is surprising that, while a great deal of research effort has been invested in comparisons of auditory and visual modes, so few comparisons have been carried out between direct lecturing and recorded lectures by the same teacher. One study (Popham, 1962), using graduate and undergraduate students, was unable to find any discernible differences in achievement and retention between the two presentation modes. This finding has since been confirmed by Menne and his colleagues (1969), who have additionally highlighted the freedom and flexibility that taped lectures can give to both teachers and students.

Unfortunately, it is still too early to do more than draw provisional generalizations about situations in which auditory learning aids are likely to be optimal. Almost all the work that has been carried out in this regard is of a descriptive nature, and few adequately controlled experiments seem to have been carried out. Nevertheless, a number of trends are discernible in the research literature. Audio learning aids seem to be optimal in signal, chain, and multiple-discrimination tasks which involve skills in language and music. They have also been shown to be useful for learning diagnostic skills involving sounds and sound-patterns. It is unlikely that learning tasks involving concepts and principles will be helped to any great extent by the use of these same aids, but their relative cheapness and flexibility may necessitate their use, particularly with more able students.

SIMPLE VISUAL AIDS

Simple visual aids, like pictures, diagrams, and graphical representations, are standard aids to learning; the aids are used either in the form of pictures and wallcharts or as slides, filmstrips, and overhead projector transparancies*. Like audio aids, they are inexpensive, often simple to use, and, above all, clear and impressive in their presentation. Unfortunately, little research has been carried out into their relative effectiveness, although there is a large body of evidence available to show that people do learn from them. Such a result is really not surprising, for pictures have traditionally been worth a thousand words. The teacher's difficulty, however, lies not in being convinced that simple aids work, but in deciding when visual rather than audio aids are optimal and when pictures should be used rather than diagrams.

There is a tendency to think that learning proceeds from the concrete to the abstract, and for this reason pictures are generally believed to be optimal for young children and more abstract diagrams and graphs for older, more educated people. This view has a great deal to commend it, but research has shown that it is a gross oversimplification. Modern perception theory is sufficiently well advanced to support the view that perception, at least in part, is learnt. Arnheim, for instance, does not view perception as a mechanical recording of stimulus material. Perception for him is 'a grasping of structural features', which enable students to generalize so as derive concepts and principles (see Norberg, 1962).

While teachers will accept that visual presentations are generally preferable to purely verbal ones, many teachers use simple visuals to consolidate what

* One important variable that is often overlooked is the size of the screen. However, Ter Louw (1961), in an informal investigation, suggests that when a large projection screen, rather than a small projection screen, is employed for showing slides, students spend *more* time viewing the picture and are better able to answer questions on the picture details and relationships.

they have already taught. Research by Gropper (1966) suggests that conceptual learning is significantly greater and quicker when pictorial presentations precede verbal or printed ones. These findings underline the power of visual materials in the learning process, and reemphasize their advantage over words in tasks involving conceptual learning.

Despite the preference that many teachers have for pictures over other simple visual aids, the evidence is not too favourably disposed towards them. Black (1962) found that simple line drawings were more effective than pictures for learning visual discriminations, mainly because the pictures contained too much detail. However, pictures can be used to teach visual discriminations, provided they contain a large number of relevant cues and a small number of irrelevant ones. Vernon (1953) found that pictures, while they were less thorough and led to a less objective grasp of argument than illustrated printed texts, were successful in arousing emotions and strong attitudes towards the subject.

An impressive study has been carried out by Dwyer (1967) who compared oral presentations involving simple line drawings, detailed shaded drawings, realistic photographs, and oral presentations containing no visual aids at all. He found that realistic photographs were the least effective media of all, regardless of the objective to be realized. On the other hand, his results demonstrated the following:
1. Simple line drawings were optimal for promoting total student understanding of the concepts involved, the location, structure, and position of parts, and for promoting transfer or the ability to identify and locate parts on a 3D model.
2. Verbal presentations, without visuals, were optimal for learning the names of parts and for developing new views and organizations.
While the detailed line drawings were not as effective as the simple line drawings, they were more effective than pictures and verbal presentations for tasks involving the acquisition of concepts, multiple-discriminations and transfer. Similar results have been reported by Swanson, Lumsdaine, and Aukes (1956), who found that the effectiveness of simple visual aids depended upon the objectives to be realized.

In some ways, overhead projector transparencies can be considered apart from other simple visuals. One transparency can be superimposed on another, while animation or movement is also possible. One study by Chance (1960) compared the use of a blackboard and overhead projector in teaching engineering drawing, and significant differences were found in favour of transparencies. Demonstration time was reduced by as much as 20 per cent (thereby allowing more time for questions, discussion, and practical work, or for reducing the amount of instruction necessary). Similar, but not quite so considerable, time-savings have been reported from studies dealing with other subjects. Other studies have demonstrated the positive effects that can come from using animated rather than static transparencies, and from teachers using the same drawing equipment as students rather than the awkward and less accurate blackboard equipment. The most important advantage of overhead projector transparencies, however, is the ability to teach multiple-discriminations by means of overlays.

One other variable which has been shown to be important is the actual ability of the students involved in the task. Vernon (1952) reports that more able children are better able to cope with abstract visuals like graphs, whereas less able students require some assistance in the form of explanations and supporting textual material. The same investigator also reports that there is no evidence that graphs (which are preferable for trends) and numerical charts (which are better at communicating factual data) help to teach material that would 'otherwise be beyond the comprehension of the reader'. Concrete illustrations, like simple pictures, have also been found to be more effective with lower ability students, whereas high ability students seem to be able to profit equally well from either abstract or concrete visual aids (Leith, 1968).

While a great deal more research still needs to be carried out, a review of the research literature does reveal a number of trends. Generally speaking, signals, multiple-discriminations, concepts, and principles are best presented by means of simple line drawings. Although realistic photographs can also realize this task, they are best reserved for realizing affective objectives. On the other hand, less able students prefer more concrete visual aids, while able students can cope equally as well with abstract as with concrete visuals.

THREE-DIMENSIONAL MODELS

Three-dimensional models are usually the show pieces of most audiovisual aid exhibitions, where they normally attract a great deal of interest and attention. They include such visual aids as mock-ups, cutaways, and enlarged versions of real objects, like slide rules and micrometers. Usually they are beautifully made, but cumbersome and unwieldly to use. Furthermore, they are often extremely expensive to manufacture or purchase.

Little research evidence is available as to their effectiveness, for no more than around a dozen studies seem to have been carried out. One well known investigation by Swanson (1954) examined the effectiveness of a wide range of visual aids (mock-ups, diagrams, and realistic pictorial charts) depicting the same equipment, destined for use as part of a lecture presentation. No significant differences were obtained, and Swanson concluded that the advantages of three-dimensional models were small in relation to their high cost. A later study by Swanson, Lumsdaine, and Aukes (1956) found that mock-ups were only superior to symbolic diagrams on a test involving recognition of parts. Large models, however, may be useful for teaching the actual manipulation of such equipment as micrometers, verniers, calculators, and slide rules.

A review of the research dealing with three-dimensional models was carried out by Allen (1960), who concluded that the advantages of such visual aids are small in relation to their overall cost. A further review of the research findings suggests that three-dimensional models may be useful in the learning of signal tasks and chains. However, the cost of the equipment may well outweigh even these two advantages.

FILMS AND TELEVISION

To a very large extent, films and television can be regarded as substantially identical media, although the two forms of presentation tend to be used rather differently. Television, on the whole, tends to be used either as an alternative to live teaching or as a means of allowing students to observe themselves or others at work. On the other hand, films are used for a much wider range of situations, although there is still a tendency to restrict them to dramatic or theatrical presentations, field trips or travelogues, and demonstrations of particular phenomena. Films are still largely regarded by instructors and teachers as optional entertainment, to be used if there is time; television, on the other hand, is seen to be more useful from the educational or training viewpoint.

Several studies have been carried out comparing live lectures with televised or videotaped lectures, and in most cases the results have shown no significant differences between the two presentations. However, one of the major objections to television has come from the lack of opportunity for students to interact with the teacher. In situations where this has been made possible through the use of two-way communication systems, the results have been no better than with conventional one-way televised lessons. Students, though, seem to prefer the two-way communication system (Carpenter and Greenhill, 1958).

One particularly interesting study (Taylor *et al.*, 1969) has examined the possibility of televising both lecture content and student-teacher interaction. The results of the investigation suggest that there are no differences between the two conditions. However, the most effective situation for low ability students was found to be a combination of televised interaction and live interaction, and this was found to be more effective than either live interaction alone or televised interaction alone. This rather surprising result was also obtained by Carner (1962), working with elementary pupils learning to read.

The importance of student-teacher interaction has also been demonstrated by Gropper (1967), using televised lessons to teach high school physics. His work suggests that, while lesser goals may be realized with the conventional type of television lesson, higher goals may be realized if the televised lessons contain situations which cause students to actively respond to the programme. There is no reason why students should be shown, or told, everything in a real or televised lesson; they can also be made to predict the outcome of a particular incident, and their prediction can then be confirmed by seeing the actual outcome on the screen. Interestingly enough, Gropper (1963) also found that science demonstrations performed by children were more effective in stimulating children of the same age, than the same demonstrations performed by their own teacher.

In an incisive review of 50 years research carried out on learning from films, Hoban (1960) concluded that students do learn from motion pictures, and that most studies do not reveal reliable differences between instruction by films and instruction by conventional methods. Furthermore, retention of material learned by film is as good as when the same material is learned under conventional methods of instruction. Comparative studies that pit films against other media are rare, but film appears to be no better and no worse than television and sometimes even slides and filmstrips. However, film research does highlight once more the importance of proper task analysis, if the learning objectives are to be realized.

Many film theorists have asserted that the unique formal property of film is motion, and that such movement is, of itself, capable of producing a response in students. Furthermore, it is frequently believed that this response to motion is affective or emotional in character. Although a number of research studies have been carried out into this phenomena, little evidence has been found for any of these assertions. Miller (1969), using galvanic skin responses to measure affective activity, found that motion film was no more emotionally arousing than filmographs (still frames on motion picture film), although students preferred motion pictures.

Studies have also been carried out involving the effectiveness of animation techniques, often considered one of the great advantages of moving film. Most of the investigations indicate that animation can materially aid learning by directing student attention to relevant cues (Lumsdaine et al., 1961). However, an earlier study by Lumsdaine and Gladstone (1958) suggests that fancy embellishments, intended to stimulate interest, are actually less effective than a simple straightforward presentation. Later studies suggest that a crude, pencil sketch version of a film on elementary science may be as effective, in terms of learning, as a polished colour version of the same film costing ten times as much to make. More recent work by Kanner (1968) adds to this point, by suggesting that colour, whether on TV or film, does not confer a learning advantage over black and white, providing appropriate verbal cues are provided whenever necessary. The aesthetic effects of colour, of course, were not considered in this study. This study by Kanner also underlines the importance of the film commentary, which Laner (1955) has also demonstrated. Vernon (1952) reminds us that it may be more effective to show still pictures and diagrams with a good commentary, than to show film with an inferior one.

Finally, two studies of moving film have indicated the importance of the film medium for training in psychomotor skills. Wendt and Butts (1962) have demonstrated the effectiveness of 8 mm film loops, shown again and again, for teaching physical skills. On the other hand, the use of 'implosion' techniques, whereby different parts of a component jump into place in their proper sequence, has been shown to be particularly apt for teaching assembly skills (Sheffield, Margolius, and Hoehn, 1961).

While film and television research has an enormous literature, the only definite and unambiguous finding appears to be that students do learn from being exposed to them. Not surprisingly, it would also appear that moving film and television are likely to be superior at imparting information involving action and activity, but inferior in imparting information about objects or phenomena. For the most part, films and television are optimal for teaching concepts and principles, as well as for realizing affective objectives. The overall effectiveness of film and television in these areas can also be markedly increased by teachers properly introducing the film, and then showing all or part of the film more than once.

SIMULATORS AND LANGUAGE LABORATORIES

Simulators of one kind or another have been increasingly used by industry and the armed forces over the last 30 years, usually because of the high cost or the dangers or difficulties involved in training personnel on the real equipment. In general, a simulator is designed to represent a real situation, to provide a student with controls over that situation, and to vary conditions during training, so that the task can be made progressively more difficult. As Gagne (1965) points out, it is not necessarily the equipment itself that is simulated, only the operations or tasks that have to be accomplished.

In the past, there has been a tendency to associate simulation with training in psychomotor skills, but, today, many other types of simulation are employed. Among the most popular of these are role-playing, business games, 'in-basket' exercises, and, to a certain extent, case studies. Regardless of the form used, they all entail students following procedures or making decisions similar to those they would be expected to make in a real job situation. The use of such simulation has been found to be especially effective in those areas where the task analysis indicates that there may be learning difficulties; this is particularly the case in chain and multiple-discrimination tasks. However, the biggest problem with simulation exists in integrating simulation experience with more conservative classroom activities. Indeed, this has been at the root of one of the major criticisms of business games (McKenney, 1962).

A special type of simulation is to be found in the language laboratory. During the last 10 years, there has been a remarkable boom in the interest expressed in foreign language skills, and this has resulted in the installation of large numbers of language laboratories. The evidence would seem to suggest that this rather expensive simulator is most useful for '... sequential, cumulative and carefully recycled development of language skills, each small skill building deliberately on the preceding steps ... [It is] weakest when it is used only as an adjunct to the grammar translation type of program'. (Mathieu, 1962).

However, Carroll (1963), in reviewing the research on language teaching,

119

concluded that next to nothing was known concerning the relative effectiveness of the procedures employed in language laboratories. These conclusions seem largely true today. Some valid comparisons have been carried out between conventional methods and language laboratory teaching (e.g., Antioch, 1960), but no significant differences in achievement have been reported for either treatment. Student attitudes, though, are always more favourable to the laboratory situation and teacher-time is saved. Molstad (1964) cites a study by Lorge which does favour language laboratories. He found that high school students studying French were significantly superior in fluency and intonation to students who had not been taught in a laboratory. Finally, one interesting report by Pickrel, Neidt and Gibson (1958) suggests that non-linguists, using specially prepared tapes produced by a language specialist, can teach conversational Spanish as well as the specialist whose material they are using.

It would seem, therefore, that simulators and simulation can be useful in teaching signals, chains, and multiple-discriminations. At the same time, simulation can also help realize affective objectives. Students readily see the relevance of what they are learning, and can practise the skills involved until they reach a level of adequacy. However, the most important advantage of simulators and simulation is to be found in the immediate knowledge that a student gets of the consequences of each one of his actions.

VISITS AND FIELD EXCURSIONS

Visits and field excursions, on the basis that they *are* reality, properly occupy a prominent position in many educational and training programmes. Unfortunately, they are usually expensive to make, and consume large amounts of time in travelling. In view of their importance to the programme and these associated difficulties, it is surprising that there has been so little research on their validity and effectiveness.

Generally speaking, of the dozen or so comparative studies available (see Allen, 1960), about half of them are favourable and about half unfavourable. In some of the studies, films, filmstrips, and slide illustrated lectures seem to be just as effective, and certainly considerably cheaper. Looking at the literature as a whole, however, three trends are just discernible. It would seem that visits and field excursions are useful in realizing both cognitive and particularly affective objectives. They can also be usefully employed for teaching chains, concepts, and principles, and have been found especially so for summarizing and consolidating material initially presented by more normal methods.

Choosing Appropriate AV Aids

Once the role of audiovisual materials is fully appreciated, the problems associated with their selection are somewhat simplified. However, the choice is still a difficult one. As we have seen, there are a large number of aids to choose from, there are many new ideas about methods of instruction to influence the selection, and there seems to be a general lack of agreement among teachers and instructors concerning the relative effectiveness of the materials. Despite these difficulties, the foregoing discussion of the research literature has revealed a number of principles which can be used as a basis for decision-making. In this way, many of the problems and anxieties that teachers and instructors experience, as well as the complexities of some of the new aids, can be partly abated.

It is still too early to do more than suggest a criterion for decision-making, but the foregoing discussion suggests that two yardsticks are available:
1. The nature of the learning objectives to be realized.
2. The structural properties of the task.
These two criteria, used together, appear to yield a key to the selection process.

LEARNING OBJECTIVES AND AV MATERIALS

The major trends we have discerned in the research literature are summarized in Fig. 7.1. It will be seen that, depending on the actual specific circumstances, of course, the following generalizations can be made:

AUDIOVISUAL AIDS	CLASSES OF LEARNING OBJECTIVES		
	COGNITIVE	AFFECTIVE	PSYCHOMOTOR
Radios / Record-players / Tape-recorders	▓	▓	▓
Line drawings / Still pictures / Transparencies	▓	▓	
Mock-ups / Cutaways / Large models	▓		▓
Films / Television / 8mm Concept films	▓		
Simulators / Language laboratories	▓	▓	▓
Visits	▓		▓

Fig. 7.1 Objectives for which the use of varying types of audiovisual aids are likely to be optimal

1. Cognitive objectives can be realized by all A-V materials.
2. Affective objectives are best realized by audio aids; pictures, films, and television; simulators and language laboratories.

3. Psychomotor objectives are best realized by audio aids; large models of of reality; simulators and language laboratories; field excursions and visits.

TASK STRUCTURES AND AV MATERIALS

Figure 7.2, which is complementary to Fig. 7.1, summarizes the major generalizations that can be drawn concerning the conditions under which the use of varying types of audiovisual aids are likely to be optimal. Three major trends are discernible:

1. Signals and chains can be realized by most AV materials: radios, films, and television are *not* optimal for signal learning tasks.

AUDIOVISUAL AIDS	TYPES OF LEARNING STRUCTURE				
	SIGNALS	CHAINS	MULTIPLE-DISCRIMIN-ATIONS	CONCEPTS	PRINCIPLES
Radios Record-players, Tape-recorders,	X	X	X		
Line drawings Still pictures Transparencies	X		X	X	X
Mock-ups Cutaways Large models	X				
Films Television 8mm Concept films		X		X	X
Simulators Language laboratories	X	X	X		
Visits		X		X	X

Fig. 7.2 Conditions under which the use of varying types of audiovisual aid are likely to be optimal

2. Multiple-discriminations can best be realized by audio aids, simple visual aids, simulators and language laboratories.

3. Concepts and principles can best be realized by simple visual aids, films and television, visits and field excursions.

Conclusion

The literature dealing with audiovisual aids has been largely unhelpful to the practical teacher forced to make decisions about the relative effectiveness of particular aids. To a very large extent, the literature has been either anecdotal in character or far removed from the realities of the classroom. However, a number of principles are available in the research data, which can be used as a basis for decision-making, once the outmoded idea that audiovisual materials should be as realistic as possible has been abandoned. More meaningful criteria for the selection of AV aids would seem to be the nature of the learning objectives to be realized and the structural properties of the task.

Posttest 7

ANSWER ALL QUESTIONS

1. Distinguish between 'realism theories' and 'task theories'.

2. Distinguish between 'optional or enrichment media' and 'necessary or obligatory media'.

3. List the five properties of audio-visual materials.

4. Distinguish between 'criterion media' and 'mediating media', in terms of both teaching and learning processes.

5. List the three broad generalizations that can be drawn from a review of the whole of the field of AV research.

6. Write short notes on the research findings dealing with:
   (a) audio aids
   (b) simple visual aids
   (c) 3-D aids
   (d) films and television
   (e) simulators and language laboratories
   (f) visits and field excursions.

7. State the two criteria against which audio-visual materials can be selected.

8. Draw a table, or use words, to state the conditions under which the use of varying classes of AV aids are likely to be optimal.

9. Choose a subject, carry out a task analysis, identify the training need, write the learning objectives, recognize the learning structures involved, and select appropriate AV materials so as to enable the students to achieve mastery.

References and Reading List

ALLEN, W. H. (1960) Audio-visual communication research. In C. W. Harris, ed., *Encyclopedia of Educational Research*. New York: Macmillan, 115–37.

ANTIOCH COLLEGE (1960) *Experiment in French Language Instruction*. Second Report, 1959–1960. Yellow Springs, Ohio: Antioch Press.

BLACK, H. B. (1962) *Improving the Programming of Complex Pictorial Materials: Discrimination Learning as Affected by Prior Exposure to and Relevance of the Figural Discriminanda*. Bloomington, Indiana: University of Indiana School of Education Memorandum, June 1962, 111–12.

BRIGGS, L. J., CAMPEAU, P. L., GAGNE, R. M., and MAY, M. A. (1967) *Instructional Media: A Procedure for the Design of Multi-Media Instruction, A Critical Review of Research, and Suggestions for Future Research*. Pittsburgh, Pennsylvania: American Institute of Research.

BROWN, J. W., LEWIS, R. B., and HARCLEROAD, F. F. (1969) *AV Instruction: Media and Methods*. New York: McGraw-Hill.

BROWN, J. W. and THORNTON, J. W. (1963) *New Media in Higher Education.* Washington, DC: National Education Association.

BRUNER, J. S., GOODNOW, J. J., and AUSTIN, G. A. (1956) *A Study of Thinking.* New York: John Wiley.

CARNER, R. L. (1962) *An Evaluation of Teaching Reading to Elementary Pupils Through Closed-Circuit Television.* Dissertation Abstracts 23, 160–1.

CARPENTER, C. R. and GREENHILL, L. P. (1958) An investigation of closed-circuit television for teaching university courses. In *Instructional Television Research Project No.* 2. University Park: Pennsylvania State University.

CARROLL, J. B. (1963) Research on teaching foreign languages. In N. L. Gage, ed., *Handbook of Research on Teaching.* Chicago: Rand McNally, 1060–1100.

CHANCE, C. W. (1960) The overhead projector and the teaching of engineering drawing. Abstracted in *A-V Communication Review.* 9, 4, A17–A18.

COGSWELL, J. F. (1952) *Effects of a Stereoscopic Sound Motion Picture on the Learning of a Perceptual-Motor Task.* Pittsburgh: Pennsylvania State University. Instructional Film Research Program.

DALE, E. (1964) *Audio-Visual Methods in Teaching.* New York: Holt, Rheinhart and Winston.

DAVIES, I. K. (1971) Presentation strategies in programmed learning. In J. Hartley, ed., *Programmed Learning and Educational Technology.* London: Iliffe.

DAY, W. F. and BEACH, B. R. (1950) *A Survey of the Research Literature Comparing Visual and Auditory Presentation of Information.* Wright Patterson, AFB, Air National Command: US Air Force Technical Report No. 5921.

DWYER, F. M. (1967) Adapting visual illustrations for effective learning, *Harvard Educational Review,* 37, 2, 250–63.

DWYER, F. M. (1970) Exploratory studies in the effectiveness of visual illustrations, *A-V Communication Review,* 18, 3, 235–249.

GAGNE, R. M. (1965) Simulators. In R. Glaser, ed., *Training Research and Education.* New York: John Wiley.

GROPPER, G. L. (1963) Why is a picture worth a thousand words? *A-V Communication Review,* 11, 4, 75–95.

GROPPER, G. L. (1966) Learning from visuals: some behavioural considerations, *A-V Communication Review,* 14. 2, 75–85.

GROPPER, G. L. (1967) Does programmed television need active responding? *A-V Communication Review,* 15, 1, 5–22.

GROPPER, G. L. (1970) The design of stimulus materials in response orientated programs, *A-V Communication Review,* 18, 2, 129–159.

HINZ, M. (1969) Effect of response mode on learning efficiency, *A-V Communication Review,* 17, 1, 77–83.

HOBAN, C. F. (1960) The usable residue of educational film review. In W. Schramm, ed., *New Teaching Aids for the American Classroom,* Stanford: Institute for Communication Research, 95–115.

KANNER, J. H. (1968) *The Instructional Effectiveness of Colour Television.* Stanford, California: Stanford University, ERIC Clearinghouse of Educational Media and Technology.

LANER, S. (1955) Some factors influencing the effectiveness of an instructional film, *British Journal of Psychology,* 46, 280–292.

LEITH, G. O. M. (1968) Learning from abstract and concrete visual illustrations, *Visual Education,* January, 13–15.

LUMSDAINE, A. A. (1963) Instruments and media of instruction. In N. L. Gage, ed., *Handbook of Research on Teaching.* Chicago: Rand McNally, 583–682.

LUMSDAINE, A. A. and GLADSTONE, A. (1958) Overt practice and audiovisual embellishments. In M. A. and A. A. Lumsdaine, eds., *Learning from Films.* New Haven, Connecticut: Yale University Press, 58–71.

LUMSDAINE, A. A. and MAY, M. A. (1965) Mass communication and educational media, *Annual Review of Psychology*, 16, 475–534.

LUMSDAINE, A. A., SULZER, R. L., and KOPSTEIN, F. F. (1961) The effect of animation cues and repetition of examples on learning from an instructional Film. In A. A. Lumsdaine, ed., *Student Response in Programmed Instruction: A Symposium.* Washington, DC: National Academy of Sciences – National Research Council Publication No. 943.

MATHIEU, G. (1962) Language laboratories, *Review of Educational Research*, 32, 168–78.

McKENNEY, J. L. (1962) An evaluation of a business game in an MBA curriculum, *Journal of Business*, 35, 3, 278–86.

MENNE, J. W., HANNUM, T. E., KLINGENSMITH, J. E., and NORD, D. (1969) Use of taped lectures to replace class attendance, *A-V Communication Review*, 17, 1, 42–6.

MILLER, N. E., ed. (1957) Graphic communication and the crisis in education. *A-V Communication Review*, 5, 1–20.

MILLER, W. C. (1969) Film movement and affective response and the effect on learning one attitude formation. *A-V Communication Review*, 17, 2, 172–81.

MINOR, E., and FRYE, H. (1970) *Techniques for Producing Visual Instructional Materials.* New York: McGraw-Hill.

MOLSTAD, J. (1964) Summary of A-V research, *Audio-visual Instruction*, 9, 492–7.

MUNSTERBERG, H. and BIGHAM, J. (1894) Studies from the Harvard Psychological Laboratory. *Psychological Review*, 1, 34–8.

NORBERG, K. (1962) Perception theory and A-V education, *A-V Communication Review*, 10, 3–108.

PEARCE, G. L. (1970) Alternate versions of overhead transparency projectuals designed to teach elementary statistical concepts, *A-V Communication Review*, 18, 1, 65–71.

PICKREL, G., NEIDT, C., and GIBSON, R. (1958) Tape recordings are used to teach seventh grade students in Westside Junior-Senior High School, Omaha, Nebraska, *National Association of Secondary School Principals Bulletin*, 42, 81–93.

POPHAM, W. J. (1962) Tape recorded lectures in college classrooms, *A-V Communication Review*, 10, 2, 94–101.

POPHAM, W. J. (1969) Pictorial embellishments in a tape-slide instructional program. *A-V Communication Review*, 17, 1, 29–35.

POWELL, L. S. (1968) *Communication and Learning.* London: Pitman.

ROMISZOWSKI, A. J. (1968) *The Selection and Use of Teaching Aids.* London: Routledge, Kegan Paul.

SAETLER, P. (1968) *A history of instructional technology.* New York: McGraw-Hill.

SHEFFIELD, F. D., MARGOLIUS, G. J., and HOEHN, A. J. (1961) Experiments on perceptual mediation in the learning of organizable sequences. In A. A. Lumsdaine, ed., *Student response in Programmed Instruction: A Symposium.* Washington, DC: National Academy of Sciences – National Research Council, Publication No. 943.

SCHIVITZGEBEL, R. L. (1970) Multi-sensory educational tools. *Educational Technology*, 10, 8, 19–21.

SILVERMAN, R. E. (1958) The comparative effectiveness of animated and static transparencies. Abstracted in *A-V Communication Review*, 6, 3, 238–9.

SWANSON, R. A. (1954) *The Relative Effectiveness of Training Aids Designed for Use in Mobile Training Detachments.* Lackland Air Force Base, Texas: Air Force Personnel and Training Research Center, Research Review, AFPTRC–TR–54–1.

SWANSON, R. A., LUMSDAINE, A. A., and AUKES, L. E. (1956) Two studies in evaluation of maintenance training devices. In G. Finch and F. Cameron, eds., *Symposium on Air Force Human Engineering, Personnel and Training Research*. Washington, DC: National Academy of Sciences – National Research Council Publication No. 455.

TAYLOR, D. R., LIPSCOMB, E., and ROSEMIER, R. (1969) Live versus videotaped student-teacher interaction. *A-V Communication Review*, 17, 1, 47–51.

TER LOUW, A. (1961) Personal communication. See D. Perrin (1969), A theory of multiple-image communication. *A-V Communication Review*, 17, 4, 376.

TRAVERS, R. M., McCORMICK, M. C., VAN MONDFRANS, A. P., and WILLIAMS, F. E. (1964) *Research and Theory Related to Audio-visual Information Transmission*. Utoch: Bureau of Educational Research, University of Utah.

TRAVERS, R. M. and ALVARADO, V. (1970) The design of pictures for teaching children in elementary schools, *A-V Communication Review*, 18, 1, 47–64.

UNWIN, D., ed. (1969) *Media and Methods: Instructional Technology in Higher Education*. London: McGraw-Hill.

VERNON, M. D. (1952) The use and value of graphical methods of presenting quantitative data, *Occupational Psychology*, 46, 11–17.

VERNON, M. D. (1953) The Value of Pictorial Illustration, *British Journal of Educational Psychology*, 23, 29–37.

VERNON, M. D. (1962) *The psychology of perception*. London: University of London Press.

WENDT, P. R. and BUTTS, G. K. (1962) Audio-visual materials, *Review of Educational Research*, 32, 141–55.

WITTICH, W. A. and SCHULLER, C. F. (1968) *Audio-visual Materials. Their Nature and Use*. New York: McGraw-Hill.

8 Selecting an appropriate class size

Learning Objectives

COGNITIVE OBJECTIVES

After carefully reading this chapter, you will be able to:

1. State the two opposing points of view about optimal class size that have to be balanced or reconciled by teachers and administrators.

2. Draw a simple diagram or state the effects that class size can have in terms of group expectations, and in terms of the expectations of individual students making up that group.

3. Summarize the major research findings regarding optimal class sizes.

4. Discuss the problem of 'span of control' in relation to different sizes of learning group.

5. Summarize the major research findings regarding the effects of different seating patterns on a learning group.

6. State the effects that can result from increasing the size of a learning group.

7. Select an optimal class size for realizing a given set of learning objectives.

AFFECTIVE OBJECTIVES

After reading this chapter, the author intends that you will:

1. Be aware of, and value, the importance of relating the size of a class or learning group to the class of objectives to be realized.

2. Incorporate this principle, whenever possible, into your organization of managerial strategies, so that it becomes characteristic of your teaching style.

> 'As Galilee found to his cost, it is always difficult and can be dangerous to operate in a field where research results come into conflict with a system of beliefs.'
>
> *Joan Woodward*

The pressure on education and training resources is now acute, so that the problem of determining the optimum size for a class or learning group has become a pressing one. However, it is not an easy problem to resolve. So many factors enter into a learning situation, that it is difficult to isolate and identify the effects of this one variable. Furthermore, most discussions on class size seem to have largely concerned themselves with the 'optimum interrelation of syllabus, training patterns (intake size, duration, and frequency) and cell splits,' as well as teacher-manning requirements, equipment availability, programming difficulties, and the physical size of classrooms. No one would deny the importance of these variables, but it is rather surprising that so little regard seems to have been given to the learning needs of students and the nature of the objectives it is hoped to realize. Since these *are* important, optimum class size must necessarily be taken into account when a teacher or instructor is organizing his resources for learning.

Educational Practice

The general complaint of most teachers and instructors is that classes are too large, and many believe that an immediate improvement can be brought about in the quality of instruction by decreasing class size. On the other hand, administrators and financiers, conscious of the cost of education and training, tend to be concerned about the small size of many classes. They point out that both the cost and the pressure on resources could be immediately relieved by increasing the number of students allocated to each teacher and instructor. The problem for both the teacher and the administrator, accordingly, is to balance or reconcile these two very different points of view.

In practice, there is an enormous variation in class size from institution to institution. Some 48 per cent of the lectures given in British universities have audiences of over 20 students (Hale, 1964), whereas 74 per cent of the classes in technical colleges have enrollments of between 11 and 15 (Pilkington, 1966). In children's schools, classes of 40 primary children and 30 secondary children seem to be the preferred upper limits, although classes, in practice, are sometimes much larger.

However, whenever improvements in class size are considered, there is usually an amazing unanimity of agreement. Most experts recommend an 'ideal' class size of 24.* Despite this remarkable agreement, there is no

---

* A class of 24 students is also administratively 'ideal,' since it can be split into sets or cells of 2, 3, 4, 6, 8, or 12 for laboratory, practical, or project work.

128

experimental evidence in favour of such medium-sized groups. Indeed, the only authority for the statement, which has been handed down in successive educational textbooks, seems to be a remark in the fifth century Talmud!

EDUCATIONAL THEORY

From the standpoint of educational theory, the size of a class or a learning group could be expected to have a number of discernible effects. These are highlighted in Fig. 8.1 in terms of group expectations and the expectations of individual students. Some of these effects are concerned with the task; for example, group productivity and individual knowledge of results. Other

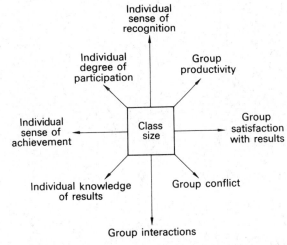

Fig. 8.1 Schematic representation of some of the effects that class size can have on the group and the individual student

effects are concerned with the relationships between members making up the group: for example, group conflict, individual sense of recognition, etc. The effectiveness of the group or class in realizing its learning objectives is a product of its task and relationship orientations.

As the size of a learning group increases, various changes are likely to occur:

1. The resources of the group are enlarged, in terms of knowledge, experience, and approaches to problem-solving. (This condition is less important, of course, in situations where student participation is not effectively utilized, for instance, as in lecture presentations).

2. The group becomes less able to utilize and exploit these resources. Since discussion time is necessarily limited, significant contributions are likely to be difficult to obtain from every student. It is also more difficult for members to make their contributions at an appropriate time, before the impact of their viewpoint has been lost to the discussion.

3. Satisfaction with the quality of the contributions tends to decrease.

This is partly because it becomes more and more difficult to keep track of the discussion, while still keeping contributions in mind, and also because there is a feeling that it is impossible to come to grips with a problem in a large group.

4. Individual differences between members become more marked. Accordingly, it becomes more and more difficult to reach a consensus, and there is also a marked likelihood that members will break into conflicting subgroups.

5. More students are kept waiting, while the rest of the group attempt to catch up with them in their learning. (In small groups, students can be more evenly matched, so that individual members are rarely held up for any length of time.)

6. More students feel a constraint against participating in the discussion. As a consequence, the group tends to become dominated by fewer and fewer people.

Theoretically, therefore, the size of a class or learning group does appear to be a significant variable, although the effects of group size seem to be of greater relevance to classes employing discussion methods than to classes employing more formal strategies, like lecture presentations. As we shall see later, all of these predictions are borne out, in fact, by the research findings.

A further factor, which arises out of the foregoing discussion, concerns the relative cost of student and teacher time. When a teacher is instructing students who are highly paid (as can happen in management training, where students are often as highly or more highly paid than their teacher), it can be argued that classes ought to be small. Since student time is more valuable than that of the teacher, it is especially important that they should progress at their own learning rate. Indeed, this may be one of the reasons for smaller classes being more characteristic of adult education, and larger classes being more characteristic of children's education.

Optimal Class Size: Research Findings

The literature on optimal class and group size has been periodically reviewed by Hudelson, 1928; Goodlad, 1960; Marklund, 1963; Thomas and Fink, 1963; McKeachie, 1963; Davies, 1966; and Hardinge, 1967. Although it is a widely held opinion that small classes are more conducive to superior attainment in learning, it would appear that the situation is rather more complex. A summary of the major trends in the research literature is set out in Fig. 8.2.

It will be seen that there is no such thing as one optimal class size for all situations. Instead, optimal class size is related to the nature of the learning objectives that are to be realized. The research data suggests that three broad generalizations can be made:

LARGE CLASSES
* Small classes are generally NOT superior to large classes, if use is made of traditional tests of achievement for measuring the acquisition of information.
* The optimum size of a class for realizing lower-order cognitive objectives is largely a matter of administrative convenience. It does *not* appear to be a significant variable in learning.
* In groups of 12 or more, leadership skills become more important. Accordingly, the teacher-leader exerts greater influence on group decisions, and the greater is the tolerance of leader-centred or dominant behaviour.

SMALL CLASSES
* Small classes are optimal when use is made of criterion measures which test high-order cognitive and affective objectives.
* In such situations the optimal size of group appears to be 5, but a larger group of 7 can be usefully employed if the students are more mature and experienced.
* One-to-one tutorials are optimal when very high-order cognitive and affective objectives are to be realized, and when students are required to work and progress at their own pace under exacting conditions.

* Both students and teachers, rationally or irrationally, generally prefer small classes.

Fig. 8.2 Optimum class size: a summary of the research findings

1. If lower-order cognitive objectives and affective objectives are to be realized, large classes are NOT inferior to small classes.
2. If higher-order cognitive objectives and affective objectives are to be realized, small classes of five or seven students are optimal.
3. If only the very highest order cognitive objectives (evaluation) and affective objectives (characterization) are to be realized, one-to-one tutorials are superior to small classes.

Thus, teachers and instructors must select a class size on the basis of the learning objectives to be accomplished. For lower-order learning objectives, class size is a matter of administrative convenience; for higher-order learning objectives, class size is a professional matter.

However, large classes also have two subsidiary effects:
1. Large classes place a heavier teaching load on instructors and teachers, since more preparation is necessary.
2. Large classes place greater restrictions upon a teacher's freedom to vary his methods of presentation.

While neither of these effects are insurmountable, they are matters of professional concern.

SPAN OF CONTROL

Optimal class size is also related to a teacher's span of control; in other words, it involves the number of subordinates a teacher-manager can effectively supervise. Graicunas (1937) has analysed subordinate-superior relationships, and has demonstrated the narrow limits within which a manager can effectively work. He has shown that an arithmetical increase in the number of subordinates results in an exponential increase in the

NUMBER OF STUDENTS	NUMBER OF POSSIBLE RELATIONSHIPS
1	1
2	6
3	18
4	44
5	100
6	222
7	490
8	1 080
9	2 376
10	5 210
11	11 374
12	24 708
18	2 359 602

Fig. 8.3 Possible number of relationships with various numbers of students

number of relationships.* This is illustrated in Fig. 8.3. It will be seen that a teacher with 4 students is inside a network of 44 possible relationships, all of which require managerial attention. If a fifth student is added to the class, the number of possible relationships for which he is responsible increases by 127 per cent in return for a 25 per cent increase in group size. Increasing the class from 12 to 18 students, increases the number of possible relationships for which a teacher is responsible from almost 25 000 to almost 2 500 000. In the learning situation, in which students are requiring a knowledge of interpersonal relationships and skills, Graicunas's data demonstrate the difficulties involved in groups consisting of more than 6 or 7 students. Obviously this data must be used with some caution, for the number of relationships possible is less important than the frequency of these relationships, their character, and the nature of the demands they make on the teacher's time. Nevertheless, Graicunas has effectively demonstrated the complexity of managing more than about half a dozen students, and highlights one of the problems associated with increasing class size.

SEATING ARRANGEMENTS WITHIN THE SMALL GROUP

One other variable related to the number of relationships that occur within a learning group, concerns the actual seating arrangements. In a review of the research data, Howells and Becker (1962) found that:

1. The most centrally situated member of a group is likely to emerge as the group leader.
2. Leaders are most likely to emerge on that side of the table around which is seated the fewest participants.

* In order to calculate the number of all possible relationships, Graicunas developed the formula:

$$n(2^n/2 + n - 1) \text{ or } n[2^{n-1} + (n - 1)],$$

where n equals the number of subordinates.

3. When communication is free:
(*a*) The maximum number of communications will be made between people seated opposite to one another.
(*b*) The minimum number of communications will be made between people seated side by side.
In other words, communication will tend to flow across rather than around the table.

Thus, seating arrangements do affect the flow of discussion, and this, in turn, influences the emergence of leadership patterns within the group.

Teachers and instructors can use these findings with advantage. Shy, retiring students can be seated in positions which are likely to cause them to contribute more than they would under normal circumstances, while talkative, out-going students can be seated in positions which are likely to limit the number of contributions they are able to make. Furthermore, teachers and instructors can ensure, to a certain extent, who will exercise the leadership function, by positioning a student in the centre of the group and on the side of the table around which is seated the least number of participants.

CONSEQUENCES OF INCREASING GROUP SIZE

Generally speaking, research demonstrates that the size of a group does have a number of other important consequences. All other things being equal, the larger the group:

1. The greater the demands upon the teacher, and the less the demands on the student to make use of his skills.

2. The greater the group's tolerance towards direction by the teacher-leader, the more differentiated he becomes from membership of the group as a whole. In other words, the more centralized the situation becomes.

3. The greater the tendency for the more active members to dominate the interaction within the group.

4. The greater the tendency for the less active members to become inhibited in their participation, and the less exploratory and adventuresome or creative the group's discussion becomes.

5. The greater the tendency for the group's atmosphere to become less intimate, the more anonymous the actions, and the generally less satisfied the members become with the results of their discussion.

Of the five major research reports investigating these phenomena, most seem to demonstrate a watershed for most of these tendencies in problem-solving situations at around the five to seven group membership mark that we have discussed earlier. Beyond this point, formality in leadership emerges rapidly, tension decreases, attitude changes become less marked, resistance to new ideas is reinforced, and group solidarity increases (Bales *et al.*, 1957).

Optimum Size For Tutorials

One further problem still remains for discussion, the optimal size for tutorial groups. Apart from Cottrell's paper (in Hale, 1964), hardly any research has been carried out into the effect of group size on the efficiency of tutorial teaching. Yet, university practice varies considerably: 61 per cent of the tutorials at Oxford, for instance, are given to one student, compared with only 32 per cent at Cambridge (Hale, 1964). Indeed, the one-to-one tutorial was severely criticized by the 1963 Report of the Robbins Committee on Higher Education, primarily on three grounds:
1. They consider that it was too exacting for most students, who, they argued, would gain more from being members of a group of three or four.
2. They considered it was extremely wasteful of the teacher's time, since it involved him repeating a great deal of his material.
3. They considered the method was too costly a teaching strategy.
These criticisms would only seem to be justified when tutorials are being used to realize lower-order cognitive objectives.

It is not the primary function of the one-to-one tutorial to provide factual information to the student; the primary aim is to develop the students' ability for analysis, synthesis, and evaluation. Repetition of subject matter is, therefore, an irrelevant issue. While it is certainly true that one-to-one tutorials may be expensive when taken by themselves, cost can only be properly considered, by looking at the whole instructional system. Indeed, the use of one-to-one tutorials should result in less formal teaching, since the student is required to work, to a great extent, by himself. Finally, to describe any form of tutorial as 'too exacting' seems to misconceive the real purpose of the tutorial strategy – which is to be as exacting as possible. The great merit of the one-to-one tutorial lies in the fact that it *is* a one-to-one operation; something is certainly lost if a second student is present. Each student can move at his own pace, makes overt rather than covert responses, and has an immediate knowledge of results. Furthermore, the student can be fully extended by the tutor, making the situation as exacting as possible, so as to realize the very highest-order learning objectives.

Conclusion

The problem of optimal class size has long troubled educators, just as the sister problem of 'span of control' has long troubled supervisors in industry. As Allen (1964) has pointed out, 'The more people each manager can effectively manage, the smaller the total number required to attain given end results.' This simple statement is really the key to the whole problem of class size, for the only criterion that can be used is the number of students a teacher can effectively *manage* in a learning situation. In other words, optimum class size is determined by the number of people a teacher must organize, lead, and control, so as to realize the learning objectives of the task. Viewed in this way the search for one overall optimal class size is a delusion. Different classes of objectives require different class sizes, if the learning objectives are to be realized in as efficient and effective a manner as possible.

Posttest 8

ANSWER ALL QUESTIONS

1. State the two opposing views about optimal class size that have to be balanced or reconciled by teachers and administrators.

2. Draw a simple diagram or state the effects that class size can have in terms of group expectations, and in terms of the expectations of individual students making up the group.

3. Summarize the major research findings regarding optimal class sizes.

4. Discuss the problem of 'span of control' in relation to different sizes of learning group.

5. Summarize the major research findings regarding the effects of different seating patterns on a learning group.

6. State the effects that can result from increasing the size of a learning group.

7. Select, and justify, an optimal class size for realizing any set of learning objectives that you have available.

References and Reading List

ALLEN, L. A. (1964) *The Management Profession.* New York: McGraw-Hill.

ARGYLE, M. (1957) *The Scientific Study of Social Behaviour.* London: Methuen.

BALES, R. F. and BORGATTA, E. F. (1955) Size of group as a factor in the interaction profile. In A. P. Hare, ed., *Small Groups: Studies in Social Interaction.* New York: Knopf, 396–413.

BALES, R. F., HARE, A. P., and BORGATTA, E. F. (1957) Structure and dynamics of small groups: A review of four variables. In J. B. Fittler, ed., *Review of Sociology: Analysis of a Decade.* New York: John Wiley, 391–422.

DAVIES, I. K. (1966) *Class Size: An Analysis of the Research Findings.* Brampton, Huntingdon: HQ RAF Technical Training Command, Research Branch Report No. 237.

DAVIES, I. K. (1970) Optimum class size, *Industrial Training International*, 5, 4, 176.

EIFERMANN, R. R. (1970) Level of children's play as expressed in group size, *British Journal of Educational Psychology*, 40, 2, 161–170.

GOODLAD, I. I. (1960) Classroom organization. In C. W. Harris, ed., *Encyclopaedia of Educational Research.* New York: Macmillan, 221–5.

GRAICUNAS, V. A. (1937) Relationships in organization. In L. Gulick and L. Urwick, eds., *Papers on the Science of Administration*. New York: Institute of Public Administration, 181–7.

HALE, E. (1964) *Report of the Committee on University Teaching Methods*. London: HMSO.

HARDINGE, N. M. (1967) *The Influence of Group Size on Group Effectiveness and Member Satisfaction: A Review*. London: Ministry of Defence (RAF), Science 4 Research Note No. 518.

HOWELLS, L. T. and BECKER, S. W. (1962) Seating arrangement and leadership emergence, *Journal of Abnormal and Social Psychology*, 64, 148–50.

HUDELSON, E. (1928) *Class Size at the College Level*. Minneapolis: University of Minnesota Press.

MARKLUND, S. (1963) Scholastic attainments as related to size and homogeneity of classes, *Educational Research*, 6, 1, 63–7.

MCKEACHIE, W. J. (1963) Research on teaching at the college and university level. In N. Gage, ed., *Handbook of Research on Teaching*. Chicago: Rand McNally, 1118–72.

PILKINGTON, H. (1966) *Report on the Size of Classes and Approved Further Education Courses*. London: National Advisory Council on Education of Industry and Commerce.

ROBBINS, R. (1963) *Report of the Committee on Higher Education*. London: HMSO.

THOMAS, E. J. and FINK, C. F. (1963) Effects of group size. *Psychological Bulletin*, 60, 371–84.

WOODWARD, J. (1965) *Industrial Organization: Theory and Practice*. London: Oxford University Press.

9 Selecting an appropriate strategy for communicating complex rules, procedures, and instructions

Learning Objectives

COGNITIVE OBJECTIVES

After carefully reading this chapter, you will be able to:

1. List the four strategies that can be used to communicate complex rules, procedures, and instructions.

2. Write short notes on the characteristics of each of these four strategies.

3. Distinguish between these four strategies in terms of their characteristics and properties.

4. State the three criteria that can be used to select an appropriate strategy for communicating complex rules, procedures, and instructions.

5. Select an appropriate communication strategy, on the basis of the model presented in this chapter.

AFFECTIVE OBJECTIVES

After reading this chapter, the author intends that you will:

1. Be aware of, and value, the four strategies that can be used to communicate complex rules, procedures, and instructions.

2. Incorporate an appropriate use of them into your organization of managerial strategies, so that they become characteristic of your teaching style.

Systematic decision-making and problem-solving are becoming increasingly characteristic of many education and training programmes. Frequently, these decisions and problems require students to read and understand complex rules, procedures, and instructions which are traditionally presented in the form of continuous prose. As information becomes more complex, comprehension difficulties increasingly occur, and language – the prime means of communication – becomes a barrier. The causes of this communication breakdown are diverse; sometimes, it is the complexity of the information itself, or the media that is employed; at other times, students lack the verbal and intellectual skills necessary, or else the fault lies in natural limitations on the amount of information they can assimilate and process at one time. Whatever the cause, however, the result is the same: what is really a breakdown in communication appears to be either a learning or a performance difficulty.

Communication Strategies

Once the real nature of the problem has been recognized, it is possible to consider how the communication difficulties can be overcome. There is a tendency for many teachers and instructors to rely far too heavily on the spoken or written word. Other communication strategies are available, and these must be considered by a teacher-manager so that the optimal strategy can be chosen for realizing a particular set of objectives.

Broadly speaking, four communication strategies or job aids are available for presenting complex rules, procedures, and instructions, so that decisions can be made and problems solved.

1. Strategies that do *not* guarantee that correct solutions will be selected:
   (a) *Continuous prose.* This is the most common method of presenting information.
   (b) *Heuristics.* These involve a trial and error, or discovery, process.
2. Strategies that *do* guarantee the correct solution will be selected, provided the necessary information is accurate:
   (a) *Algorithms.* These are recipes or sets of instructions, which are usually presented in a family tree format.
   (b) *Decision tables.* These are also recipes, but they are presented in the form of a set of questions which have to be answered.

Each of these strategies has particular advantages and disadvantages, for there is no universal strategy that is optimal in all situations. Factors relevant to one task may be immaterial to another, and for this reason each of the strategies must now be considered separately.

CONTINUOUS PROSE

Continuous prose is the most common and the most obvious way of presenting information. In the majority of instances, it is preferable to any other method, but it is becoming increasingly evident that prose may not be necessarily the optimal strategy for presenting complex instructions. Anyone who has tried to follow the assembly instructions that accompany most do-it-yourself kits will have experienced some of the difficulties associated with this communication strategy.

The problem can be seen most clearly in many technical manuals and government publications. The sheer density of their prose style makes communication very difficult indeed. Sometimes, the difficulty lies in the way that the information is written, but more usually the difficulty is due to the material's complexity. In 1963, for instance, the, then, Ministry of Pensions and National Insurance issued a small leaflet setting out the qualifications for a small grant payable on death:

> Contributions paid late cannot normally count for death grant (other than towards yearly average) unless they were paid before the death on which the grant is claimed and before the death of the insured person if that was earlier. But if the insured person died before the person on whose death the grant is claimed, contributions which, although paid late, have already been taken into account for the purpose of a claim for a widow's benefit or retired pension, will count towards death grant. (*Leaflet NI 48, 'Late Paid or Unpaid Contribution' MPNI, 1963.*)

Superficially, the problem appears to be one of style. Many people faced with the task of writing or rewriting such a regulation would go to considerable lengths to ensure that they choose exactly the right words and sentence arrangement so as to make its meaning crystal clear. Indeed, the impact of programmed instruction, to a very large extent, stems from its often excessively elementary, childish, and repetitive step-by-step language. Shorter sentences, simpler syntax, and more orderly presentation, of course, can result in better prose, but this is not necessarily so.

Many of the difficulties associated with understanding prose appear to stem much more from the order in which the clauses are presented, and the way in which the clauses are related to each other. A number of research findings (Miller, 1962; Miller and McKean, 1964; Wason, 1959, 1961, 1962, and 1965; Wason and Jones, 1965; Greene, 1970) suggest that the time taken to respond correctly to a sentence varies according to its grammatical structure. The results of these investigations are summarized in Fig. 9.1, and it will be seen that from a communication point of view:

1. Short, simple sentences are preferrable to more complex ones.

1. Simple sentences (which are affirmative, active, and declarative) are more rapidly identified and processed, than are more complex sentences built by combining a number of simple sentences.
2. Each grammatical complication (e.g., negatives, passives, and qualifications, etc.), when added to a simple sentence, creates an increment of difficulty which delays correct identification and processing.
3. Semantic and pragmatic factors in language, relating to the way in which logical connectives are ordinarily used, interact with syntactic factors so as to inhibit or facilitate understanding.
4. Negative qualifications, except in simple instructions, can appreciably affect the efficiency of understanding.
5. In the absence of context, it takes longer to respond to negative statements than to affirmative ones, even when the amount of information conveyed by the statements is equal.
6. It takes longer to match sentences expressed in the active voice with correlative sentences in the passive voice.
7. Connectives, such as 'except', 'or', 'if', and 'unless' (which are difficult to avoid in continuous prose) can appreciably affect the efficiency of performance.
8. The time taken to evaluate the truth of a sentence is affected more by its syntax (affirmative or negative) than by its truth value (true or false).
9. Sentences which are ambiguous are not always recognized as such. Students tend to make decisions about meaning, rather than perceive ambiguities – a matter of some importance in courts of law when evidence is being taken.
10. When a number of sentences of different grammatical structure are strung together into continuous prose, any comprehension difficulties are likely to be cumulative in effect.

Fig. 9.1   Continuous prose: a summary of the research findings

2.   Qualifications, conjunctions, and the passive voice should be avoided whenever possible.

3.   Negative sentences should not be used.

In a great deal of prose, these recommendations can be followed with little or no difficulty. However, it is quite a different story when it comes to complex rules and instructions, and for this reason continuous prose is rarely optimal for tasks involving this type of information.

HEURISTICS

Renewed interest in heuristics can largely be traced to the publication in 1945 of Polya's book *How to solve it* and Duncker's essay *On Problem Solving*. In essence, an heuristic strategy involves a trial and error, or discovery, process. It has been nicely described in the following manner:

If we try to short-cut the systematic Plan* by guessing, asking for help, trying to remember when we last saw it, etc., the Plan we follow is said to be an 'heuristic'. A systematic Plan, when it is possible, is sure to work, but it may take too long or cost too much. An heuristic Plan may be cheap and quick, but it will sometimes fail to produce the intended result. (Miller, Galanter, and Pribram. 1960).

* In this context, a Plan is a hierarchy of instructions which control the order in which a sequence of operations is to be carried out.

Some years ago, Turing demonstrated the effectiveness of such an heuristic approach when he calculated that in order to solve a simple children's puzzle, which involved sliding coloured squares in a particular way, almost twenty-one billion possible arrangements would need to be considered.

In situations which involve such a large number of alternatives, an heuristic strategy is really the only practical method of realizing the task. Any other strategy would involve a systematic search through an enormous number of possible solutions until the correct one had been identified. This is an eminently reasonable approach when the number of possible outcomes is limited, or when the solution is so important that it is not possible to chance or risk an incorrect solution. In any other situation, however, an heuristic is likely to be much more effective and efficient.

Generally speaking, heuristic or discovery strategies are optimal when:
1. The number of possible outcomes is very large indeed.
2. The number of possible interactions is very large and their relationships complex.
3. The underlying structure of the task is unknown.
4. The risks involved in following an incorrect solution can be accepted.
In situations involving fault-finding on a passenger aircraft, an heuristic strategy might be used to teach the task, but it could not be used to find an operating fault. Any risk of an incorrect solution would be unacceptable in such a context.

ALGORITHMS

Unlike an heuristic plan, an algorithm is a systematic plan; if it is correctly followed, a successful solution is guaranteed. An example of an algorithm is shown in Fig. 9.2. The technique was initially developed by Wason and Jones at London University for expressing government rules and regulations, and by Lewis, Gane, and Horabin of Cambridge Consultants for industrial and commercial situations.

As Lewis (1967) has pointed out, the special merit of an algorithm is that, 'it reduces a problem-solving task to a series of comparatively simple operations, and indicates (for a variety of contingencies) the order in which these operations should be carried out'. A further advantage of the algorithmic approach is that a student or trainee need only work through that part of a regulation or procedure that is directly relevant to his problem. In this way, time spent in making a decision is sytematically reduced, and the job is accordingly simplified.

Any set of rules can be logically presented in the form of an algorithm, although they are best employed when the number of interactions and outcomes is limited. As these increase in size and complexity, an algorithm can become very large and quite unwieldly to use. However, algorithms have repeatedly been shown to be very successful indeed for dealing with such chain structures as procedures and routines, in which the number of decision

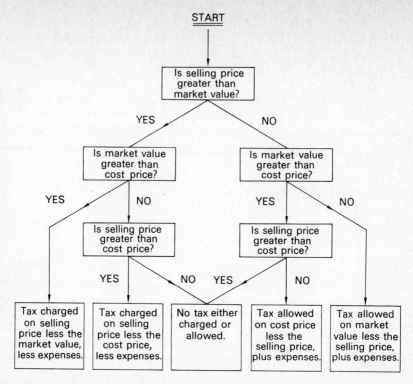

Fig. 9.2 An algorithm for the capital gains tax (Reproduced with permission from Lewis, B. N. and Woolfenden, P. J. (1969) *Algorithms and logical trees: A self-instructional Course.* Cambridge: Algorithms Press)

points is limited. They are less successful for multiple-discrimination tasks, such as are commonly encountered in functional checks and fault-finding. Many examples of algorithms will be found in an excellent instructional programmed text by Lewis and Woolfenden (1969).

DECISION TABLES

Since the publication by Grad in 1961, the use of what are now known as 'logic' or 'decision' tables has increasingly interested systems analysts and computer programmers. Packer and Davies (1969), however, have also demonstrated their application, outside the computer area, to the communication of complex rules and instructions. Figure 9.3 shows such a decision tree, and it will be seen that it is a very much simpler version of the death grant regulation discussed earlier; in use, the decision table is actually even simpler than it appears. Only two conditions disqualify (rules 2 and 3), and so, if these do not apply, all other permutations of answers *must* qualify.

In essence, a decision table capitalizes upon two parameters implicit in all information: the questions that have to be answered, and the decisions that

CONDITION STUB	CONDITION ENTRIES					
Q1 Were the contributions paid late?	No	Yes	Yes	Yes	Yes	Yes
Q2 Were the contributions paid before the death of the subject of the claim?	—	No	Yes	Yes	Yes	Yes
Q3 Is the insured person alive?	—	—	No	No	No	Yes
Q4 Were the contributions paid before the insured person died?	—	—	No	No	Yes	—
Q5 Have the contributions already been taken into account for a claim for a widow's or retirement pension?	—	—	No	Yes	—	—
ACTION STUB	**ACTION ENTRIES**					
Death grant is payable.	*			*	*	*
Death grant is NOT payable.		*	*			
Rules	(1)	(2)	(3)	(4)	(5)	(6)

(A dash in the condition entry column indicates that either a yes or a no answer is acceptable. In other words, the answer to the question does not affect the final outcome.)

Fig. 9.3 Decision table for the death grant regulation

have to be taken on the basis of those answers. As a result, a decision table has one great advantage over both continuous prose and algorithms. Not only is it possible to search serially or sequentially through the information, discarding particular elements or areas as irrelevant, but it is also possible to employ a different and simpler kind of search. This consists of simply answering the questions, and then matching the resulting pattern of answers with the patterns on the decision table until an identical line is located. At the foot of this line will be found the correct solution or decision to the problem.

Decision tables have a number of other distinct advantages over continuous prose and algorithms in the field of diagnostic testing:

1. They ensure complete exposition of every eventuality, and so minimize possible sources of error due to oversight.

2. They help to define the problem and clarify causal and effectual relationships between conditions and actions.

3. They are one of the few strategies available which allow major amendments to the logic of the instruction to be carried out without introducing hidden and undesired consequences.

Furthermore, in constructing a decision table, structure can often be imposed upon information where it has been previously lacking or unknown, so that the problem is significantly simplified and the demands of the task reduced.

Selecting an Appropriate Strategy

There are four convenient strategies available for expressing the internal logic of complex rules, procedures, and instructions. No one method is optimal for all situations, so that the actual choice of an appropriate strategy is often extremely difficult. However, the nature of the task is a useful and meaningful criteria, since:

1. Some tasks are essentially procedural (chains), while others are diagnostic (multiple-discriminations) in character.

2. Some tasks are relatively simple, while others are more complex.

3. Some tasks contain risks that can be accepted, in the sense that while error should be avoided, a mistake would not be regarded as catastrophic. In other tasks, the decision is too important or critical for the possibility of error to be entertained.

CONDITION STUB	CONDITION ENTRY				
Is the task basically diagnostic in character (as opposed to procedural)?	Yes	Yes	No	No	—
Is the task complex?	—	Yes	Yes	No	No
Is the risk of a wrong decision being made acceptable?	No	Yes	—	No	Yes
ACTION STUB	ACTION ENTRY				
Decision table	X				
Heuristic		X			
Algorithm			X	X	
Continuous prose					X
Rules	(1)	(2)	(3)	(4)	(5)

Fig. 9.4 Decision table for deciding upon optimal decision-making strategies

Figure 9.4 summarizes the conditions under which different communication strategies are optimal in problem-solving or decision-making tasks. It will be seen that broadly speaking:

1. *When risks can be taken*
   (a) Continuous prose is optimal if the task is simple.
   (b) Heuristics are optimal if the task is both complex and diagnostic.
   (c) Algorithms are optimal if the task is both complex and basically, although probably not entirely, procedural.

2. *When risks cannot be taken*
   (a) Decision tables are optimal if the task is basically diagnostic.
   (b) Algorithms are optimal if the task is basically, although not necessarily entirely, procedural.

Conclusion

Teaching students to solve problems and make decisions on the basis of complex rules, procedures, and instructions has often presented considerable difficulties to both students and teachers. Although the problem is essentially a communication one, it has often been wrongly diagnosed as a learning difficulty and training has been accordingly lengthened. Replacing continuous prose, however, with job aids such as heuristics, algorithms, and decision

144

tables has usually reduced the problem, and diminished the need for formal instruction.

Posttest 9

ANSWER ALL QUESTIONS

1. List the four strategies that can be used to communicate complex rules, procedures, and instructions.

2. Write short notes on the characteristics of each of these four strategies.

3. Distinguish between these four strategies in terms of their characteristics and properties.

4. State the three criteria that can be used to select an appropriate strategy for communicating complex rules, procedures, and instructions.

5. Select a set of rules, procedures, or instructions, and represent the data in a form other than continuous prose. Justify your choice of strategy.

References and Reading List

DAVIES, I. K. (1970) Algorithms: a strategy for overcoming communication problems – a review, *Psychology Today*, April 1970.

DUNCKER, K. (1945) On problem-solving. In L. S. Lee, trans., *Psychological Monographs*, No. 270.

GRAD, B. (1961) Tabular form in decision logic, *Datamation*, 7, 7, 22–6.

GREENE, J. M. (1970) The Semantic function of negatives and passives, *British Journal of Psychology*, 61, 1, 17–22.

JONES, S. (1968) *Design of Instruction*. London: HMSO Training Information Paper No. 1.

LEWIS, B. N., HORABIN, I. S., and GANE, C. P. (1967) *Flow charts, logical trees and algorithms for rules and regulations*. London: HMSO.

LEWIS, B. N., HORABIN, I. S., and GANE, C. P. (1967) *Case Studies in the Use of Algorithms*. Oxford: Pergamon.

LEWIS, B. N. and WOOLFENDEN, P. J. (1969) *Algorithms and Logical Trees: a Self-Instructional Course*. Cambridge: Algorithms Press.

MILLER, G. A., GALANTER, E., and PRIBRAM, K. H. (1960) *Plans and the Structure of Behaviour*. New York: Henry Holt.

MILLER, G. A. (1962) Some psychological studies of grammar, *American Psychologist*, 17, 748–762.

MILLER, G. A. and McKEAN, K. O. (1964) A chronometric study of some relationships between sentences, *Quarterly Journal of Experimental Psychology*, 16, 297–308.

PACKER, D. G. and DAVIES, I. K. (1969) *Communication problems: a note on the use of decision tables.* Unpublished paper given to the Ergonomic Research Society Conference on *Anticipating Training.* London, 30 October 1969.

POLYA, G. (1945) *How to solve it.* Princeton: Princeton University Press.

WASON, P. C. (1959) The processing of positive and negative information, *Quarterly Journal of Experimental Psychology*, 11, 92–107.

WASON, P. C. (1961) Response to affirmative and negative binary statements, *British Journal of Psychology*, 52, 133–42.

WASON, P. C. (1962) *Psychological Aspects of Negation.* Report of the Communication Research Centre, London: University College, London.

WASON, P. C. (1963) Negatives: denotation and connotation, *British Journal of Psychology*, 54, 299–307.

WASON, P. C. (1965) The contexts of plausible denial, *Journal of Verbal Learning and Verbal Behaviour*, 4, 7–11.

WASON, P. C. and JONES, S. (1965) *The Logical Tree Project.* Report of the Department of Psychology. London: University College, London.

SECTION THREE
Leading

People are the energizing element in any organized group. Good people can get results even without proper planning and organization; backed by sound plans and organization, good people become outstanding.

Louis A. Allen

The leading function of the teacher-manager

Leading is the work a teacher does to motivate, encourage, and guide students, so that they will readily realize agreed learning objectives.

When a teacher-manager leads, he attempts to:

1. Harness student motivation.

2. Select an appropriate teaching strategy, for all ages, so as to realize cognitive, affective, and psychomotor objectives.

In this sense, leadership is not so much a personal quality, but an aspect of organization. A leader, by his very position, is obliged to be effective, and his effectiveness depends, to a very large extent, upon his sensitivity and style. He must balance the needs of the learner and the demands of the learning task, and still get the right things done.

10 Harnessing student motivation

Learning Objectives

COGNITIVE OBJECTIVES

After carefully reading this chapter, you will be able to:

1. Define the term motivation.

2. Briefly summarize the principle features of Maslow's hierarchy of human needs.

3. Distinguish between, and write short notes upon, intrinsic motivation and extrinsic motivation.

4. Write a short description of Herzberg's motivation-hygiene theory.

5. State what is meant by the term 'task enrichment'.

6. State how the motivation-hygiene theory can be meaningfully applied to a learning situation.

7. Design a learning task so as to harness student motivation.

AFFECTIVE OBJECTIVES

After reading this chapter, the author intends that you will:

1. Be aware of, and value, the importance of harnessing student motivation.

2. Incorporate the principle of 'task enrichment' into your organization of managerial strategies, so that it becomes characteristic of your teaching style.

> Each period has its own problems, and its own needs. Yet they
> are all aspects of the same person.
>
> *Teilhard de Chardin*

Motivation is the hidden force within us which impels us to behave in a
particular way. Sometimes, the force is purely instinctive, at other times, it
arises from a rational decision; more usually, the force is a mixture of both
processes. However, regardless of its source, harnessing student motivation
is such an obvious aspect of a teacher's leadership role, that it is surprising
that so little helpful work appears to have been carried out. Although
educators and psychologists have made detailed studies of cognition during
the last 50 years, little progress appears to have been made on studies of
motivation. Furthermore, what little work has been accomplished, has
largely been concerned with animals and young children, so that it is rarely
of immediate relevance to teachers faced with making decisions about the
organization of a learning task.

The Nature of Motivation

It is probably a mistake to think of motivation as a necessary prerequisite
for learning. A more useful way of thinking about this force is to regard
motivation as a general willingness to enter into a learning situation. However,
it is unnecessary to postpone learning until appropriate classes of motivation
are available. Frequently, the best strategy is to ignore any initial motivational
states and to concentrate on presenting the subject material in such a way
that student motivation is developed and harnessed during the learning
process.

MASLOW'S HIERARCHY OF HUMAN NEEDS

When a person is actually motivated he is in a state of tension, and is ready
to undertake a course of action consistent with his feelings. Motivation, in
effect, involves fulfilling a set of needs, which Maslow (1954) has classified
into a fivefold hierarchy:
1. Physiological needs (e.g., thirst, hunger, sex).
2. Safety needs (e.g., survival, security, order).
3. Needs to belong (e.g., identification, friendship, love).
4. Esteem needs (e.g., success, self-respect, confidence).
5. Needs for self-actualization (e.g., desire to fulfill oneself).
As the lower needs are satisfied, higher level motives are released; however,
a need does not have to be completely satisfied before the next need emerges.
Even the most untalented student will seek to fulfill himself, once his other
needs have been more or less satisfied.

Maslow's classification is of obvious interest to a classroom teacher, but it fails to indicate which strategies are likely to be optimal in fulfilling human needs. Furthermore, there is an important difference between Maslow's first three needs, and the two higher order needs for esteem and self-actualization. It is useful, therefore, to distinguish between two general classes of motive in terms of the strategies involved in realizing them:

1. *Intrinsic motivation*. These refer to *content* factors, and are inherent in either the task itself or the student himself. Intrinsic motivation is the basis of most modern educational theories concerning activity and discovery, since exploration and curiosity are intrinsic to most people.

2. *Extrinsic motivation*. These refer to *context* factors, and are imposed on the task or the student by a teacher or other external agent. Extrinsic motivation usually takes the form of rewards or punishments of one type or another. To a very large extent, intrinsic motivation is associated with Maslow's two higher order needs, whereas extrinsic motivation is associated with his three lower order needs. Morrison and McIntyre (1969) argue that most teachers tend to be more interested in extrinsic motivation; a concern that is apparent, for instance, in the perennial arguments over the place of punishment and other classroom sanctions. Accordingly, the real power of intrinsic motivation has often been overlooked or too readily associated with permissive styles of teaching.

The Motivation-Hygiene Theory

Some years ago, Frederick Herzberg and his colleagues, at the University of Pittsburgh, conducted a large number of interviews with such diverse people as accountants, engineers, farm-workers, nurses, and kitchen-hands. As each person was interviewed, they were asked to recall specific incidents in their work which had made them feel either particularly good or particularly bad about the job they were doing, and what effects these feelings had had on their attitudes and their performance. Herzberg found that, generally speaking, good feelings were associated with events that indicated that they were doing their work particularly well, whereas bad feelings were associated with background events about how they were being treated.

These studies led Herzberg to a new and sophisticated theory of motivation which he published in 1966. Although the theory is presented only from the point of view of industry and commerce, it has a great deal of relevance to the teacher-leader whose duty it is to release and serve the motivational needs of his students. Herzberg's motivation-hygiene theory helps to systematize a teacher's role in providing compensatory conditions for poorly motivated students, and helps him to assess the relevance and importance of the actions that he takes.

On the basis of his interviews, Herzberg concludes that people have two contrasting sets of needs:

1. *Motivators.* When present, motivators make a person happy; they have a general uplifting effect upon his performance and his attitudes towards a task. In other words, motivators give rise to feelings of satisfaction and to increased productivity above the norm usually associated with the job. These feelings, furthermore, are long-lasting, and are always present within the content of work itself.

2. *Hygiene factors.* When hygiene factors are at some low level, they make a person unhappy; they have a general depressing or limiting effect on both his performance and his attitudes towards a task. In other words, hygiene factors give rise to feelings of dissatisfaction, and tend to decrease productivity below the norm usually associated with the job. These feelings, furthermore, are not especially long-lasting, and are usually present within the environment rather than within the task itself.

Both motivators and hygiene factors are important, but hygiene factors are limited in their capacity to influence behaviour, whereas motivator factors are capable of longer and more lasting effects. To a very large extent hygiene factors can be identified with McGregor's theory X and motivators with theory Y, discussed in the next chapter.

As a result of his studies, Herzberg found that hygiene factors consist, for the most part, of company policies and administration; supervision; working conditions; interpersonal relations; money, status, and security. When these needs are not met, an individual can feel that the situation in which he works is unfair, unpleasant, dissatisfying and, perhaps, even insulting to his sense of worth. As a result, he can become disinterested and passive, or even embittered and antagonistic. The term 'hygiene' is used to suggest prevention rather than cure; attention to these factors will prevent a man from feeling *unhappy*, but they will not make him feel *happy*. In other words, hygiene removes causes of dissatisfaction from the environment, it represents a replenishment need that goes back to zero when it is satisfied. Hygiene factors are the prerequisite of effective motivation, but they are not themselves motivating. If they are not continually looked after, man will become dissatisfied and will limit production once more.

Motivators, on the other hand, are *not* the opposites of hygiene factors. They are concerned with work itself, rather than with the environment within which work takes place. Herzberg found that motivators involve those feelings of accomplishment, recognition, responsibility, personal growth, and development that come from work which offers sufficient challenge, scope, and autonomy, and in which people are pushed to the limits of their capabilities. While the absence of motivators will not cause workers to be necessarily unhappy, their presence is a powerful force, indeed. They can cause people to work far beyond their normal level of productivity, to adapt a creative approach, and enjoy feeelings of high job satisfaction.

Methods of Harnessing Student Motivation

Teachers generally have always made a more or less organized attempt to harness student motivation through the actual content of their teaching, the sanctions they use, and their personal relationships with their students. The distinction, therefore, between hygiene factors and motivators makes considerably sense in a classroom context, as is suggested in Fig. 10.1. Obviously, it is pleasant for students to work in modern, well-planned classrooms, workshops, and laboratories. Schools, training departments, colleges, and universities ought to be well organized and administered; teaching styles should be as relaxed and as permissive as the circumstances will allow. Good interpersonal relationships between staff and staff, staff and students, students and students should be encouraged and nurtured, and students must be treated in such a way that they develop a sense of personal dignity, status and individual worth. The motivation-hygiene theory, however, offers a ready explanation of a particularly puzzling phenomena. Why should certain schools, colleges, and training departments possessing all these advantages still fail to measure up to institutions

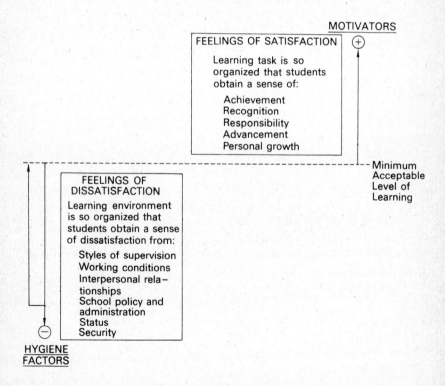

Fig. 10.1 The motivation-hygiene theory applied to learning and teaching

possessing few of them? Herzberg's assertion that work itself can be a powerful motivator represents an important contribution to learning theory, for traditionally work has been considered an unpleasant necessity – with the result that extrinsic forms of motivation have long been considered necessary.

A teacher has an essential leadership role in terms of learning productivity. He has a responsibility to create an environment which is compatible with both student needs and the needs of the task. A student is rarely aware of precisely why he feels free to give so freely of himself, but he is, to a very large extent, reacting to 'a general atmosphere created by a managerial style that symbolizes a supportive attitude' (Gellerman, 1963). A reaction that is best nurtured by teachers adopting a strategy of 'task enrichment'*, a technique that is also largely synonymous with what Lloyd Homme (1969) has called contingency contracting.

Task enrichment implies that both teachers, and instructors have a clear responsibility to design learning tasks in such a way that students have an opportunity to experience a sense of personal achievement, recognition, responsibility, autonomy, advancement, and growth. Apathy and minimal effort are the natural hallmarks of learning tasks that offer little satisfaction. Inbuilding more hygiene factors, such as closer supervision and better communication, are only likely to produce a temporary improvement. Task enrichment, on the other hand, can serve to produce both a lasting increase in satisfaction, motivation, and learning productivity.

Conclusion

There is increasing evidence that we are not realizing the full potential of our students and trainees. Indeed, there is a tendency to design learning tasks so as to take advantage of only the minimum performance that students are actually capable of investing. All too often we have tended to motivate students by appealing to their basic needs and thereby imposing extrinsic forms of motivation and encouragement. These involve only one of the many strategies available to teachers and instructors, and students need for autonomy and self-actualization have been largely ignored – mainly because it has not been readily apparent how learning tasks can be organized so as to realize them for the majority of students. The work of Frederick Herzberg, however, suggests a model that is both useful and relevant to learning, for its emphasis on task enrichment supplies teachers and instructors with a powerful strategy for developing and harnessing student motivation.

* The term 'enrichment' does *not* imply that the strategy is optional or peripheral to the objective to be realized. It is unfortunate that the term has this meaning in the context of audiovisual materials. In the context of this chapter, 'enrichment' involves the fundamental quality of the learning experience, and is, therefore, a key concept in the harnessing of student motivation.

Posttest 10

ANSWER ALL QUESTIONS

1. Define the term 'motivation'.

2. Briefly summarize the principle features of Maslow's hierarchy of human needs.

3. Distinguish between, and write short notes on, the twin concepts of 'intrinsic motivation' and 'extrinsic motivation'.

4. Write a short description of Herzberg's motivation-hygiene theory.

5. State what is meant by the term 'task enrichment'.

6. State how the motivation-hygiene theory can be meaningfully applied to a learning situation.

7. Select a learning task and state how you would structure it so as to harness student motivation.

References and Reading List

BIRCH, D. and VEROFF, J. (1969) *Motivation: A Study of Action*. Belmont, California: Brooks Cole.

COFER, C. N. and APPLEY, H. M. (1964) *Motivation: Theory and Research*. New York: John Wiley.

FRIEDLER, B. C. (1970) Motivator: least developed of teacher roles, *Educational Technology*, 10, 2, 28–36.

GELLERMAN, S. W. (1963) *Motivation and Productivity*. New York: American Management Association.

HEBRON, M. E. (1966) *Motivated Learning*. London: Methuen.

HERZBERG, F., MAUSNER, B., and SNYDERMAN, B. (1959) *The Motivation To Work*. New York: John Wiley.

HERZBERG, F. (1966) *Work and the Nature of Man*. Cleveland, Ohio: World Publishing.

HILGARD, E. R. (1963) Motivation in learning theory. In S. Koch, ed., *Psychology: A Study of A Science*. New York: McGraw Hill.

HOMME, L. (1969) *What Behavioural Engineering Is*. Albuquerque, New Mexico: Westinghouse Learning Corporation.

MASLOW, A. H. (1954) *Motivation and Personality*. New York: Harper.

MCCLELLAND, D. C. (1953) *The Achievement Motive*. New York: Appleton-Century-Crofts.

MCCLELLAND, D. C. (1965). Towards a theory of motive acquisition, *American Psychologist*, 20, 326–33.

MORRISON, A. and MCINTYRE, D. (1969) *Teachers and Teaching*. London: Penguin.

RETHLINGSHAFER, D. (1963) *Motivation as Related to Personality*. New York: McGraw-Hill.

SEARS, P. S. and HILGARD, E. R. (1964) The teacher's role in the motivation of the learner. In E. R. Hilgard, ed., *Theories of Learning and Instruction*. Chicago: University of Chicago Press, 182–209.

SMITH, J. M. (1970) Age differences in achievement motivation, *British Journal of Social and Clinical Psychology*, 9, 2, 175–6.

VERNON, M. D. (1969) *Human Motivation*. Cambridge: Cambridge University Press.

VROOM, V. H. and DECI, E. L., ed. (1970) *Management and motivation: selected readings*. London: Penguin Books.

11 Identifying an appropriate teaching strategy

Learning Objectives

COGNITIVE OBJECTIVES

After carefully reading this chapter, you will be able to:

1. Distinguish, in the context of teaching, between theory X and theory Y.

2. Explain what is meant by the term 'self-fulfilling prophecy', and relate this concept to education and training.

3. List the two broad conclusions that can be drawn from a review of the whole field of research into the effectiveness of different teaching strategies.

4. Write short notes on the research findings dealing with: lectures; lesson-demonstrations; group discussions; tutorials; role-playing, case studies and gaming; brain-storming; programmed learning and computer-assisted instruction; independent study; leaderless groups; and sensitivity training.

5. Distinguish between the three criteria against which teaching strategies can be selected. Explain how each has to be balanced against the others in terms of the requirements they make.

6. Select appropriate teaching strategies, so as to enable a student to achieve mastery in the most efficient and effective way possible.

AFFECTIVE OBJECTIVES

After reading this chapter, the author intends that you will:

1. Be aware of, and value, the importance of choosing appropriate teaching strategy against the three criteria discussed.

2. Incorporate this principle into your organization of managerial strategies, so that it becomes characteristic of your teaching style.

> The whole duty of the teacher is epitomized by two sayings from the Fourth Gospel: 'I came that they may have life', and 'It is expedient for you that I go away'.
>
> *H. G. Stead*

The decisions that a teacher-manager has made up to now have been largely tactical in character. To a very large extent, they have centred on choosing between alternatives, such as between retrogressive chaining and progressive chaining, simple line drawings and realistic pictures, large classes or small groups. In each case, the answer involves problem-solving, and fortunately solutions have been readily available. Now we have to look at an entirely different order of decisions. These are strategic in character, and involve the broad framework within which teachers and students must work. Strategic decisions, therefore, are decisions that matter. They are less concerned with solving problems, and more concerned with style.

Teaching Style

Douglas McGregor (1960) has pointed out that behind every managerial decision there are assumptions or theories about the nature of man: 'Our assumptions are frequently implicit, sometimes quite unconscious, often conflicting; nevertheless, they determine our predictions that, if we do *a*, *b* will occur. Theory and practice are inseparable.' McGregor then goes on to distinguish between two broad sets of assumptions that managers traditionally make, and labels these with the non-emotive titles of theory X and theory Y. The underlying assumptions of these two theories are summarized in McGregor's own words in Fig. 11.1. It will be seen that while theory X is traditional and autocratic in character, theory Y is essentially progressive and participative.

On the surface, the distinction between the two sets of assumptions is seemingly very simple, but the reasoning behind the distinction is subtle. As Warren Bennis has pointed out, the two theories are essentially statements of 'how one person's influence on another person's behaviour is believed to take place'. Since our behaviour as teachers is usually consistent with the assumptions we make about students, the teaching style we adopt will broadly indicate our philosophy. This is particularly important because of what McGregor calls the *self-fulfilling prophecy*.

SELF-FULFILLING PROPHECY

When we make assumptions about our students, they will often tend to behave in a way that is consistent with these assumptions. In other words, they fulfil the prophecies we make about them. Students who are treated as trouble-makers become trouble-makers, students who we regard as irre-

THEORY X	THEORY Y
The average human being has an inherent dislike of work and will avoid it if he can.	The expenditure of physical and mental effort in work is as natural as play or rest.
Because of this human characteristic of dislike of work, most people must be coerced, controlled, directed, threatened with punishment to get them to put forth adequate effort toward the achievement of organizational objectives.	External control and the threat of punishment are not the only means for bringing about efforts toward organizational objectives. Man will exercise self-direction and self-control in the service of objectives to which he is committed.
	Commitment to objectives is a function of the rewards associated with their achievement.
The average human being prefers to be directed, wishes to avoid responsibility, has relatively little ambition, wants security above all.	The average human being learns, under proper conditions, not only to accept but to seek responsibility.
	The capacity to exercise a relatively high degree of imagination, ingenuity, and creativity in the solution of organizational problems is widely, not narrowly, distributed in the population.
	Under the conditions of modern industrial life, the intellectual potentialities of the average human being are only partially utilized.

Fig. 11.1 An outline of the underlying assumptions behind theory X and theory Y (Reproduced with permission from McGregor, D. (1960) *The Human Side of Enterprise*. New York: McGraw-Hill)

sponsible do us the courtesy of behaving irresponsibly; students who are viewed as failures, behave as failures. The self-fulfilling prophecy, of course, also works in the opposite direction. Students who are regarded as able, mature, responsible, and successful often behave in a way as to vindicate our prediction. It is for this reason that teaching style is a matter of great importance, as Rosenthal and Jacobson (1968) have shown in their important book *Pygmalion in the Classroom*. Style affects the very environment in which students learn.

THEORY X

A teacher-leader who adopts a teacher style consistent with theory X is more concerned with his students behaviour as it is, than with growth and development. He regards the capacities of his students as largely static, unimprovable, and not very impressive. Accordingly, a theory X teacher will seek to compensate for his student's weaknesses and deficiencies by adopting one of two teaching styles based on a carrot and stick approach to motivation:
1. *A hard approach*. This involves coercing students to learn by using teaching strategies that are essentially autocratic and teacher-centred. These

will enable him to discipline, control, punish, threaten, and cajole students, as well as to exercise constant surveillance over their work.

2. *A soft approach*. This involves coaxing students to learn by using teaching strategies that are essentially permissive and student-centred. These will enable him to reward, praise, blame, love, and bribe students, as well as to ensure that students' initiative is not stifled.

Both these approaches are based on the assumption that students dislike and will avoid learning, and must, therefore, be manipulated, controlled, or conditioned so as to get them to invest the necessary effort. It is true that there is an essential difference between the task centred and the human relations centred approaches, but the result is the same. Extrinsic motivation in the form of control or love is used as a vehicle to cause students to work. Coercing a student to learn, however, will tend to lead to resistance, apathy, and minimum effort: coaxing a student to learn may well lead to comfortable relationships in the classroom, but is unlikely to lead to anything but the minimum effort in furthering learning objectives.

THEORY Y

A teacher-leader who adopts a teaching style consistent with theory Y is less concerned with the abilities of his students as they are, and more concerned with their potentialities for growth and development. Instead of looking at students as a *given* in the educational process, they are seen as a *variable* which has to be considered and nurtured. In other words, theory Y seeks to explore the limits of human capacity, and consequently any teacher who adopts this style of leadership is constantly involved in change and innovation. There can be no one way of operating; no one methodology that is optimal for all objectives, all tasks, and all students.

A theory Y teacher is sometimes misrepresented as someone who believes that students will work harder if left to their own devices, rather than firmly led. This is as naïve as it is untrue. McGregor simply implies that, under the right conditions, *many* people will find sufficient satisfaction in their work, that they will invest more effort than if they are coerced or coaxed. Teachers, however, have to set up the right conditions for this to happen, and it is here that a teacher-leader has to exercise his great skill, experience, and sensitivity. It is certainly not easy to so structure a learning situation so that students will obtain a sense of personal achievement and personal growth. But, as we have seen in the previous chapter, student motivation can be harnessed by enriching the learning experience. In any case, intrinsic motivation is considerably more powerful and sustaining, over a longer period, than extrinsic motivation, and, furthermore, is more closely aligned to the real aims of education and training.

A theory Y approach also supplies a teacher with a much broader range of strategies. He can still be autocratic when necessary, or completely permissive if the situation requires it, or he can operate anywhere between these two extremes. In other words, a theory Y teacher regards his students as natural decision-makers and problem-solvers, and he attempts to harness these potentialities by adopting a style that is most likely to realize the learning objectives of the moment. This demands a certain degree of flexibility of style, as well as a highly developed sensitivity, so that the needs of students and task can be properly explored and assessed.

The importance of such sensitivity and flexibility of style has been repeatedly emphasized by Flanders (1964). His work indicates that teachers, working with students whose achievement and attitudes are superior, tend to be sensitive enough to diagnose situation needs, able to match their diagnosis with action, and flexible enough to change their style spontaneously and at will. Less successful teachers, on the other hand, appear to be restricted to a limited number of roles, and unable to vary their style from one situation to another. However, the problem still remains as to how decisions affecting style can best be made, and accordingly we must now examine the research findings concerning the effectiveness of different teaching methods.

A Review of the Research Literature

A casual examination of the many textbooks that are available on the techniques of teaching will demonstrate the great variety of instructional strategies available to a teacher. However, in an analysis and investigation of teaching methods, Wallen and Travers (1963) drew two firm conclusions from the research:
1. 'There has not been much research. In view of the quantity of heated debate over these issues, one might have expected more.'
2. 'Teaching methods do not seem to make much difference, or to phrase it more appropriately, there is hardly any direct evidence to favour one method over another. Perhaps one should not have expected research to discover consistent differences between methods in the first place.'
These conclusions have largely been reiterated by Dubin and Taveggia (1968). Across mountains of data and seventeen reviews of research they proclaim one key point THERE ARE NO DIFFERENCES. Yet, after four decades of research effort in comparative studies of teaching methods, the persisistent belief remains that significant differences do exist.

The explanation of this rather surprising finding may be rather simpler than it seems. In an important article Egon Guba (1969) comments that:

Innovations have persisted in education not because of the supporting evidence of evaluation, but despite it. A recent dramatic example is afforded by the Higher Horizons programme in New York City. Test data failed to affirm what supervisors, teachers and clients insisted was true – that the program was making a difference so great that it simply could not be abandoned. . . . When the evidence produced by any scientific concept or technique continually fails to affirm experiential observation and theory arising from that observation, the technique itself may be called into question. . . .

This, of course, is what has probably happened in many of the research studies investigating the effectiveness of different teaching methods. No significant differences have been identified, because educational measurement typically involves student performance in final examinations or tests.

Such tests and examinations are rarely related to a definition of learning objectives, and even more rarely are they related to a task analysis. For the most part, they are concerned with measuring lower order cognitive objectives. Student attitudes, values, and beliefs are seldom evaluated. In any case, the essential difference between a lecture and a tutorial or seminar may be less a matter of a final test score and more a matter of style. Once this essential difference is realized, there are very great differences indeed between the various teaching methods in terms of leadership style and student motivation.

Human needs are complex, and while teacher-managers can so organize matters that students are forced to realize learning objectives, it is much more important that students should meet and achieve them for themselves – with the help of the teacher, and not because of him. There can be little doubt about which experience is likely to be more worthwhile, or which is most likely to exploit the student's needs for self-fulfillment. Many teaching methods do not use students to their full capacity. They achieve only minimum student performance, with the result that teachers contribute more and more to accomplish less and less, in terms of both learning productivity and the quality of the learning experience. Once this precept has been understood, it is possible to review different teaching methods in terms of their success in realizing different kinds of learning objectives and their usefulness to a theory Y approach to the management of learning.

LECTURE METHOD

The lecture method, to a very large extent, is the traditional method of teaching adults. It is essentially autocratic in form and style. Superficially, it might seem that a lecture is the easiest teaching strategy to describe and define, since the lecturer's role is apparently to transmit information. The student, typically, has few opportunities to make overt responses; questions and comments are occasionally invited during the lecture, but are more usually encouraged at the end of the presentation. Accordingly, the student is outwardly, at least, a passive participant, and the lecturer receives little feedback information. This is a great disadvantage, and can seriously hinder the course of student learning – particularly if the learner is not well motivated and the material is complex in character.

Evaluation of the lecture strategy has consisted almost entirely of comparisons with lesson-demonstration and discussion methods. Bearing in mind that one man's lecture can be another man's lesson or discussion, it is not surprising that most research workers report that there are no discernible significant differences between the techniques from the point of view of immediate mastery of factual information (see Davies, 1966 for a detailed review of the literature).

The equally important aspect of retention, however, has seldom been investigated, and what results are available tend to be conflicting. McLeish (1966), in a particularly well contrived study, found immediate recall of up to 40 per cent of the lecture material, but this fell to some 15 per cent to 20 per cent a week later. One further important study (Ward, 1956) found an interaction between retention and student ability:

1.   When a lecture method was used with adult students of lower ability, greater immediate recall and later retention of 'understanding' type material was found. (The importance to less able students of passive listening, rather than active responding has been noted before in the discussion of audiovisual learning aids.)

2.   When a discussion method was used with adult students of higher ability, greater retention of 'understanding' type material was found.

Method apparently made little difference to adult students of higher ability on tests of immediate recall, so that both lecture and discussion strategies were optimal.

When a lecture method has been evaluated from the point of view of its success in realizing higher-order learning objectives, the research evidence becomes clearer. It would seem that lectures are inferior to lesson and discussion group strategies when the objectives are concerned with attitude change, problem-solving, and topics like leadership. An investigation by Hartley and Cameron (1967), who compared the notes students took during lectures with what the lecturer actually said, arrived at two broad conclusions:

1.   Students did *not* regard the lecture primarily as a source of detailed, factual information.

2.   Students *did* regard the lecture as a means of providing them with a framework of ideas and theory, into which they could later fit material obtained by independent study.

These findings are reinforced by the work of Dwyer which was discussed in chapter 7.

In his monograph on *The Lecture Method*, McLeish (1968) distinguishes between a lecture and the lecture method, and he concludes that the lecture is open to serious criticism if it is used as an all-purpose teaching method. Furthermore, the success of a lecture or even of the lecture method (teaching only by lectures) is dependent, to a very large extent, on the expectations of the students involved. If they are favourably disposed towards the strategy, it will work: if they regard the strategy as reactionary, it will fail.

Generally speaking, however, it is possible, from a review of the research evidence, to recognize three situations in which a lecture is likely to be optimal:

1. Lectures can be successfully used to realize lower order cognitive objectives, and the method is particularly efficient if large numbers of students are involved.

2. Lectures can be successfully used to realize the very highest order cognitive objectives, by providing new views and organizations of knowledge.

3. Lectures can be successfully used to realize affective objectives (but only if the method is occasionally employed and is handled in a skilful and sensitive manner), such as when a lecturer inspires an audience with his own enthusiasm and captures their imagination.

To achieve these three sets of objectives is a skilled task, and many lecturers often fail to capitalize fully on the unique properties of the strategy that they are employing. All too often they regard the lecture as a mere communication strategy, and overlook the importance of leadership style. What should be a rewarding and enriching learning experience, often becomes a dull and insipid 'reading'.

LESSON-DEMONSTRATION METHOD

The lesson-demonstration method is the traditional schoolroom strategy, and variants of it are used in most technical schools and industrial training departments. This particular method also forms the basis of most instructional technique courses, and has been widely adopted by the military – particularly where there are problems with average and below average trainees, and a shortage of highly trained and qualified staff. As a technique, a lesson is less autocratic than a lecture, but considerably less permissive than a discussion. In essence, it consists of three successive phases. An introduction, or brief lecturette, in which the aim is stated; a development phase, which usually features a good deal of question-and-answer and other class activity; and a consolidation phase, in which the lesson material is rehearsed, revised, and tested. Variants of the strategy are employed for realizing both cognitive and psychomotor objectives.

Despite the great popularity of this teaching strategy, there is almost a complete dearth of experimental evidence. To a large extent, this may be due to the difficulty of defining the actual strategy, since it is largely transitional in character – it lies somewhere between a lecture and a discussion. One investigation (Pringle and McKenzie, 1965) compared rigidity in problem-solving between students taught by a traditional lesson approach and those taught by means of a more student-centred, progressive regime based on discussion methods. No overall difference was found between the two methods, although less able students in the lesson group tended to be more rigid in their approach than comparable students in the student-centred group. Other investigations with children by Richardson (1948) and Hallworth (1952), and with older adults by Belbin (1965), found group teaching preferable to lesson teaching in terms of motivation, morale, and greater liking for the subject being studied. However, no superiority in learning cognitive material has been clearly demonstrated by any of these studies.

Generally speaking, it would appear that the classical lesson-demonstration method is optimal as a teaching strategy for average and below average students with an untrained and inexperienced teacher. Only lower order affective objectives are likely to be realized, although both lower and middle order cognitive objectives can be achieved in skilled hands. The main advantage of the strategy, however, is to be found in the support it gives a teacher, since the successive phases and subphases of lesson development – all of which are neatly laid down in the basic textbooks – supply a model of what is expected of him as a teacher or instructor.

GROUP DISCUSSION METHODS

As with the lecture, there is really no acceptable definition of what is meant by group discussion or, even, discussion method. In essence, the strategy is always student-centred. The situation, however, can vary from a largely unstructured one, in which teachers play a non-commital or mediating role, to a largely structured situation, in which teachers adopt a severe or autocratic manner. Regardless of the form, however, discussion usually centres around a specific problem, and some kind of agenda is normally agreed upon. While the actual definition of the method can be troublesome, a great deal of research has been carried out: indeed, the literature on the subject is voluminous. Early observations suggested that people tend to work harder when they work together, as a result of a process called 'social facilitation'. Later studies have suggested that the superiority of groups over individuals in problem-solving tasks, at least, is also due to the rejection of erroneous solutions through group discussion.

An analysis of later research on group versus individual learning indicates that students generally learn more rapidly in groups. Group experience also appears to transfer, so that students appear to learn more efficiently when they subsequently return to work on their own (Perlmutter and de Montmollin, 1952). However, there are some limitations. Some superior students do *not* benefit from group-learning experience, and for them the social processes taking place within the group actually seem to inhibit learning.

While discussion methods can be used to transmit knowledge, the real advantage of the strategy is to be found in the changes that can be brought about in motivation, emotions, and attitudes. Lewin (1958) showed, in his now classic experiments on group decision-making, that it is sometimes easier to change a group than an individual. Changes in attitude, interpersonal relations, and in the self-concept, as a result of group experience, have also been recorded by many other investigators (see Davies, 1966).

It would also appear that group discussion permits certain types of social learning to occur which are not possible in a lecture situation. Students are reported to be significantly superior in role-flexibility and self-insight, while discussion methods also facilitate the development of group membership skills (Gibb and Gibb, 1952). Indeed, McKeachie (1954) reports significant changes in student attitude towards other races and to criminals as a result of discussion strategies, while Pelz (1959) found that discussion could persuade students to volunteer for tasks when they thought (sometimes wrongly) that the other participants would also volunteer.

It is not possible to summarize completely all the findings of research studies carried out on group discussion methods here, but a number of generalizations can be made (see, for instance, Lorge, Fox, Davitz, and Brenner, 1958):

1. Group decisions involving an element of risk tend to be more radical than individual decisions on the same problem.

2. Group judgements tend to be more accurate than the average judgement of individual group members when there is a wide range of opinion and the material is unfamiliar. Otherwise, group judgements are not necessarily better, regardless of the criterion employed.

3. Group problem-solving tends to be superior when the material is familiar and individual members possess skills relevant to the solution. There is, though, one important qualification, group solutions are very likely to be inferior to the best individual solution. Otherwise, group problem-solving is not necessarily superior to the average solution by individual members.

4. The main advantage of a group situation seems to be more in facilitating rejection of incorrect approaches than in providing a wide range of approaches to a problem. However, one exception to this finding appears to be brain-storming.

5. Group discussion methods seem most to benefit students who tend to make the poorest individual judgements or solutions.

6. When group superiority has been established, it has largely been shown to be a function of the quality of the individual members making up the group. A group is only likely to solve a problem if at least one group member could have solved it alone.

7. In terms of time taken, group methods are usually less efficient. However, if group members trust one another and can work well together, groups can then work more rapidly than individuals working alone.

8. The presence of outsiders does influence individual performance in the group: it can be beneficial if the group are working harmoniously together and an outsider joins the group. The effect of an observer, however, is deleterious when the group is not harmonious, or when he merely observes or constitutes an audience. This, indeed, is one very sound argument for closed circuit television in teacher-training.

9. Group discussion methods are far more effective than direct attack in changing expressed attitudes. Discussion is also the best way of introducing change or innovation of any kind.

10. Groups tend to be more creative than individuals when they use a decision-making structure appropriate to the task, when they have enough time to explore ideas, and when there is a non-evaluative climate in the group. These circumstances, of course, are typically found in the brain-storming strategy.

The results of this overview of research seem to support the assumptions with which this discussion on group method began. Group discussion is not optimal for realizing lower-order cognitive objectives, any superiority that this strategy possesses is to be found in realizing higher-order cognitive objectives, as well as affective ones.

TUTORIALS

Tutorials are generally held to be one of the most valuable educational experiences, and yet the strategy has received virtually no attention from research workers. The term itself covers a wide range of activities of which the most common are:

1. *Supervision tutorials.* These are commonly employed in our older universities, and are now becoming excessively popular in America. They consist of a regular meeting of student and teacher during which the former reads an essay and defends it in argument. The strategy can provide an exceptionally able student with an excellent opportunity to deepen his understanding of a subject while advancing his mastery of the basic skills of scholarship. However, the technique depends for its success on a well-informed and sympathetic tutor, and a student who has thoroughly prepared himself for the encounter. If any of these factors are absent, then the whole business can become a time-wasting embarrassment.

2. *Group tutorials.* These tutorials arose out of the need to make a more efficient use of staff and to provide for the needs of less exceptional students. There is no evidence that the strategy arose out of any real conviction about the intrinsic advantages of working with small groups (Powell, 1964). Indeed, Griend (1963) has suggested that, since only a handful of tutors are sufficiently familiar with social psychology as to be able to exploit the full potentialities of a small group, the striking developments that have been made in the last 15 years in group dynamics have been largely ignored by educationalists.

3. *Practical tutorials.* These are commonly employed, either on a group or an individual basis, to realize psychomotor skills in a laboratory, workshop, gymnasium, rehearsal room, etc. This subject will be dealt with more fully in a later chapter, but it is important to recognize that the essential basis of the teaching of physical skills is largely a variant of the tutorial method.

It has also been suggested that a major obstacle to any wider use of supervision is the excessive demands that the strategy makes on both student and tutor time, and the need for student and tutor to be broadly equated in terms of ability. Group tutorials, accordingly, are more generally favoured and and employed in adult teaching.

One particularly notable feature of the group tutorial is the wide variability of individual contribution: some participants say very little, while others say too much. One investigator (Bloom, 1953) reports that, contrary to what they themselves believe, most tutors monopolize discussion time and give students little opportunity to participate. In such circumstances, the tutorial can become a lecture, and the proposition that students are decision-makers and problem-solvers is forgotten or ignored.

Both Bloom (1953) and Axelrod (1948) suggest that the quality of group tutorials can be enhanced by ensuring that discussions are problem-centred rather than competitive, and that tutors act as mentors rather than judges. The need for careful preparation by both staff and students is paramount, and it has been clearly demonstrated that some knowledge of group processes is of value to all. Providing these requirements are fulfilled, it is quite evident that a tutorial strategy is particularly useful for realizing higher-order cognitive and affective objectives.

ROLE-PLAYING, CASE STUDIES, AND GAMES

Role-playing is a technique which is widely used to rehearse cognitive skills which have been acquired by other methods, and to bring about changes in attitude. Although it is usually only possible to simulate the experience, it does seem possible to make that experience seem real, so that trainees take on some of the attitudes and feelings normally associated with the role. The strategy is rapidly gaining in popularity, although it seems to be most fashionable in two extreme situations: in primary schools and on business courses. However, regardless of the situation involved, the technique is essentially concerned with problem-solving; instead of talking about the problem, though, students 'play out' solutions.

There is an essential difference between role-playing and case studies, although one can be used in conjunction with the other. One investigator (Solem, 1960) has pointed out that role-playing places the problem in a lifelike setting, involves problems with on-going processes, and deals with problems involving the participants themselves. Case studies, on the other hand, present a problem for discussion, derive the problem from previous events and typically deal with problems involving other people. The emphasis in role-playing is on feelings, while case studies emphasize the importance of facts. Accordingly, the two strategies realize different cognitive objectives. Case studies are primarily concerned with the higher-order classes of analysis, synthesis, and, particularly, evaluation, while role-playing is primarily concerned with the lower- and middle-order classes of knowledge, comprehension and application.

Both role-playing and case studies are effective at promoting real attitude change. Janis and King (1954) found that students playing a role tend to shift their private opinion in the direction of that role rather more than students watching the activity. Other investigators (see Davies, 1966) have reported similar findings, and, while attitude change can also be induced by discussion groups, it is clear that the change is greater when students are called upon to play an active part. Indeed, whatever form the participation takes the rule appears to be quite simple – the more personal the involvement becomes, then the greater the attitude change (Knutson, 1960). However, students can resent role-playing as a childish exercise, so that very careful preparation is necessary before the strategy is employed.

Case studies have probably one of the most disappointing research literatures of any teaching strategy. Although there are many excellent descriptive books available, of which Pigors and Pigors (1961) is one of the most useful, the technique has largely been accepted on its face value. Grattino and Volpe in Italy (see Smith, 1968) have reported a decrease in stereotyped judgements and interpretation as a result of case study techniques, and an increase in analysis of situations in terms of the facts presented. A number of American studies have also been carried out, and the general consensus of their findings seems to point to an increased concern with human relations. However, the acceptability of case studies is largely a matter of their credibility and face validity, and it is not surprising, therefore, that they are reported to be more successful in changing attitudes than realizing lower-order cognitive objectives.

Business games are, in many ways, a specialized form of role-playing. They attempt to simulate the rather more complex features of organization life, and play is usually divided into a number of operating periods during which participants have to make a wide range of decisions. Some of the games can be played in a few hours, others take many weeks, even months, to play, and involve the use of a computer. The practice that students get in decision-making and the use of decision-assisting tools is invaluable, but evaluation studies of the game strategy are scarce. Two studies of games have been made in this country: Fairhead (1965), rather surprisingly, found that attitudes were not changed by nine hours of gaming, nor was there any change in the attitudes of his control group who attended lectures instead. On the other hand, an unpublished study by BEA suggests that students who gamed for two weeks did as well on an examination of cognitive knowledge as students who had followed a six months' directed reading programme. However, students who excelled on the course underwent both training programmes.

BRAIN-STORMING

Brain-storming is completely permissive in style. The strategy is based upon the assumption that a group of people can produce more ideas than individuals working by themselves. The technique, in essence, consists of a problem-solving situation, in which participants are given a problem and then asked to bring into the discussion any ideas which come to mind – no matter how outlandish. In this way, the group encourages, rather than discourages, strange and unusual suggestions, and these are then analysed, synthesized, and evaluated. A unique and practical solution, accordingly, is then fashioned from what may have been originally, a rather bizarre idea.

Although the basis of this method appears to be both psychologically and educationally sound, what little experimental evidence there is available appears to be contradictory. One study (Taylor, Berry, and Black, 1958) suggests that brain-storming may actually inhibit rather than facilitate creative thinking, since the instruction to 'let go' and express all ideas may have a deleterious effect upon group members. On the other hand, Parnes and Meadow (1959) report significantly more good-quality ideas from brain-storming than from groups simply instructed to come up with good ideas. To a large extent, however, the problem may well lie in what is meant by *creative* ideas, and, for this reason, the Parnes and Meadow study, which used the well-known Hanger and Brown AC tests of creativity, may be a more meaningful evaluation of the strategy.

PROGRAMMED LEARNING AND COMPUTER-ASSISTED INSTRUCTION

Programmed learning is based upon laboratory investigations into learning by Professor B. F. Skinner of Harvard and the teaching strategies developed by Norman Crowder for the United States Air Force. Although programmed learning takes many forms and may involve the use of a teaching machine or even a computer, all forms have a common characteristic. They elicit and systematically reinforce correct, and only correct, responses. The development of this learning technique, as we saw in the first chapter, has also had a considerable impact upon educational and training practices (see Ofiesh, 1965; Hartley, in press). Indeed, it has given birth to the wider concept of an educational technology. The advantages of the method are many, but among the most important are active student responding, immediate knowledge of results, self-pacing (i.e., students can progress at their own speed), and a low error rate.

A very great number of investigations have been carried out, and the results certainly demonstrate that programmed learning can reduce training time without loss in either achievement or retention. The results of comparisons between students taught by programmed methods and those taught by means of conventional class teaching vary from experiment to experiment. Although the results alone tell us very little, taken together a number of trends are discernible. These have been summarized by Williams (1966):

1. Human teachers seldom prove to be *more* effective than programmed materials.
2. Frequently, no difference in effectiveness is to be found.
3. More often than not, the programme outshines the human teacher.
4. Even where no significant differences in terms of level of subsequent performance is found, programmed instruction usually takes less time.
5. These results hold for long-term, as well as for short-term retention.

The most detached review of 15 years of programmed learning, and its most valued tenets of belief, has been carried out by Leith (1969).

To a very large extent, it is unfortunate that programmed learning has tended to be used primarily for realizing lower-order cognitive objectives. By far the greater proportion of the programmes available on the commercial market are concerned with teaching basic facts and formulaes, almost as if these were the tasks teachers were most willing to offload on the programmer. Such programmes tend to be boring and uninspiring, and it would be very wrong to think that such materials need be characteristic of the strategy. Extremely successful programmes have been written for medical diagnosis, art and poetry appreciation, and good listening, to name but a few. Indeed, it is quite clear that the full potentiality of programmed learning has yet to be realized: indeed, it is capable of realizing middle-order cognitive and affective objectives – particularly when more flexible approaches, such as computer assisted instruction, (CAI) are employed. Whereas the student is completely programmed or controlled in a conventional programmed text, CAI gives him complete freedom to select and decide what he will see and do next. In other words, the programme a student studies is completely personalized, and depends upon his particular needs and progress (Hickey, 1968).

INDEPENDENT STUDY

Teachers have long been critical of the practice of spoon-feeding students, and particularly of the assumption that learning bears a close relationship to the frequency with which students sit in front of an instructor. Recent developments, however, are beginning to do more than to challenge this 'packaging theory of education'. An increasing number of schools, colleges, and training departments have been successfully experimenting with independent study programmes as part of their regular teaching procedures, with a view to developing student initative, responsibility, and understanding for what they study. In this way, it is hoped to fashion an educational experience that will provide for its own continuous renewal.

Independent study, which is more usually called 'project work', has been defined by Baskin (1961) in his now classic booklet as, '. . . independent work or reading, sometimes on one's own, sometimes in small groups, but with such work taking place in the absence of the teacher and in lieu of certain regularly scheduled class meetings'. In all instances, however, the programme is characterized by precisely defined objectives, and the successful accomplishment of an associated criterion test. Until now, such programmes have usually been held to be the special prerogative of the superior student. What is new is the use of independent study as part of a teacher's regular teaching repertoire, and its employment with *all* students within a particular class or on a particular course.

The results of such programmes have been varied. While they do not support the contention that independent study is significantly superior to more conventional strategies, the data do demonstrate that students perform just as well on conventional tests of achievement. In addition, there is convincing evidence that students who have undergone independent study programmes are more interested and enthusiastic in their attitude to the subject, more independent and less restricted in their thinking, and significantly more resourceful in their overall approach to learning. Teachers, on the other hand, who have used this approach have reported that, while their work was significantly different to that under conventional teaching programmes, it was no less difficult or exacting (Antioch College Report, 1961, 1963).

Even more encouraging results have been reported in the industrial training area by Mager and McCann (1961), who replaced a six month's orientation course for engineers with an independent study programme. Each student was given a detailed statement of learning objectives, but was free to decide for himself what he needed to learn, how much time he would devote to the different topics, and how the material should be sequenced. The results were most encouraging. Training time was reduced by some 65 per cent, and there was also a significant increase in the standards obtained. So it would seem that independent study programmes can, in certain circumstances, be optimal not only for realizing affective objectives, but for realizing cognitive ones as well.

LEADERLESS GROUPS

The primary purpose of a leaderless group is to encourage students to solve problems on their own through mutual participation, criticism, and correction. This does not mean that a teacher is redundant; the group is leaderless for the very simple reason that a teacher's presence would not help the realization of the learning objectives. Unfortunately, many teachers and instructors seem to be very reluctant to employ the technique, even though the educational issues are clear and encouraging. Simon Stuart (1969), in a remarkable book, has demonstrated its effectiveness for teaching of English in a secondary modern school. As he himself writes, '. . . "Say" was the signpost to my insistence that the pupils had to do the work. "Say" meant a refusal on my part to ask questions – for to ask questions was to suggest answers. . . .'

It is already accepted that participation in small groups offers learners educational and psychological advantages:
1. Anxiety can be reduced.
2. Argument can be readily understood and appreciated due to increased possibilities for feedback.
3. There is an absence of authority likely to compel the acceptance of otherwise unsupported statements and opinions.
4. There is a greater degree of freedom, so that emotional feelings, which can block problem-solving, can be fully expressed.

5. There is an increased opportunity for practising a wide variety of intellectual and social skills.

In the absence of a teacher, these processes can develop without hindrance and restraint, and middle-order cognitive and affective objectives realized.

Two serious objections, however, are often raised against the use of leaderless groups. Worthwhile discussion may not develop in the absence of a teacher stimulus and students may not be able to perceive and challenge fallacious arguments and error. An investigation by Powell and Jackson (1963) revealed that these objections might be ill-founded. One word of warning is appropriate, though; it is quite useless to assign students to leaderless groups and tell them to discuss. Careful preparation, detailed briefing, and concrete outcomes, are all essential if the learning objectives are to be realized.

SENSITIVITY TRAINING

Sensitivity training is almost as difficult to define as the discussion method, for it is a generic term embracing a wide variety of techniques. However, the strategy which uses a small group with a trainer, has three principal goals (Martin, 1969):

1. To increase the ability to appreciate how others react to one's own behaviour.
2. To increase the ability to gauge the state of relationships between others.
3. To increase the ability to carry out skilfully the behaviour required by the situation.

Groups meet either full-time for one or more, usually two, weeks or once a week for about three months. There is no fixed agenda for discussion. Instead, the participants focus their attention on the problems they are experiencing here and now in their interpersonal relationships with their fellow participants. The trainer does *not* take part in the discussion; his role is merely to point out what is happening in the group. Put quite simply, sensitivity training (sometimes called 'T-group training', 'laboratory training', or 'group dynamics') is a technique which employs group participation in such a way as to help participants become aware of how they affect others and others affect them.

Unfortunately, the problems of evaluating sensitivity training are very great indeed, and the clearest evidence still largely consists of the very positive statements of support which come from people and organizations who have undergone the experience as part of their leadership and management training. Since its original conception in a training laboratory at Bethel, Maine, in the summer of 1947, the T-group has been regarded as an important social development which deserves study for its own sake, as well as for the sake of providing a special setting in which problems of individual and group functioning can be studied. The research that has been undertaken, therefore, has always tended to have a double aim, and this has been its undoing.

Research on sensitivity training suggests a large checkerboard, incomplete and uneven. The general concensus of most studies (see Smith, 1969) seems to suggest that something like 60–75 per cent of the people who have been exposed to the technique have benefited. Changes of attitude certainly occur, and both Elliott (1958) and Smith (1969) report changes implying increased flexibility of behaviour after sensitivity training. In one important study by Bunker (1965), comparing 200 participants in sensitivity training, eight months after their course, with 200 controls who had not been trained, it was found that T-group participants had:

1. A better diagnostic understanding of self and others in the group, as well as in group processes.
2. A greater openness, receptivity, and tolerance of differences.
3. An increased operational skill in interpersonal relationships, and a greater capacity for collaboration.

Boyd and Ellis, whose results are reported in Bunker (1965), compared T-group participants with students undergoing training in interpersonal relationship by means of lecture and discussion strategies and found similar results in favour of sensitivity training.

Research is also available to show that all of the following qualities have been positively influenced: various perceptions of self, affective behaviour, congruity between self-precept and ideal self, self-insight, sensitivity to the feelings or behaviour of others, role flexibility, sensitivity to group decisions, behavioural skill, self-confidence, and the ability to diagnose organization problems (Bradford, Gibb, and Benne, 1964). This is only a partial list, but these factors do seem to have been changed for some people, under certain conditions. The danger, however, is to be found in the fact that, since sensitivity training differs little from group therapy, the effects could be positively harmful unless handled by sensitive and properly trained people.

Choosing an Appropriate Teaching Strategy

Choosing an appropriate teaching strategy is very much a matter of teacher effectiveness. Fortunately, as Peter Drucker (1967) has pointed out, effectiveness can be learnt. This involves learning how to manage five talents: managing time; choosing what to contribute; knowing where and how to apply your strength to the best effect; setting up the right priorities and, then, knitting all these together by making effective decisions. When a teacher decides upon a particular teaching strategy all these points should have been considered. There are times when he could do the job more quickly himself by lecturing than by students working independently. The problem is to decide when he should give them the information they require, and when he should leave them to discover that information for themselves.

Generally speaking, three basic criteria can be used by a teacher-leader in order to choose the appropriate teaching method:

1. The nature of the learning objectives to be realized.
2. The need to enrich the learning experience, so as to harness intrinsic as well as extrinsic motivation.
3. The ability of the students involved in the task.

The actual decision as to which strategy should be employed is a function of the interaction of these three variables. Great skill and expertise is needed to balance one requirement against the other, but the essential difference between a theory X teacher and a theory Y teacher is to be found in this process. A theory X teacher has no real decisions to make; autocracy or permissiveness are, for him, a way of life.

OBJECTIVES TO BE REALIZED

In the review of research findings on different teaching methods, we have seen that, very broadly speaking, there are no discernible differences between different teaching strategies from the point of view of realizing cognitive objectives. However, this is an oversimplification. Figure 11.2, which summarizes the major trends in the research literature, suggests that the following more helpful generalizations can also be drawn from the same data:

1. *Cognitive objectives.* All teaching strategies can be employed to realize cognitive objectives. However,

   (a) low order cognitive objectives can best be realized by lectures, lesson-demonstrations, programmed-learning, and computer-assisted instruction;

TEACHING STRATEGY	CLASSES OF LEARNING OBJECTIVE					
	COGNITIVE		AFFECTIVE		PSYCHOMOTOR	
	LOW	HIGH	LOW	HIGH	LOW	HIGH
Lectures Lesson-demonstration	▓	▓			▓	▓
Group discussion Tutorial		▓	▓		▓	▓
Role-playing Case studies Games		▓	▓	▓		
Brain-storming		▓	▓			
Programmed learning Computer-assisted learning	▓	▓				
Independent study Leaderless groups Sensitivity training	▓	▓	▓	▓	▓	▓

Fig. 11.2 Objectives for which the use of varying types of teaching strategy are likely to be optimal

(b) high-order cognitive objectives can be realized by all teaching strategies.

2. *Affective objectives.* All teaching strategies, except, apparently, gaming, can be employed to realize affective objectives. However,
(a) Low-order affective objectives can be realized by all teaching strategies
(b) High-order affective objectives can best be realized by group discussions, tutorials, role-playing, case studies, brain-storming, computer-assisted instruction, independent study, leaderless groups, and sensitivity training.

3. *Psychomotor objectives.* Lesson-demonstrations, practical tutorials, and independent study, are the only teaching strategies most likely to realize psychomotor objectives.

NEED TO ENRICH THE LEARNING EXPERIENCE

Research in motivation and the many developments in curriculum reform have all focused attention on the importance of enriching learning experiences so as to make them worth while and intrinsically motivating. This, as we have seen in the previous chapter, is best accomplished by ensuring that the teaching strategy employed allows students to experience feelings of achievement, recognition, responsibility, and personal growth. The teaching methods most likely to realize these objectives are permissive rather than autocratic in style, but it would be foolish to believe that students unused and ill-prepared for permissive strategies would necessarily benefit from them.

Figure 11.3 summarizes the relationship between each teaching strategy and the degree of control a teacher or student can expect to exercise. It will be

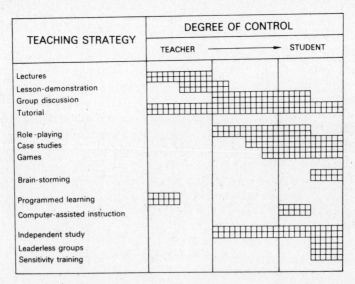

Fig. 11.3   Relationships between teaching strategy and teacher-student control

seen that some teaching methods, for example, the tutorial, can be used in either an autocratic or a permissive mode. Generally speaking, teaching strategies can be classified under the following headings:

1. *Autocratic styles include:*
   (a) Lectures.
   (b) Lesson-demonstrations.
   (c) Tutorials.
   (d) Programmed learning.
2. *Permissive styles include:*
   (a) Tutorials.
   (b) Group discussions.
   (c) Role-playing, case studies, and gaming.
   (d) Brain-storming.
   (e) Computer-assisted instruction.
   (f) Independent study.
   (g) Leaderless groups.
   (h) Sensitivity training.

It is as well to remember that autocratic styles do realize rather different objectives than do more permissive styles, although they may use exactly the same information content. Autocratic styles, as is shown in Fig. 11.2, tend to realize cognitive objectives, while permissive styles tend to realize affective ones. However, there are other important differences. There is now abundant evidence available (see Davies, 1966, for references) that the following distinction can be drawn:

1. *Autocratic or teacher-centred modes.* These tend to be more conventional in style: content is determined by the teacher, emphasis is upon intellectual changes, and there is little or no attempt to develop or use group cohesiveness.

2. *Permissive or student-centred modes.* These tend to be less conventional in style, content is largely determined by the participants, emphasis is upon attitudinal changes, and attempts are made to develop and use group cohesiveness.

Accordingly, autocratic modes are characterized by their subjectivity and conventional approach, while permissive modes are characterized by their objectivity and creative approach. So that selecting a particular mode depends upon the nature of the objectives to be realized, and the teacher's view of the task. In many instances, it will be necessary to employ a teacher-centred style to lay the basic framework and teach the basic facts, and then employ more permissive styles to realize the higher-order cognitive and affective objectives.

ABILITY OF THE STUDENTS INVOLVED

As we have seen in the discussion on research findings into teaching methods and audiovisual learning aids, there is a recurring suggestion that there is an important interaction between student ability and optimal teaching strategy. It would seem that:

1. Very able students prefer, and appear to benefit from, permissive teaching strategies that are less group and more individual orientated.
2. Able students prefer, and appear to benefit from, more permissive teaching strategies.
3. Less able students prefer, and appear to benefit from, more autocratic teaching strategies.

What a student prefers, however, may not be necessarily what is best for him in the long term.

However, regardless of the teaching strategy employed, textbooks and other reading materials provide a common link between the different styles. Dubin and Traveggia (1968) suggest that the lack of significant differences between the different teaching strategies in realizing cognitive objectives may, in fact, be due to the powerful effect that reading may have in cancelling anything the teacher may or may not do. As Thorndike pointed out some sixty years ago, it might be more fruitful to examine the differences between textbooks than the differences between teaching methods.

Conclusion

If teaching is worth doing, it is worth doing well; magnificent buildings and expensive equipment can never compensate for dreary and lifeless instruction. From the point of view of making teaching easy, it is unfortunate that no significant differences are discernible between the different teaching strategies from the point of view of realizing cognitive objectives. However, teaching is *not* easy. It is a highly complex and professional activity, and for the very simple reason that while there may be no comfortable and direct relationship between teaching and learning, there *is* a direct relationship between teaching, motivation, and learning productivity.

Leaders are necessary in any organization so as to ensure that objectives are realized. It is quite true that some people can work without them, but it is also true that all people work better with them. So it is with teachers. Students follow a teacher because of what he *is*, as well as because of what he *does*. A teacher is largely responsible for the effectiveness of his class and of his individual students. Accordingly, the style that he adopts will have a great deal to do with the ultimate success that his students experience in learning. The teacher-leader, therefore, has a responsibility to ensure that he selects those teaching strategies that are likely to be effective, otherwise he will not get the right things done.

Posttest 11

ANSWER ALL QUESTIONS

1. Distinguish, in the context of teaching, between theory X and theory Y.

2. Explain what is meant by the term 'self-fulfilling prophecy', and relate this concept to education and training.

3. List the two broad conclusions that can be drawn from a review of the whole field of research into the effectiveness of different teaching strategies.

4. Write short notes on the research findings dealing with:
    (a) Lectures.
    (b) Lesson-demonstrations.
    (c) Group discussions.
    (d) Tutorials.
    (e) Role-playing, case studies, and gaming.
    (f) Brain-storming.
    (g) Programmed learning and computer-assisted instruction.
    (h) Independent study.
    (i) Leaderless groups.
    (j) Sensitivity training.

5. Distinguish between the three criteria against which teaching strategies can be selected. Explain how each has to be balanced against the others in terms of the requirements that they make.

6. Select a learning task, and state the teaching strategy you would employ so as to enable students to achieve mastery in the most efficient and effective way possible. Justify your selection of strategy.

References and Reading List

ANTIOCH COLLEGE (1961) *Experiments in Independent Study* 1956–1960. Yellow Springs, Ohio: Antioch College Report.

ANTIOCH COLLEGE (1963) *Using Groups in Independent Study.* Yellow Springs, Ohio: Antioch College Report.

AXELROD, J. (1948) The technique of group discussion in the college class, *Journal of General Education*, 26, 200–07.

BASKIN, S. (1961) *Quest for Quality: Some Models and Means.* Washington, DC: US Department of Health, Education and Welfare. New Dimensions in Education, No. 7.

BASS, B. M. and VAUGHAN, J. A. (1966) *Training in Industry: The Management of Learning.* London: Tavistock Pbns.

BELBIN, R. M. (1965) *Training Methods.* Paris: OECD.

BLOOM, B. S. (1953) Thought-processes in lectures and discussions, *Journal of General Education*, 7, 160–9.

BRADFORD, L. P., GIBB, J. R., and BENNE, K. D. (1964) *T-Group Theory and Laboratory Method*. New York: John Wiley.

BUNKER, D. R. (1965) Individual applications of Laboratory Training, *Journal of Applied Behavioural Science*, 1, 131–48.

COOPER, C. L. and MANGHAM, I. L. (1970) T-group training: before and after, *The Journal of Management Studies*, May 1970, 224–239.

DAVIES, I. K. (1966) *Training Methods: An Analysis of the Research Findings*. Brampton, Huntingdon: HQ RAF Technical Training Command, Research Branch Report No. 234.

DAVIES, I. K. and HARTLEY, J., eds. (1971) *Contributions to an Educational Technology*. London: Iliffe.

DRUCKER, P. F. (1967) *The Effective Executive*. London: Heinemann.

DRUCKER, P. F. (1969) *The Age of Discontinuity*. London: Heinemann.

DUBIN, R. and TAVEGGIA, T. C. (1968) *The Teaching-Learning Paradox: A Comparative Analysis of College Teaching*. Eugene, Oregon: University of Oregon, Center for Advanced Study of Educational Administration.

EDLING, J. V. (1970) *Individualized instruction: a manual for administrators*. Cornwallis, Oregon: Continuing Education Publications.

ELLIOTT, A. G. P. (1958) *An Experiment in Group Dynamics*. Mimeographed report by Simon Engineering Ltd.

FAIRHEAD, J. (1965) The validation of business exercises, *Bulletin of the Association of Teachers of Management*, 19, 1–16.

FELDMAN, D. H. (1970) Effects of computer-assisted instruction on children's behaviour, *Educational Technology*, 10, 3, 11–14.

FLANDERS, N. A. (1964) Some relationships among teacher influence, pupil attitudes and achievement. In B. J. Biddle and W. J. Ellena, eds., *Contemporary Research on Teacher Effectiveness*. New York: Holt, Rinehart and Winston, 196–231.

GIBB, L. M. and GIBB, J. R. (1952) The effects of the use of participitative action groups in a course in General Psychology, *American Psychologist*, 7, 247.

GRIEND, P. C. (1963) Teaching, Training and Group Dynamics. In J. A. Lauwerys *et al.*, *The Yearbook of Education*, 1963. Yonkers, New York : World Book Company, 178–93.

GUBA, E. C. (1969) The Failure of Educational Evaluation, *Educational Technology*, May 1969, 29–38.

HALLWORTH, H. J. (1952) *A Study of Group Relationships Among Grammar School Boys and Girls Between the Ages of Eleven and Sixteen Years*. London: University of London Library, unpublished MA thesis.

HARTLEY, J., ed. (in press) *Strategies for Programmed Instruction: An Educational Technology*. London: Iliffe.

HARTLEY, J. and CAMERON, A. (1967) Some Observations on the Efficiency of Lecturing, *Educational Review*, 20, 1, 30–7.

HICKEY, A. E. (1968) *Computer-Assisted Instruction: A Survey of the Literature*. Newburyport, Massachusetts: Entelek Incorporated.

JANIS, I. L. and KING, B. T. (1954) The Influence of Role Playing on Opinion change, *Journal of Abnormal and Social Psychology*, 49, 211–18.

KNUTSON, A. L. (1960) Quiet and vocal groups, *Sociometry*, 23, 36–49.

LEITH, G. O. M. (1969) *Second Thoughts on Programmed Learning*. London: National Council for Educational Technology.

LEWIN, K. (1958) Group decision and social change. In E. Maccoby, T. Newcomb, and E. Hartley, eds., *Readings in Social Psychology*. New York: Holt, 197–211.

LORGE. I., FOX, D., DAVITZ, J., and BRENNER, M. A. (1958) A Survey of Studies Contrasting the Quality of Group Performance and Individual Performance, *Psychological Bulletin*, 55, 337–72.

MAGER, R. F. and McCANN, J. (1961) *Learner Controlled Instruction.* Palo Alto, California: Varian Associates.

MARTIN, A. O. (1969) Foreword. In P. B. Smith, *Improving Skills in Working with People in the T-group.* London: HMSO, Training Information Paper No. 4.

McGREGOR, D. (1960) *The Human Side of Enterprise.* New York: McGraw-Hill.

McKEACHIE, W. J. (1954) Individual conformity to attitudes of classroom groups, *Journal of Abnormal and Social Psychology*, 49, 282–289.

McLEISH, J. (1966) *Student Retention of Lecture Material.* Cambridge Institute of Education Bulletin, 3, 3, 2–11.

McLEISH, J. (1968) *The Lecture Method.* Cambridge: Cambridge Institute of Education, Monograph on Teaching Methods No. 1.

MORRIS, J. F. and LUNZER, E. A. (1969) *Contexts of Education.* London: Staples.

MORRISON, A. and McINTYRE, D. (1969) *Teachers and Teaching.* London: Penguin.

OFIESH, G. D. (1965) *Programmed Instruction: A Guide for Management.* New York: American Management Association.

PARNES, S. J. and MEADOW, A. (1959) Effects of 'brainstorming' instructions on creative problem-solving by trained and untrained subjects, *Journal of Educational Psychology*, 50, 171–6.

PERLMUTLER, H. V. and MONTMOLLIN, G. DE (1952) Group learning of nonsense syllables, *Journal of Abnormal and Social Psychology*, 47, 762–9.

PELZ, D. C. (1959) Some factors in group decision. In E. E. Maccoby, T. M. Newcomb, and E. C. Hartley, eds., *Readings on Social Psychology.* London: Methuen.

PIGORS, P. and PIGORS, F. (1961) *Case Method in Human Relations: The Incident Process.* New York: McGraw-Hill.

POWELL, J. P. (1964) Experimentation and teaching in higher education, *Journal of Educational Research*, 7, 3. 179–91.

POWELL, J. P. and JACKSON, P. (1963) Learning through unsupervised discussion, *Hermathena*, 107, 99–105.

PRINGLE, M. L. and McKENZIE, I. R. (1965) Teaching method and rigidity in problem solving, *British Journal of Educational Psychology*, 35, 1 50–9.

RICHARDSON, J. E. (1948) *An Investigation into Group Methods of Teaching English Composition.* London: University of London Library, unpublished MA thesis.

ROSENTHAL, R. and JACOBSON, L. (1968) *Pygmalion in the Classroom.* New York: Holt, Rinehart and Winston.

SMITH, P. B. (1968) Training and developing executives. In D. Pym, ed., *Industrial Society: Social Sciences in Management.* London: Penguin.

SMITH, P. B. (1969) *Improving Skills in Working With People: The T-Group.* London: HMSO, Training Information Paper No. 4.

SOLEM, A. R. (1960) Human relations training: Comparison of case study and role playing, *Personal Administration*, 23, 29–37.

STUART, S. (1969) *Say: An Experiment in Learning.* London: Nelson.

TAYLOR, D. W., BERRY, P. C., and BLACK, C. H. (1958) Does group participation when using brainstorming facilitate or inhibit creative thinking? *Administrative Science Quarterly*, 3, 23–47.

WALLEN, N. E. and TRAVERS, R. M. W. (1963) Analysis and investigation of teaching method. In N. L. Gage, ed., *Handbook of Research on Teaching.* Chicago: Rand McNally, 448–505.

WARD, J. N. (1956) Group versus lecture-demonstration method in physical science instruction for general education college students, *Journal of Experimental Education*, 24, 197–210.

WILLIAMS, J. D. (1966) Programmed Instruction Not Yet Proven? *New Society*, 7, 173, 8–13

12 Teaching older students

Learning Objectives

COGNITIVE OBJECTIVES

After carefully reading this chapter, you will be able to:

1. List the five difficulties that older people experience in learning.

2. Recognize these difficulties when they occur.

3. State the characteristics of and choose an appropriate teaching strategy, optimal course length, and lesson duration.

4. Choose appropriate job aids for older workers.

5. Identify an appropriate sequence of subject material for older students.

6. State the importance to older students of advance organizers, behavioural objectives, and over-learning.

AFFECTIVE OBJECTIVES

After reading this chapter, the author intends that you will:

1. Recognize and accept the difficulties that 'older' people experience in learning.

2. Incorporate the techniques of overcoming these difficulties into your repertoire of teaching strategies, so that they become characteristic of your teaching style.

> A man has rights, has a knowledge, has a position, which must be taken for granted and respected; that he must under no circumstances be put on a first form, and turned into a child. You cannot do it; you have no business to attempt it. The world has been teaching him – I must add with all reverence, God has been teaching him – whatever you have been doing.
>
> *Frederick Denison Maurice, 1855*

Today, with the application of recent and novel advances in science, there has emerged a new technology based upon a great variety of man-machine systems. This has created difficulties in the education and training of operatives, technicians, technologists, and managers. At the same time, the labour force is tending to age, in the sense that the average age of the working population is gradually rising. Already half the labour force in this country is over the age of 40, and, by 1980, it is estimated that in the United States there will be more than 33 million men and women over the age of 45 – almost 6 million more than at the present time.

Traditionally, older people are regarded as less flexible and less mobile, so that further training and retraining can present a number of very acute problems – both to management and to the individuals concerned. The demands for such training and retraining, however, are gradually increasing as techniques and skills become outmoded through new inventions and insights into the nature of organization and work. Something of the enormity of the problem can be gauged by the fact that something like half our present working population will change their jobs three or four times during their lifetime.

In the past, ideas have tended to live longer than people, but, today, people live much longer than ideas. Change and innovation are becoming so characteristic of our society that the very nature of education and training is undergoing renewal. No longer can we conceive of education and training as being primarily concerned with communicating the traditions and skills of the past. In the present age of discontinuity, education and training are also concerned with preparing people for change and conflict.

Problems of Teaching Older People

In an earlier chapter, dealing with the identification of training need, an important distinction was made between teaching children and teaching adults. Another distinction can also be made between teaching younger adults and older adults. As people mature through the exercise of independence and self-reliance, and as the so-called ageing process takes its toll, so forms of learning based upon imitation and memorization become less and less important. Older people learn more by synthesis and evaluation, more by independent methods of study and discovery. Teaching methods that are optimal with younger people, therefore, are not necessarily optimal with older people. Out of this very simple statement has largely arisen the mythology that older people are more difficult to train and retrain. It would be more accurate to say that it is not age that causes the difficulties, but inappropriate teaching strategies and teacher credibility.

The term 'older' person can also give rise to some misconceptions. It is very difficult to be precise, but learning difficulties tend to be experienced, on account of age, by people over the age of 35. Some American studies, however, suggest that the effects of age in certain engineering operations can be experienced much earlier. Difficulties have been reported (see Birren, 1959) with people over the age of 25 on punch-press operations and over the age of 19 on coil-winding. On the other hand, certain individuals over 50 years of age have learnt new tasks as easily and as well as considerably younger men. The general rule, however, is that differences between people in terms of skilled performance tend to widen with each succeeding age group (Welford, 1958; Kay, 1951).

LEARNING DIFFICULTIES OF OLDER PEOPLE

Older people tend to experience a number of learning difficulties that are peculiarly characteristic. To a large extent, these can be summarized under the following five headings.

1. *Motivational problems.* A mythology has sprung up that older people are more difficult to train, are less adaptable to change, and are too old to learn. These assumptions usually lead to a self-fulfilling prophecy, in the sense that older people tend to behave in a way which is consistent with what people expect of them. This phenomena is one of the root causes of many of the motivational problems that older people experience, and leads to a wholesale waste of valuable talent and experience.

2. *Problems of 'unlearning'.* Many older people experience great difficulty in casting off errors and mistakes once they have occurred; they tend to make the same mistake again and again and again (Kay, 1951). Similarly, the more people know, and the more experience they have, the greater is the difficulty to 'unlearn' what is no longer appropriate in a new situation or job. Entwisle (1959) has demonstrated how, in a programme for the conversion of brewery drivers from horse-drawn to motor vehicles, experience of drivers below the age of 40 was advantageous, while the experience of drivers over the age of 40 was disadvantageous to learning the new skill.

3. *Problems associated with forgetting.* Although it is often considered that older people tend to have poor memories, research has shown that this is a gross oversimplification. Bromley (1958) has demonstrated that in three matched groups, composed of people aged between 17 and 76, age made no difference to scores in a test involving the short-term memory (i.e., in a test involving *immediate* rather than long-term recall). However, Belbin (1968),

in an important review of the problems associated with the retraining of older workers, shows that there is a good deal of evidence to suggest that, while there may be no differences under ideal conditions, disturbances and interference from unrelated events can, and do, increasingly affect the performance of the short-term memory of older people. In other words, under ideal conditions, there are no discernible differences in terms of the short-term memory between younger and older people; when conditions are not ideal, older people tend to have difficulty remembering.

4. *Resistance to change and innovation.* Older people tend to have great difficulty in accepting new ideas, methods, concepts, and principles. It is as if they are handicapped by what they already know and believe, and so they appear rigid and unyielding. To a very large extent, this resistance to change comes from feelings of insecurity and difficulties in relationships with younger people, and they accordingly tend to adopt an autocratic style as a defence mechanism.

5. *Problems of adjustment.* After training or retraining has been successfully accomplished, Newsham (1969) has reported that there is a rather critical period of adjustment to the new work situation and environment. This period can occur immediately after training has been completed, but might even be delayed a few weeks. In any case, it is during this settling-in phase that older people experience the problems of adjustment most acutely, so as to make them more prone to leave the organization than are their younger colleagues.

While many of these difficulties are cognitive in character (in the sense that older people forget more easily and have difficulty in unlearning), it is the attitudinal component that lies at the real root of their problem. It is also important to remember that the difficulties affect not only their orientation or attitude towards the task or job, but also their orientation towards or concern for people. Older people hold values, reinforced over the years, which tend to make them inflexible, defensive and resistant to innovation. Given the necessary encouragement, however, these difficulties are not as insurmountable as they might at first appear, particularly if they are allowed to make the change for themselves in a supportive atmosphere.

Optimal Teaching Strategies for Older People

Although the difficulties that older people experience in learning are very real, good teaching can do a great deal to militate against the worst effects of age. For this reason, it is possible to argue that no special educational and training programmes are necessary. Unfortunately, good teaching is less characteristic of a great deal of our instruction than many of us are ready to admit. Good teachers are in short supply, their time is necessarily limited, there are often heavy constraints on what they can do, and classes are often larger than is consistent with the objectives that have to be realized. While every student, regardless of age, has the right to expect skilled and sym-

1. *When tasks involve the need for short-term memory:*
   (a) Avoid the need for conscious memorizing. This may often be accomplished by making use of 'cues' which guide the trainee.
   (b) When possible use a method which involves learning a task as a whole. If it has to be learned in parts, these parts should be learned in cumulative stages.
   (c) Ensure consolidation of learning before passing on to the next task or to the next part of the same task. (Importance of self-testing and checking.)

2. *When there is 'interference' from other activities or from other learning:*
   (a) Restrict the range of activities covered in the course.
   (b) Employ longer learning sessions than is customary for younger trainees.
   (c) Vary method of learning rather than the content of the course.

3. *When there is need to translate information from one medium to another:*
   (a) Avoid the use of visual aids which necessitate a change of logic or a change in the plan of presentation.
   (b) If simulators or training devices are to be used, they must be designed to enable learning to be directly related to practice.

4. *When there is need to 'unlearn' something for which the older learner has a predilection:*
   (a) Ensure 'correct' learning in the first place.
   (b) Employ an automatic feedback system to convince the older learner of his errors.

5. *When tasks are 'paced':*
   (a) Allow the older learner to proceed at his own pace.
   (b) Allow him to plan his programme within certain defined limits.
   (c) Aim at his beating his own targets rather than those of others.

6. *As tasks become more complex:*
   (a) Allow for learning by easy stages of increasing complexity.

7. *When the trainee lacks confidence:*
   (a) Use written instructions.
   (b) Avoid the use of production material too soon in the course.
   (c) Provide longer induction periods. Introduce the trainee very gradually both to new machinery and to new jobs.
   (d) Stagger the intake of trainees.
   (e) Avoid formal tests.
   (f) Don't give formal time limits for the completion of the course.

8. *When learning becomes mentally passive:*
   (a) Use an open situation which admits discovery learning.
   (b) Employ meaningful material and tasks which are sufficiently challenging to an adult.

Fig. 12.1 Suggestions for adapting training programmes to suit 'older' learners
(Reproduced with permission from Belbin, E (1965). Problems of Learning for for the Over 40's. *Gerontologia, 7.*)

pathetic teaching, it is quite clear that older students are more affected than younger students by poor teaching practice and style.

A concise summary of how the learning difficulties of older people can be overcome is given in Fig. 12.1. The table has been constructed by the staff of the Industrial Training Research Unit of University College, London. Most of the major points of the table can be summarized under the following three headings:

187

1. Selecting an optimal teaching strategy.
2. Selecting optimal teaching tactics.
3. Selecting an optimal course length and lesson duration.

OPTIMAL TEACHING STRATEGIES

The Industrial Training Research Unit has investigated the relationship between teaching methods and the willingness of older adults to remain with their firms. Their results indicate that informal teaching methods, such as on the job training, are no more effective, when measured by manpower turnover/retention figures, than systematic methods employing more formal teaching strategies, such as lectures, lessons, and practical demonstrations. However, teaching methods involving discovery learning are optimal, in the sense that they are followed by a markedly higher long-term survival rate (Martin, 1969).

The discovery or heuristic strategy is a remarkably difficult method to pin down, since it can mean many things to different people. In essence, however, it calls for a teacher to direct a student's attention to some information, object, or problem, and require him to reach some conclusions. The teacher does not tell the student what he must discover; the student discovers it for himself. What distinguishes this method so dramatically from the formal or tell and do methods (lecture, lesson, and practical demonstration, etc.) is the teacher's use of student feedback. This is clearly shown in Fig. 12.2, where the roles of both student and teacher, under the two broad teaching strategies, are briefly summarized using Bales' (1950) categories of group behaviour as a means of contrasting the various interactions. The reasons why discovery methods are optimal and more acceptable for adults are also clearly discernible.

A teacher's main role in discovery learning is, 'To diagnose the level of accomplishment of the trainee, to administer the appropriate task out of a number of graded tasks, to check the results, to ask the right question at the right time, and to act as consultant to the trainee only when help is sought.' (E. and R. M. Belbin, 1968).

Typically, discovery learning involves not only discovery in the true sense of the term, but also project work, seminars, T-groups, case studies, discussion groups, assignments, and open-ended exercises. The technique, in fact, involves what we have called 'learning by objectives', in which the teacher manages by exception.

In a sense, discovery methods are the same for both student and teacher. A teacher's responses or interventions are determined, in part, by the inferences he makes about a student's behaviour, just as a student's responses are determined, in part, by the inferences he makes about the data. Both teacher and student cooperate in the process; both entertain hypotheses from the data available to them, and both converge on, or discover, a solution. Such a teaching strategy, therefore, helps realize both cognitive and affective

	TEACHER	CHARACTER OF TEACHER INTERVENTION		STUDENTS	CHARACTER OF STUDENT INTERVENTIONS	
		TELL AND DO	DISCOVERY		TELL AND DO	DISCOVERY
TASK PROCESS	Gives orientation (clarifies, informs, repeats, confirms)	Often	Seldom	Ask for orientation	Seldom	Often
	Gives opinion (evaluates, analyses, expresses a feeling or wish)	Often	Seldom	Ask for opinion	Seldom	Often
	Give suggestions (directions, hints, proposals, information)	Often	Seldom	Ask for suggestions	Seldom	Often
GROUP PROCESS	Agrees with decision (accepts, understands, concurs, complies)	Seldom	Often	Disagree with decision	Often	Seldom
	Releases tension (jokes, laughs, helps, advises)	Seldom	Often	Show tension	Often	Seldom
	Shows solidarity (helps, rewards, defends, raises other's status)	Seldom	Often	Show antagonism	Often	Seldom

Fig. 12.2   Content and process for two broad teaching strategies showing the varying character of teaching-student interventions

189

objectives, and nothing can be more helpful to accepting new ideas than discovering them for yourself.

OPTIMAL TEACHING TACTICS

Once an optimal, discovery teaching strategy has been selected, it is important to consider a number of detailed tactical problems. Discovery methods certainly avoid the need for imitation and memorization, and involve a minimum amount of explanation. However, they can increase the possibility of error, and, as we have already seen, mistakes once made are very difficult to unlearn. Adults are also easily upset and disturbed by failure, and are quick to feel that they are getting nowhere. Teachers, therefore, must guard against the possibilities of continuous and overwhelming failure, and it is for this reason that programmed books and teaching machines can often be so effective with older students.

One particular source of difficulty with older people is following complex verbal instructions, procedures, and orders. The difficulties, as we have seen earlier, arise not so much from the choice of words, but from the order in which the clauses are presented and the way in which they are related. These grammatical difficulties delay correct identification, and result in information-processing problems for the short-term memory. The solution does not necessarily involve rewriting or simplification; sometimes, this will help, but more often than not the very complexity of the information makes continuous prose an inefficient communication media. On such occasions, heuristics, algorithms, and decision tables can provide very effective job aids.

It is also important to give older people a most detailed description of what is actually expected of them. Advance organizers can serve as conceptual frameworks, precisely written objectives enable the student to plan his work and evaluate progress, while constant revision and consolidation of ongoing lessons before new material is introduced ensures continued readiness and success. Abundant evidence (see Morrisett and Hovland, 1959) is available to confirm the proposition that learning is not transferable to new learning tasks until it has first been overlearned.

The sequencing of material can also present problems to older adult students. Logical sequences are not always optimal for learning, and student preferred sequences tend to differ from traditional teaching sequences in a number of ways (Mager, 1961). Initial student interest tends to be in the concrete rather than in the abstract, in things rather than in theory, in how rather than in why. Students also tend to proceed from a simple whole to a more complex whole, and for this reason some audiovisual aids can, in fact, interfere with, rather than assist, the learning process. Further work has also demonstrated that when a responsible learner is provided only with behaviourally stated objectives and is permitted to instruct himself, in any way and in any order that he chooses, then he can considerably reduce the time taken to realize those objectives by dovetailing what he needs to know with what he already knows.

Time is an important variable in the teaching of older people, and in some ways its effects are greater than with younger students. Generally speaking, older trainees prefer somewhat longer training periods or lessons: whereas the optimal learning time for younger students appears to be about 45 to 60 minutes, older students tend to prefer somewhat longer training sessions – usually about 90 minutes. If the training session is intensive, there is a suggestion that younger people prefer 30 minute sessions and older people 60 minute sessions.

Neale, Toye, and Belbin, (1968), using a teaching machine to teach map-reading, found that 'with trainees in their thirties and forties, results from 5 one-hour sessions on the 5 consecutive days were significantly better than from the 10 shorter (i.e., half-hour) sessions.' This preference for longer training sessions is probably related to the need of older people to constantly revise and consolidate what they have learnt, so that the effects of interference can be lessened. It is for this reason that the Belbins (1968) stress the importance of the cumulative – part-learning method for the over thirty-fives, whereby each link in the chain is continuously rehearsed as the next link is added. The alternative strategy is to learn each link separately, before they are chained together.

Research also suggests that the length of a course of training is significantly related to labour turnover/retention figures – either actually during training, or soon afterwards. Three trends are discernible (see Newsham, 1969) for men over the age of 35:

1. They are *most* likely to succeed in those jobs requiring training courses of from 10 to 13 weeks' duration.
2. They survive *less* well in jobs requiring either longer training courses or very short training courses.
3. They survive *least* well in jobs requiring training courses of from 6 to 8 weeks' duration.

In other words, whenever possible, very short, short, and long training courses should be avoided; medium length courses, of about three months' duration, appear to be optimal.

Conclusion

Training and retraining older people is becoming increasingly characteristic of our society. Sometimes it involves formal management training or development programmes, sometimes it involves learning an entirely new job as when personnel leave the armed services, and sometimes it involves the learning of new techniques and procedures like metrication and decimalization. Whatever its cause, the problems are very similar. Most of the difficulties are associated with motivation, unlearning, forgetting, resistance to change and innovation, and problems of adjustment. The best indicator of success, however, is evidence that the trainee has continued to learn in a formal setting since leaving school.

Older people learn more readily by discovering things for themselves. They react badly to tell and do methods, such as following spoken or written instructions, listening to oral instruction, and reading books. Their learning experiences must also be so structured that memorization, interruptions, and failure are all avoided. The old saying that 'nothing succeeds like success' is as true of teaching older students as it is of teaching children. Learning difficulties do occur with older people, but the difficulties can be overcome by employing appropriate teaching strategies matched by sensitivity and understanding.

Posttest 12

ANSWER ALL QUESTIONS

1. List the five difficulties that older people experience in learning.

2. State how you would recognize and diagnose these difficulties when they occur.

3. State the characteristics of, and choose an appropriate teaching strategy for, a learning task that you could teach to older students. State how your teaching strategy would change if you taught the same topic to younger students.

4. State the importance to older students of advance organizers, behavioural objectives, and overlearning.

References

BALES, R. F. (1950) *Interaction Process Analysis: A Method of the Study of Small Groups.* New York: Addison-Wesley.

BELBIN, E. and R. M. (1968) Retraining and the older worker. In D. Pym, ed., *Industrial Society: Social Sciences in Management.* London: Penguin, 152–67.

BELBIN, E. and WATERS, P. (1967) Organised home study for older re-trainees, *Industrial Training International*, 2, 5, 196–8.

BELBIN, R. M. (1969) *The discovery method in training.* London: HMSO Training Information Paper No. 5.

BELBIN, R. M. (1969) How do they learn? In J. Rogers, *Teaching on Equal Terms.* London: BBC Publications, 22–31.

BIRREN, J. E., ed. (1959). *Handbook of Ageing and the Individual.* Chicago: University of Chicago Press.

BROMLEY, D. B. (1958) Some effects of age on short-term learning and remembering, *Journal of Gerontology*, 13, 398–406.

CLEUGH, M. F. (1962) *Educating Older People*. London: Tavistock Press.

ENTWISLE, D. B. (1959). Ageing: the effects on previous skill on training, *Occupational Psychology*, 3.

KAY, H. (1951) Learning of a serial task by different age groups, *Quarterly Journal of Experimental Psychology*, 3, 166–83.

LONSDALE, K. (1967) Physics and ageing, *The Advancement of Science*, 24, 119, 11–30.

MAGER, R. F. (1961) On the sequencing of instructional content. *Psychological Reports*, 9, 405–13.

MARTIN, A. O. (1969) Learning in industry. In J. Rogers, *Teaching on Equal Terms*. London: BBC Publications, 32–44.

MORRISETT, L. and HOVLAND, C. I. (1959) A comparison of three varieties of training in human problem solving, *Journal of Experimental Psychology*, 58, 52–5.

NEALE, J. G., TOYE, M. H., and BELBIN, E. (1968) Adult training: the use of programmed instruction. *Occupational Psychology*, 42.

NEWSHAM, O. B. (1969) *The Challenge of Change To the Adult Trainee*. London: HMSO Training information Paper No. 3.

WELFORD, A. T. (1958) *Ageing and Human Skill*. Oxford: Oxford University Press.

13 Teaching psychomotor skills

Learning Objectives

COGNITIVE OBJECTIVES

After carefully reading this chapter, you will be able to:

1. List the six classes of industrial tasks recognized by Seymour.

2. State the four aims of skills analysis training.

3. Distinguish between, and write short notes upon, the knowledge content and skill content of a job, stating the importance of each.

4. List four important factors that can affect the rate at which a skill is acquired, and indicate the nature of their influence.

5. Name, and distinguish between, the three learning phases involved in acquiring a physical skill, demonstrating the characteristics and the appropriate training strategies for each phase.

6. Briefly discuss the importance of job aids to both teachers and trainees.

7. Identify and use appropriate teaching strategies for psychomotor skills.

AFFECTIVE OBJECTIVES

After reading this chapter, the author intends that you will:

1. Be aware of, and value, the importance of identifying an appropriate strategy for teaching psychomotor skills.

2. Incorporate the principles presented in this chapter into your organization of managerial strategies, so that they become characteristic of your teaching style.

> Unless we have analysed and understood the skills and knowledge
> which are used by the experienced worker, and have based our
> training upon such an understanding, then any training results
> which are achieved will be haphazard and not systematic.
>
> *W. Douglas Seymour*

It is sometimes assumed that realizing psychomotor objectives, like learning to operate a capstan lathe or playing a piano, is considerably more difficult than realizing cognitive objectives. Some teachers and instructors believe that the teaching tactics and strategies involved are also quite different. These two assumptions, however, are far from the real truth of the matter. All the stages that we have detailed so far are also relevant and meaningful to the teaching and learning of physical skills; while the emphasis may be different, the procedures are broadly similar.

CLASSES OF INDUSTRIAL TASKS

The successful accomplishment of any skilled performance involves acquiring both a knowledge and a skills component, for, as Seymour points out, every job has both a 'knowing' and a 'doing' side. While the relative proportions of these two components will vary from task to task, skills analysis over a wide range of jobs suggests that certain industrial skills have similar structural characteristics or properties. Seymour (1966), on the basis of these, recognizes six main classes of work:

1. *Handwork*. This involves manual work with the operator's own hands, e.g., hand-sewing, lace-making, finishing.
2. *Handwork with tools*. This involves manual work with the help of hand-tools, e.g., most types of assembly work.
3. *Single-purpose machine work*. This involves the use of mechanically or electrically driven machines for a single, specific purpose, e.g., coil-winding, pie-packing, typing.
4. *Multipurpose machine work*. This involves the use of power-driven machines which can be easily adapted for a wide variety of different purposes, e.g., industrial sewing, capstan lathe work.
5. *Group machine work*. This involves an operator being responsible for the output from a number of semiautomatic or automatic machines, e.g., automatic weaving and spinning work, automatic capstan lathe work.
6. *Non-repetitive work*. This involves work which is specialized and non-repetitive in character. There is, usually, a high degree of responsibility attached to such tasks, e.g., machine setting and maintenance, fault-finding and rectification, loom-overlooking.

The proportion of knowledge and skill will vary, of course, within each of these six classes of work. In both handwork and non-repetitive work, for instance, the skill component is very large indeed, whereas the size of the knowledge component varies. It is large in non-repetitive work and small in handwork. Similar variations exist among the other classes. Once these are identified, it is possible for teachers and students to assess the varying importance of knowledge and skill, and plan their training accordingly.

Skills Analysis Training

It is important to distinguish between the classical way of teaching psycho-motor skills and the systematic method suggested by Douglas Seymour on the basis of a lifetime's research and investigation. Seymour bases his training strategy on a detailed job and skills analysis, and for this reason his approach is usually referred to as 'skills analysis training'. This approach has four basic aims which characterize the whole process:
1.   To enable new trainees to become competent and confident workers.
2.   To achieve this goal with the least waste of time and resources.
3.   To facilitate the integration of trainees into the socio-technical system of the factory and workplace.
4.   To assist trainees, who have changed their job and are being retrained, to regain their economic and social status with the least possible delay.
All too often in conventional training, the critical interactions between men, machine, job, and organization are overlooked or ignored. Skills analysis training, however, seeks to redress this balance by systematically analysing the requirements of the job in both its social and technical setting.

KNOWLEDGE CONTENT OF THE JOB

In teaching or learning any physical skill, it is necessary to consider the information or knowledge component of the task. This cognitive content broadly involves three quite different kinds of information, and all three must be learnt if the trainee is to reach the level of proficiency of the experienced worker:
1.   Information about the actual factory itself, and the work place where the task will be performed. This will involve knowing how his output fits into, and contributes to, the overall production system.
2.   Information about the actual job itself. What is done, why it is done, and how it is done.
3.   Information about the quality of work expected. This will involve knowing the name of faults, their appearance, cause, and effects, whose responsibility they are, what can be done to rectify them, and how they can be prevented.
All this information, of course, is readily available from a job and skills analysis, and these important documents must form the basis of an instructor's lesson plan. While most training programmes set out to teach a man information necessary to the job itself, too few of them set out to emphasize information about quality. Skills analysis training, however, sets out to

redeem this balance, for without systematic instruction on fault avoidance and fault analysis a skill cannot be performed at mastery level.

SKILL CONTENT OF THE JOB

The structures involved in teaching the skill content of a job largely consist of signals, chains, and multiple-discriminations, and the tactics discussed in the last section are still relevant and meaningful. Probably, the greatest difference between teaching cognitive and psychomotor skills is that the latter make far greater demands on the teacher. Indeed, this is probably one of the reasons for the increasing use of training devices and simulators in the area of physical skills, since these aids enable both teachers and students to use their time more effectively and efficiently (see Glaser, 1962).

Teaching the skill content of any job largely involves getting a student to *do* things, and this means that a teacher must exercise five broad responsibilities:

1. He must demonstrate the skill to the trainees as a complete cycle of operations.

2. He must break down the skill into related, but separate, subroutines, and demonstrate these just as a skilled worker would perform them.

3. He must tell, and then show, trainees how a skilled worker actually obtains his results.

4. He must allow trainees to continuously practise each of these subroutines until they learn the skill beyond the criterion, i.e., they overlearn the task.

5. He must then ensure that these subroutines are chained together

FACTOR	RESEARCH FINDINGS
Improvement on basic skill motions	Not all basic skill motions (therbligs) improve equally. Stationary acts, like grasp and position, tend to improve more rapidly than movement acts, like reach and move. This difference is probably due to the fact that stationary therbligs involve a greater degree of perception.
Rate of progress	Progress tends to be rapid initially (because it is associated with the cognitive aspects of the task), but this is then followed by a much longer period of gentle progress (associated with the motor aspects of the task.)
Plateaux	Plateaux, or periods of no improvement, do not generally occur in simple tasks. In more complex tasks, they may occur at different times for different individuals. They tend to result either from subjective factors (like distractions, lack of incentives, working conditions, etc.), or from factors inherent in acquiring the actual skill concerned.
Skilled performance	Improvement in acquiring a skill continues with practice, but gradually flattens out as mastery is reached, at which point the trend approximates more and more closely to a straight line.

Fig. 13.1   **Some factors affecting the rate at which psychomotor skill is acquired**

PHASE	CHARACTERISTICS OF PHASE	APPROPRIATE TRAINING STRATEGY
Introduction	1. Importance of cognitive processes. Trainees analyse task and verbalize what they learn. 2. Importance of perceptual processes. Trainees learn what to look for, how to recognize important cues, and how to make critical discriminations. 3. Importance of tension. Trainees experience tension, and accordingly appear to be doing an excessive amount of work.	1. Tell student what to do, how to do it, what to expect, and what procedures should be used. Teach him to talk through the manoeuvres. 2. Teach him to recognize the necessary cues or signals and to make the necessary multiple-discriminations about quality. 3. Judicious use of whole-part-whole learning. Provide information about successes and failures frequently and promptly. Short training periods.
Development	1. Gradual decline of attention to cognitive and perceptual processes. 2. Correct patterns of behaviour gradually fixed and errors reduced. 3. Coordination begins to develop and rhythm begins to appear. 4. Strategies involving judgement, decision-making, and planning begin to appear.	1. Play down cognitive and perceptual processes. Concentrate on physical skills involved. Fade out talking through manoeuvres. 2. Give extensive practice on each of sub-routines. Then gradually chain these together and practise complete skill. Constantly feedback information about errors – both their cause and effect. 3. Emphasize importance of proper coordination and rhythm. Longer training periods. 4. Introduce strategies of judgement, decision-making, and planning, Demonstrate their importance.
Consolidation	1. Tension begins to fade away. Work requires less effort and trainees begin to find that they have all the time they need for the job. 2. Gradual increase in the speed of performance. Resistance to stress and interference from other activities. Skill becomes automatic. 3. Gradual shift from relying on visual feedback to reliance on feedback from other senses.	1. Practise complete skill beyond criterion, so that it is overlearned. Concentrate on rhythm and economy of movement. Much longer training periods. 2. Brief students for, and gradually transfer them to, their final workplace. Constantly check quality of their work. emphasizing subtle multiple-discriminations and signals. 3. Wean them away from visual feedback. Concentrate on trainees developing and using other senses.

Fig. 13.2 Learning phases and appropriate training strategies for acquiring complex psychomotor skills

(retrogressively or progressively), and the complete skill overlearned through constant practice.

The actual rate at which a psychomotor skill is acquired is affected by a number of factors. The more important of these are summarized in Fig. 13.1, and teachers must ensure that students are fully aware of them and of their effects. Unless trainees are warned in advance of the reasons for the apparent unevenness of their progress, they can become needlessly disillusioned and their motivation is inevitably weakened.

Training Strategies for Complex Skills

Although certain inborn abilities play an important role, performance on most psychomotor tasks is largely a function of the habits and skills acquired on the task itself (Fleishman, 1967). Furthermore, once a skill has been acquired, it is rarely forgotten – regardless of the length of the retention interval. For instance, in studying a complex radar tracking skill, Fleishman found that, even after two years, personnel could still track at a very high level of mastery, although they had had no opportunity either to practise or see the task performed during the interval. At the same time, there is no clear-cut evidence that skill acquired on one task will necessarily transfer to another, although there is a suggestion that, while practice may not transfer, training (i.e., instruction in concepts and principles) can transfer to another situation.

In acquiring any complex skill, a number of learning phases are recognizable. These are summarized in Fig. 13.2 under the titles of introduction, development, and consolidation. It is important to recognize, however, that these three phases are not as clear-cut as they appear in the diagram. Each phase overlaps, and progress from one phase to another is rarely smooth or continuous. Nevertheless, the diagram does indicate the broad course of events, and allows variations in the overall training strategy to be highlighted. The distribution of practice, always the important part of acquiring skill, needs to be varied according to the particular learning phase. Spaced practice tends to be superior to massed practice, particularly in the early phases of training. Thirty minute periods on the same task, therefore, will tend to be optimal at the start of instruction, whereas periods of up to two hours or more tend to be optimal in the development phase, and periods of up to six hours in the consolidation phase.

In the introductory phase of training, cognitive and perceptual processes tend to dominate, and for this reason students must be properly briefed. They need to know what to do, how to do it, what to expect, what needs to be specially emphasized, what procedures should be employed, and what cues they should look out for. The appropriate training strategy, therefore, for this introductory phase will largely consist of telling and showing, but trainees should still be encouraged to verbalize or talk through each of the actions and chains involved. Information should also be provided about the sources of possible error, and the necessary multiple-discriminations should be taught so that faults can be recognized and rectified.

In the development phase of training, cognitive and perceptual processes become less worrisome, and emphasis should change to the actual psychomotor processes involved. Trainees, therefore, should begin to concentrate upon the skill content of the job, in the sense that the necessary signals and chains of each subroutine are practised and overpractised until they become 'fixed'. If the task is a simple one, there is no need to break it down into a number of subroutines, but when the task is a complex or lengthy one a whole-part-whole method of learning is to be preferred. When all the parts or subroutines have been acquired, these should be chained together into the complete skill, which should then be practised as a whole. It is important to remember that, in the development phase, practice has two separate, but related, functions: first, it serves to fix the skill, and second, it helps develop coordination and rhythm. At every stage, success and error should be constantly fed back to trainees as frequently and as promptly as possible, so that, to a very large extent, instruction takes on the character of a number of short tutorials.

The final phase of training involves consolidating what has been learnt. This is accomplished by overlearning the task beyond the criterion or level of adequacy. In this way, constant rehearsal and practice of the whole skill should help to make it automatic, in the sense that trainees will become completely relaxed, no longer affected by distractions, and have sufficient stamina to maintain the pace for a complete working day, if necessary. The consolidation phase of learning should gradually be brought to an end by introducing trainees, and then actually transferring them, to their final work place. Even after this has been accomplished, however, they should continue to be visited by their instructor over the next few weeks, so that he can constantly follow up and monitor their progress.

JOB AIDS

Supplying teachers and trainees with job aids can often appreciably simplify the actual task itself. Instructors should be encouraged to develop, or be given, if necessary, instruction schedules or lesson plans based on the job and skills analysis documents. It is useful to write out such schedules under three headings (left hand, attention points, and right hand), and to include enough detail for an instructor to teach not only *what* has to be achieved, but also *how* the experienced worker achieves it. The lefthand and the righthand columns of the lesson schedule should list hand movements, while the middle column should list the sensory features that need special attention, information about quality and any safety procedures that may be necessary.

Trainees, of course, will also often benefit from being given such instruction schedules. Job aids for workers, however, normally take the form of procedural guides, checklists, algorithms, and decision tables, all written in a form that is relevant and meaningful to the job. Such guides have been shown to improve the speed and accuracy of not only inexperienced, but also experienced and skilled operators.

Conclusions

Realizing psychomotor objectives is broadly similar, in terms of the teaching strategies and tactics employed, to realizing cognitive and affective objectives. The major differences are ones of emphasis rather than of kind. As with all education and training programmes, analysis and synthesis are the foundations of effective teaching and learning. However, acquiring a physical skill is obviously an individual rather than a group matter, and, for this reason, good teaching has always tended to be characteristic of this area of endeavour. Modern developments in skills analysis training, however, are reemphasizing the importance of the knowledge content in physical skills, for, as Professor Harry Kay has pointed out, skilled performance involves obtaining the maximum information out of the minimum number of cues.

Posttest 13

ANSWER ALL QUESTIONS

1. List the six classes of industrial task recognized by Douglas Seymour.

2. State the four aims of skills analysis training.

3. Distinguish between, and write short notes on, the twin concepts of 'the knowledge content of a job' and 'the skill content of a job'. State the importance of each.

4. List the four factors that can affect the rate at which a skill is acquired, and indicate the nature of their influence.

5. Name, and distinguish between, the three learning phases recognizable in the acquisition of a physical skill. State the characteristics of each phase, and detail the appropriate teaching strategy.

6. Briefly discuss the importance of job aids to both teachers and students.

7. Select a learning task involving the acquisition of a physical skill, and state what teaching tactics and strategies you would employ.

References and Reading List

BASS, B. M. and VAUGHAN, J. A. (1966) *Training in Industry*. London: Tavistock Pbns.

BIEL, W. C. (1963) Training programs and devices. In R. M. Gagne, ed., *Psychological Principles in System Development*. New York: Holt, Rinehart and Winston, 343–84.

FITTS, P. M. (1962) Factors in complex skill training. In R. Glaser, ed., *Training Research and Education*. New York: John Wiley, 177–97.

FLEISHMAN, E. A. (1967) Individual differences and motor learning. In R. M. Gagne, ed., *Learning and Individual Differences*. Columbus, Ohio: Charles E. Merrill.

GLASER, R. M. (1962) *Training Research and Education*. New York: John Wiley.

LEGGE, D., ed. (1970) *Skills: selected readings*. London: Penguin Books.

SEYMOUR, W. D. (1954) *Industrial Training for Manual Operations*. London: Pitman.

SEYMOUR, W. D. (1959) *Operator Training in Industry*. London: Institute of Personnel Management.

SEYMOUR, W. D. (1966) *Industrial Skills*. London: Pitman.

SEYMOUR, W. D. (1968) *Skills Analysis Training*. London: Pitman.

SINGER, E. J. and RAMSDEN, J. (1969) *The Practical Approach to Skills Analysis*. London: McGraw-Hill.

SECTION FOUR
Controlling

A continuing need of every manager is to check up to make sure that plans are being carried out effectively, that organization is sound, and that leading is effective.

Louis A. Allen

The controlling function of the teacher-manager

Controlling is the work a teacher does to determine whether his organizing and leading functions are successfully realizing the objectives which have been set. If the objectives are not being realized, then a teacher must reassess and regulate the situation — he should not change his objectives.

When a teacher-manager controls, he attempts to:

1. Evaluate the learning system.

2. Measure learning.

3. Manage by learning objectives.

In this way, the teacher-manager tries to determine whether events conform to plans, and to change failure into success: only his effectiveness can convert resources into results.

14 Evaluating a learning course

Learning Objectives

COGNITIVE OBJECTIVES

After carefully reading this chapter, you will be able to:

1.   Distinguish between a criterion test and a test of educational achievement, in terms of their objectives, construction, and pattern of scores.

2.   State four reasons for the former lack of evaluation in most educational and training programmes.

3.   State the five functions of a criterion test.

4.   List, and write short notes on, the three characteristics of an efficient and effective learning experience.

5.   Construct an appropriate criterion test from a statement of learning objectives.

AFFECTIVE OBJECTIVES

After reading this chapter, the author intends that you will:

1.   Value the concept of evaluation.

2.   Incorporate the technique into your repertoire of teaching strategies, so that it becomes characteristic of your teaching style.

> If a man will begin with certainties, he shall end in doubts: but if he will be content to begin with doubts, he shall end in certainty.
>
> *Francis Bacon*

Once the objectives of a learning situation have been carefully isolated and identified, it is possible to begin formulating the tests or examinations that will be used to decide whether or not they have been realized. As Mager once remarked, if you have gone to the trouble of going through all the stages that we have been discussing, it *matters* whether your students can actually do the things that you have planned for them. At the same time, evaluation can encourage teachers and instructors to improve on their own professional skills, as well as help them to obtain better facilities and resources for learning.

Criterion tests are often confused with the achievement tests or examinations more usually associated with education and training, and it is important, therefore, to recognize that the two are quite different in function.

> Measures cast in terms of such criterion standards (i.e., behaviourally defined objectives) provide information as to the degree of competence obtained by a particular student which is independent of reference to the performance of others. . . . In instances where a student's relative standing is the primary purpose of measurement, reference need not be made to criterion behaviour. Educational achievement examinations, for example, are administered frequently for the purpose of ordering students in a class or school, rather than for assessing their attainment of specified curriculum objectives. (Glaser, 1965).

Indeed, the character of scores obtained by students completing the two tests are quite different. In an achievement test, most of the scores tend to be normally distributed (a few students will do very well, a few will do badly, and the majority will cluster around the average); whereas in a criterion test, most of the scores tend to cluster in the upper regions. After all, if a teacher sets out to realize 10 objectives, he would be very disappointed if students only realized 50 per cent of them, for the very simple reason that no teacher or instructor is in the failure business.

The Nature of Evaluation

Until recently, tests and examinations measuring the realization of objectives have not been a serious concern of teachers and instructors. Education and training programmes have been permitted to stand on their assumed merits, and there has been little or no demand for evaluation. This has probably been due to four main difficulties: the lack of a suitable conceptual evaluation framework, the general lack of precision in statements of educational and training objectives, the difficulties involved in any form of educational measurement, and the very nature of most educational and training programmes. However, in view of the increasing investment now being made in educational and training systems, some form of responsible audit or evaluation is becoming more and more necessary.

Evaluation can take two general forms: it can either concern itself with the teacher teaching (measuring such variables as voice, mannerisms, humour, personality, blackboard work, question technique, class activity, audiovisual aids, teaching strategies, etc.), or it can concern itself with the learner learning (realizing objectives). This discussion is concerned only with the latter approach.

THE IMPORTANCE OF EVALUATION

There are many cogent reasons, other than fashion, for the present importance of evaluation. Despite the fact that the measurement of learning can never be accurate – simply because we cannot measure learning directly, but must measure signs or indicants of it – it does provide useful information concerning the efficiency, effectiveness, and utility of what has been accomplished. In other words, it enables us to:

1. Measure the competence or capability of students in terms of whether or not they have realized their agreed objectives.
2. Determine which particular objectives have *not* been realized, so that appropriate remedial action can be taken.
3. Decide the relative class order (or ranking) of the students, in terms of their success in realizing the agreed objectives.
4. Inform the teacher or instructor of the appropriateness of his teaching strategy, so that the strengths and weaknesses of the course can be determined.
5. Devise procedures so as to improve course design, and determine whether or not additional learning resources are necessary.

In other words, evaluation enables us, as teachers, to exercise our essential managerial *control* function, in the sense that it feeds back to us control information regarding the appropriateness of our organization of learning resources.

Although the most important function of the criterion test is to measure changes in student behaviour, the criterion test has an additional function in industrial training. It can be used to tell an organization exactly what a student will be able to do at the conclusion of each training stage. For this reason, an organization's review of, and agreement to, the contents of a criterion test can be one of the most crucial stages in its commitment to training. The criterion test enables the training problem to be pinned down in terms that an organization can understand, approve, and value. Training, accordingly, acquires face validity and credibility in the eyes of management, since it is seen to be intimately related to the reality of work.

Ofiesh (1965) has described how one American airline tried for a number of years to teach its sales staff to calculate the appropriate overseas fare for passengers who deviated from the standard, laid-down routings. Their training school tackled the problem conventionally, by teaching a complex mileage system of surcharges, fictitious destinations, break-points, and other complex technical matters. Despite a great deal of analysis, the training problem was never really pinned down until an effort was made to *construct* a criterion test. Immediately, the problem became clear. It was seen to involve four different, but related, decisions, and these – to the delight of the airline's management – became the total specification of the training system for dealing with this important operating problem.

SIGNS OF AN EFFICIENT LEARNING SITUATION

It is not possible to determine the quality of a learning experience from direct evidence, but a number of signs or indicants can be used. Generally speaking, it is possible to say – with all the proper qualifications – that an efficient and effective learning experience tends to be characterized by:

1. *The successful realization of objectives.* In terms of actual evaluation test scores, this means that the majority (90 per cent or more) of the students obtain the majority (90 per cent or more) of the objectives. This concept is increasingly referred to as the 90/90 criterion, although it is important to realize that 90 per cent is not an exact number, but an order of magnitude.

2. *The deliberate destruction of the normal curve of distribution.* If students are tested by a pretest, prior to undertaking the learning programme, it will be found that their pretest scores tend to follow a normal distribution. This implies that a few students will already have realized most of the objectives before they begin, a few will have realized none, and the majority will have realized some of the objectives. The teacher's aim is to destroy this normal distribution, and to replace it with the skewed distribution characteristic of the 90/90 criterion.

3. *The lack of any direct relationship between ability and learning.* There is an increasing body of evidence (see Davies, 1969) to suggest that the lack of any correlation between intelligence and learning or retention may indicate a highly efficient and effective learning experience. This happy situation is illustrated in Fig. 14.1. The series of vertical lines, representing the pretest score (bottom of line) and posttest scores (top of line) of 144 mechanical engineering apprentices, are so arranged in each group that intelligence scores increase from the left to the right. There is no statistically significant relationship between intelligence scores and posttest scores in either of the four classes. Situations such as this, of course, have always been promised by programmed learning, but the promise has rarely been fulfilled. However, 'in certain of the new curricula, there are data to suggest that aptitude measures correlate much less with end-of-course achievement than they do with achievement in early units.' (Cronbach, 1963.)

At the same time, no learning experience should be considered entirely successful if it is not characterized by a positive shift in the student's attitude

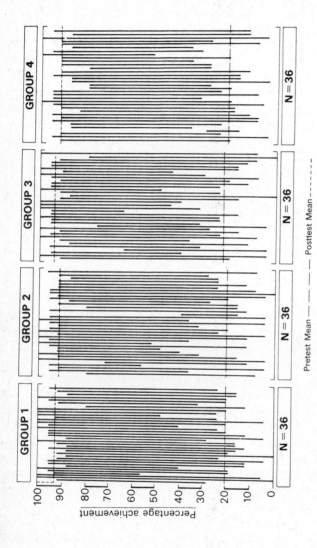

Fig. 14.1 The relationship between intelligence and learning (Each vertical line represents one mechanical engineering apprentice. The bottom of the line indicates his pretest score, the top of the line indicates his posttest score. Each of the four classes are matched on pretest scores, intelligence, mechanical aptitude, science examination marks and – where necessary – by random numbers. In each class of 36 students, the vertical lines are so arranged that intelligence test scores increase from the left to the right. There is no statistically significant relationship between intelligence test scores and posttest scores, and this is clearly visible from the diagram. The task involved learning 'the principles of operation of an automatic transmission system in automobiles.' See Davies, 1969).

211

to either the subject or to learning in general. Attitude surveys, for this reason, can fulfill a very important function in the evaluation process, as can student reactions communicated at the end of short courses, conferences, and seminars. Readers who would like to follow up this approach are particularly recommended to read Oppenheim's (1966) clear and practical handbook.

Techniques of Evaluation

Criterion testing requires no additional testing skills to those already known to the educationist, an expert summary of which is given by Dorothy Adkins-Wood (1960). Since such criterion tests are intimately related to the objectives they measure, they can either be formulated directly from the objectives, or – as some prefer – the objectives can be formulated from the criterion measure. For the unskilled, the latter approach is probably preferable, since people tend to be more skilled in asking questions than in defining objectives.

It is most important to realize, however, that the criterion test must fulfill three essential conditions, if it is to do its job properly. This means that it must be:

1. *Appropriate*. The criterion test must be appropriate to the objectives, as well as appropriate to the subject material, the teaching strategy employed, and to the students who will respond to it.

2. *Effective*. The criterion test must perform its job of measurement. This means that the test must be reliable (i.e., its scores not dependent on chance), and valid (i.e., the test serves its purpose).

3. *Practical*. The criterion test must be practical in the sense that it is acceptable to both teachers and students, realistic in terms of the cost and time involved in administering it, and, preferably, easily used and reused.

If these three conditions are fulfilled, most of the charges levelled against educational achievement examinations will be avoided.

Evaluation, properly speaking, involves four types of test: prerequisite tests, pretests, posttests, and retention tests. The function of the prerequisite test, which is often a section of the pretest, is to determine whether or not students fulfill the necessary prior conditions for undertaking the learning commitment. Any student who fails this test should undergo immediate remedial teaching, once the real nature of his difficulty has been defined, since he cannot possibly hope to realize the agreed objectives.

The pretest fulfills a number of functions. It can indicate to the teacher which of the objectives are already in the student's repertoire; he can also use the pretest results to decide when, and at what point, the student should enter the learning system. This information is particularly important if a unit or module approach is being used, or when a remedial learning programme is being undertaken. A student's pretest score, compared with his posttest score,

Learning Objectives
At the end of this lesson, you will be able to:
1. State the names given to the number system which uses a base ten, and the number system which uses a base two.
2. Count in the binary number system.
3. Translate numbers from the decimal number system to numbers in the binary system, and vice versa.
4. Read a set of readout lights on a digital computer.

Criterion Test
Answer ALL questions. There is NO time limit.
Section A. Number systems (Objective 1)
1. What is the name given to the number system which uses a base 10?
2. What is the name given to the number system which uses a base 2?

Section B. Counting and translation (Objectives 2 *and* 3)
1. Complete the following sequence of numbers:

(a) 0001	(d) 0100	(g) ——	(j) ——
(b) 0010	(e) ——	(h) ——	(k) ——
(c) 0011	(f) 0110	(i) ——	(l) ——

2. What numbers, in the system base 10, are represented by:

(a) 10011	(c) 00111
(b) 0010	(d) 10010

Section C. Reading and translating readout (Objective 4)
1. Draw three sets of readout lights with five lights in each set:
(a) In the first set, shade in the light(s) so that the set represents an even number.
(b) In the second set, shade in the light(s) that represent the smallest number possible.
(c) In the last set, shade in the light(s) that represent 4.
(In each case, a shaded light in ON, and an unshaded light is OFF).
2. What number (base 10) is displayed by each of the following sets of lights?

(a)	○	○	●	●	○
(b)	○	●	○	○	●
(c)	●	●	○	○	○
(d)	●	○	●	●	○

(In each case, a shaded light is ON and an unshaded light is OFF).

Fig. 14.2 Set of learning objectives, and associated criterion test, for an actual lesson entitled 'How to read computer readout lights'

can also have an important motivating effect, since it helps to demonstrate that a change has indeed taken place.

The posttest, of course, is administered immediately the lesson ends. Its main function is to determine whether or not the objectives have been realized. For this reason, the test really consists of the objectives rewritten in test format; an example of this is illustrated in Fig. 14.2. Readers may also like to compare the posttest at the end of each chapter with its associated list of cognitive objectives. The use of the word 'test', in this discussion, is not intended to imply that all lessons should necessarily be accompanied by a formal question paper. On many occasions the last stage of the lesson, or even the assignment given to the student for completion before the next lesson, will cause the student to perform the total task and so constitute a true evaluation. Retention tests, of course, can take a different form to that of the posttest, but, since the aim is to determine which of the objectives still remain in the student's repertoire, it is usual for the retention test to follow the posttest in every particular.

Conclusion

Examinations have for long been the whipping boy of education; they have tended to be blamed for nearly every sin of commission and omission committed by both teachers and students. Bruner (1965), however, has pointed out that, 'It is obvious that an examination can be bad in the sense of emphasizing trivial aspects of a subject. Such examinations can encourage teaching in a disconnected fashion and learning by rote. What is often overlooked, however, is that examinations can also be allies in the battle to improve curricula and teaching.' Such an approach underlines the importance of properly constructed criterion tests. Not only are they measuring instruments, but, in a very real sense, they are also aids to improving the overall quality of learning experiences.

Posttest 14

ANSWER ALL QUESTIONS

1. Distinguish between a criterion test and a test of educational achievement in terms of their objectives, construction, and pattern of scores.

2. State four reasons for the former lack of evaluation in most education and training programmes.

3. State the five functions of a criterion test.

4. List, and write short notes on, the three characteristics of an efficient and effective learning experience.

5. Select a learning task for which you have a list of behavioural objectives, and construct an appropriate criterion test. Justify the test.

References and Reading List

ADKINS-WOOD, D. (1960) *Test construction.* Columbus, Ohio: Charles E. Merrill.
BRUNER, J. S. (1965) *The process of education.* Cambridge, Massachusetts: Harvard University Press.
CRONBACH, L. J. (1963) Course improvement through evaluation, *Teachers College Record*, 64, 672–83.

DAVIES, I. K. (1969) *Mathetics: An Experimental Study of the Relationship Between Ability and Practice in the Acquisition of Basic Concepts in Science.* Unpublished PhD thesis, University of Nottingham.

GLASER, R. (1965) Toward a behavioural science for instructional design. In R. Glaser, ed., *Teaching Machines and Programmed Learning. II: Data and Directions.* Washington, DC: Department of Audiovisional Instruction, National Education Association.

HESSELING, P. (1966) *Strategy of Evaluation Research.* Netherlands: Van Gorcum.

LIGHT, R. J. and SMITH, P. V. (1970) Choosing a future: strategies for designing and evaluating new programs, *Harvard Educational Review*, 40, 1, 1–280.

OFIESH, G. D. (1965) *Programmed Instruction: A Guide for Managers.* New York: American Management Association.

OPPENHEIM, A. N. (1966) *Questionnaire Design and Attitude Measurement.* London: Heinemann.

TRACEY, W. R. (1968) *Evaluation Training and Development Systems.* New York: American Management Association.

TYLER, R. W., ed. (1969) *Educational evaluation: new roles, new means – The sixty-eighth yearbook.* Chicago: National Society for the Study of Education.

15 Measuring learning

Learning Objectives

COGNITIVE OBJECTIVES

After carefully reading this chapter, you will be able to:

1. Define the term 'measurement'.

2. List the three basic procedures that must be followed if sound measurement is to be obtained.

3. List, distinguish between, and write short notes upon the four scales of measurement.

4. Explain how the scales of measurement can be used to select appropriate test statistics.

5. List, and write short notes upon, the five types of criterion power tests commonly employed as measures of learning.

6. State the relationship between the five criterion power tests and the four scales of measurement.

AFFECTIVE OBJECTIVES

After reading this chapter, the author intends that you will:

1. Be aware of, and value, the principles of measurement as applied to the work of the teacher-manager.

2. Incorporate the principles into your value system, so that they become characteristic of your teaching style.

> There is no more common error than to assume that, because prolonged and accurate mathematical calculations have been made, the application of the result to some fact of nature is absolutely certain.
>
> *A. N. Whitehead*

Once the importance of evaluation in education and industrial training has been thoroughly understood, the teacher-manager comes face to face with the very real difficulties of measuring learning. If this measurement, however, is not to become a meaningless and misleading business, its theoretical nature and assumptions must be thoroughly grasped. Unfortunately, this requirement is not always fulfilled, probably because the concept of measurement seems such a familiar and obvious one to us. Yet as Hartley (1967) has pointed out, evaluation in programmed learning, for instance, has yielded little in the way of unequivocal results, despite the importance that this strategy has traditionally placed on proper evaluation procedures. Much of the difficulty, however, in most evaluation studies seems to stem from the nature of the measurements taken, the assumptions that are made, and the selection of the test statistics for use in the subsequent analysis.

The Nature of Measurement

Although the term 'measurement' is difficult to define, Campbell (1940) has probably given the most useful and incisive formulation: 'Measurement is the assignment of numerals to objects or events according to rules.' The problem of measurement, therefore, for the teacher-manager concerned with the difficulties of evaluation becomes one of making the rules explicit.

Variables, like length, mass, and time, are relatively easy to measure, in the sense that there are several simple and clear criteria available. Unfortunately, this is rarely the case with the variables that interest the teacher and instructor, for the obvious reason that there are few 'good' rules which can be readily adopted. Nevertheless, we must have rules whatever we measure, but their limitations must be recognized and thoroughly understood if grave error in evaluation is to be avoided.

Three basic procedures should always be followed if sound measurement is to be obtained:
1. Define the object or event to be measured in the most precise form possible.
2. Define the numerical scale from which the numerals of measurement are to be assigned.
3. Ensure that the measurement procedure is analogous to reality.

Defining objects or events in physical science presents little or no difficulty; in education and industrial training, however, an operational definition of learning must normally be employed. The second procedure, defining the numerical scale or set, can be a troublesome business. In measuring height, for instance, we know precisely what is meant by a difference of two or three inches, but, in the area of learning, it is surprisingly difficult to know what a difference of 10 per cent at the lower end of a scale on a posttest means when compared with an equivalent difference on the higher end of the same scale.

Difficulties can also exist in learning evaluation with respect to analogism, particularly when we are dealing with variables like personality, motivation, and attitudes. Although we speak of measuring objects or events, we are, in fact, often speaking inaccurately. What we are really doing is to measure their properties or characteristics, and in education and industrial training even this is usually accomplished indirectly. For instance, it is *not* possible to measure achievement, retention, intelligence, attitude, or personality directly, some sign or indicant of them must be taken and their properties then inferred.

Levels and Scales of Measurement

Measurement of any kind can be classified on the basis of a set of rules, nine of which are generally recognized. These form the very foundation of measurement, and the rules or postulates are conventionally grouped in such a way as to define or form four scales (see Stevens, 1946; Coombs, 1953):

      1.   Nominal scale.
      2.   Ordinal scale.
      3.   Interval scale.
      4.   Ratio scale.

The characteristics of these four scales of measurement are summarized in Fig. 15.1. It will be seen that the four scales form a hierachy, with the nominal scale yielding the least and the ratio scale the most information.

Although rules or postulates are often assumed to be fulfilled in measurement, in education and industrial training they should *always* be tested. Most measurements in physical science, for instance, depend upon the fifth postulate shown in Fig. 15.1, but it is difficult to find a great number of situations where this postulate is completely fulfilled in the social sciences. Jones may like Smith, and Smith may like Brown, but it certainly does not follow that Jones likes Brown – yet, this conclusion would be necessary if the fifth postulate is assumed. Indeed, postulates 6, 7, 8, and 9 are rarely fulfilled outside the physical sciences, so that the majority of measurements in education and training involve only the nominal and ordinal scales. Accordingly, the range of appropriate test statistics which can be used in learning evaluation is very considerably curtailed, so much so that even the calculation of a mean score is strictly speaking inadmissable.

No.	LEVEL	PROPERTIES	RELEVANT RELATION AND NUMERICAL OPERATIONS	ASSUMPTIONS	POSTULATES	EXAMPLES
1	Nominal	Classification	Equate Not equate	(1) All members of a set are assigned the same numeral, and no two sets are assigned the same numeral	(1) Either $(a=b)$ or $(a \neq b)$, but not both (2) If $(a=b)$, then $(b=a)$ (3) If$[(a=b)$ and $(b=c)]$, then $(a=c)$	Car registration plate numbers Simple questionnaire and interview data gathered on an all-or-none basis
2	Ordinal	Classification Order	Equate Not equate	(1) As above (2) Objects can be rank ordered on the basis of an operationally defined characteristic or property	(1), (2) and (3) above (4) If $(a>b)$, then $(b>a)$ (5) If$[(a>b)$ and $(b>c)]$, then $(a>c)$	Moh's scale of hardness Most psychological and educational test scores
3	Interval	Classification Order Equal units	Equate Not equate Add Subtract Multiply Divide	(1) As above (2) As above (3) Distances on the scale represent equal intervals	(1), (2), (3), (4) and (5) as above (6) $[(a=p)$ and $(b>O)]$, then $(a+b)>p$ (7) $(a+b)=(b+a)$ (8) If $[(a=p)$ and $(b=q)]$, then $(a+b)=(p+q)$ (9) $(a+b)+c=a+(b+c)$	Temperature scales Very well validated intelligence tests, etc.
4	Ratio	Classification Order Equal units Absolute zero	Equate Not equate Add Subtract Multiply Divide	(1) As above (2) As above (3) As above (4) Scale has an absolute or natural zero	(1), (2), (3), (4), (5), (6), (7), (8), and (9) above as	Common scales of length, mass and time Sone scale of loudness

Fig. 15.1 A classification of scales of measurement

NOMINAL SCALE

The nominal scale is the most elementary form of measurement, and it imparts, therefore, the least information. Numerals on this scale (e.g., telephone numbers) are assigned as classifying labels. They do *not* respresent an amount, nor does a higher number mean more than a low one. Since only the first three postulates are fulfilled, numbers on this scale *cannot* be added or subtracted, multiplied or divided. In other words, numbers on the nominal scale can only be counted and compared, so as to measure differences and similarities; as Fig. 15.1 suggests, numbers on this scale are merely labels of classification.

SCALE	CLASSIFICATION	ORDER	EQUAL UNITS	ABSOLUTE ZERO
1. Nominal scale	Yes			
2. Ordinal scale	Yes	Yes		
3. Interval scale	Yes	Yes	Yes	Yes
4. Ratio scale	Yes	Yes	Yes	Yes

Fig. 15.2 **Properties of the four scales of measurement**

Identifying two teaching methods as 1 and 2 (or A and B) is one example of the nominal scale. The nominal scale is also widely used in simple questionnaires and interviews which collect all or none type data, like age, sex, religion, interests, etc.; the scale is also used for data collected from tests which require true/false, yes/no, agree/disagree and similar/different types of response. It has been estimated (Davies, 1970) that something like 40 per cent of all measurements taken in education and industrial training actually involve the nominal scale.

ORDINAL MEASUREMENT

Measurements on the ordinal scale involve not only:
1. the property of classification, but also
2. the property of rank order.

In other words, it is possible to determine whether one object or event has more or less of a particular trait than another. However, it is important to appreciate that the scale does not yield any information whatsoever about the amount of the actual difference involved. Measurements on the ordinal scale, therefore, *can* be equated or not equated, they can be placed in rank order, but they *cannot* be added or substracted, multiplied or divided. Since something like half the measurements involved in learning evaluation belong to the ordinal scale, this restriction is particularly severe. Indeed, most pretest, posttest and retention test scores are basically ordinal measurements, as are most intelligence, aptitude, personality, and attitude test scores (see Kerlinger, 1964; Wood, 1961).

INTERVAL SCALE

Measurements on the interval scale involve not only:

1. the property of classification, and
2. the property of rank order, but also
3. the additional property of equal interval between each numeral.

Thus, the difference between 25 and 50 on this scale is the *same* as the difference between 50 and 75. If the ordinal scale had been involved, no such information would be available, and it would only have been possible to say that one score was greater than another. The interval scale, on the other hand, enables us to calculate how much greater one score may be as compared with another, and for this reason data collected on this scale may be added and subtracted, multiplied, and divided. Thus, the whole range of test statistics can usually be employed in analysing the data. It is important to remember, however, that it is *not* the quantities or amounts that are being manipulated arithmetically, only their intervals or distances.

If two measures of the same variable are employed, for instance, a multiple-choice type of posttest *and* an essay or short answer type of posttest, an equal interval can be assumed if the two measures can be shown to be substantially related to each other. For this reason, scores on many well-constructed and validated achievement, retention, intelligence, and aptitude tests can often be regarded as approximating to the interval scale, provided a substantial relationship can be demonstrated with other measures of the same variable.

RATIO SCALE

Measurements on the ratio scale involve not only:

1. the property of classification,
2. the property of rank order, and
3. the property of equal interval, but also
4. the additional property of an absolute zero.

Thus, measurements taken on the ratio scale contain more information than on any other scale, and, for this reason, it is the ideal form of measurement for the scientist. Since the scale has an absolute zero, statements of ratio are meaningful in the sense that numbers on the scale represent the actual amount of the property being measured. Accordingly, it is possible to say that a score of 50 per cent on this scale is twice as good as a score of 25 per cent, and for this reason there is no limitation on the range of test statistics that can be employed with data collected on the ratio scale.

Unfortunately, this scale is very rarely, if ever, achieved in learning evaluations, although some close approximations are sometimes made. In most tests and examinations in education and training, an arbitrary rather than an absolute zero is employed, for the very simple reason that it is not possible to think of someone with zero intelligence, zero achievement, or even zero personality. However, objective style examinations do have a particular advantage from the ratio scale point of view. It is sometimes possible, when dealing with somewhat esoteric subject material completely unknown to the students prior to instruction, to so continuously field test and revise the examination that the scores obtained at the pretest stage closely approximate that to be expected by chance alone. If this happy state can be realized, it can be assumed, with some justification, that an absolute zero or baseline has been achieved, thus making possible a ratio scale of measurement.

Scales and the Selection of Test Statistics

Once the properties of the four scales of measurement are understood, it will be appreciated that the selection of test statistics to be employed in analysing the data requires very considerable care. This is not to say that inappropriate test statistics cannot be calculated, but only that the subsequent interpretation difficulties may be so great as to render the calculations sterile if not misleading. Unfortunately, in their haste to use sophisticated test statistics many teacher-managers fail to appreciate that the choice is largely dependent on the nature of the problem involved, the character of the distribution of the measurements obtained, and the scale of measurement that has been employed.

Three types of information are most commonly required in learning evaluation:

1. Measures of typical value.
2. Measures of variability.
3. Measures of association.

Test statistics yielding information of this kind are extremely varied, but the choice is largely dependent upon the scale of measurement involved as will be seen from Fig. 15.3. Readers who are unfamiliar with the test statistics displayed are recommended to consult the very fine book by J. P. Guilford (1965).

It will be seen from Fig. 15.3 that the only measure of typical value that can be collected from data belonging to the nominal scale is the mode, since no numerical operations of any kind are possible. A median and a mode can be calculated from data on the ordinal scale, but the mean, which involves addition and division in its calculation, can only be used for data on the interval and ratio scales. No test statistic of variability exists for the nominal scale, although partiles (such as quartiles and centiles) can be used with ordinal data. However, standard and average deviations are applicable to data collected on both the interval and ratio scales of measurement, since all four numerical operations can be employed. Measures of association or correlation are only really available to interval and ratio scale data, although a coefficient of association can be calculated for both the nominal and ordinal scales, and a ranking coefficient for the ordinal scale.

In terms of more sophisticated techniques, all classical and parametric test statistics can be used with interval and ratio measurements, with perhaps

No.	CLASSES OF TEST-STATISTIC	SCALES OF MEASUREMENT			
		NOMINAL	ORDINAL	INTERVAL	RATIO
1	*Typical value*	Mode	Mode Median	Mode Median Mean	
2	*Variability*	—	Partiles	Partiles Range Standard deviation Average deviation Standard score	
3	*Association*	Coefficient of association	Coefficient of association Ranking coefficient	Coefficient of association Ranking coefficient Simple, partial and multiple coefficients Multivariate technique	

Fig. 15.3 The relationship between scales of measurement and common test statistics

the possible exception of coefficients of variation – which ought to be reserved for ratio measures.

Within this wealth of available techniques, factor analysis, regression analysis, multiple regression analysis, and even the somewhat laborious canonical correlation, are all especially relevant. Indeed, of all the many multivariate techniques, factor analysis is probably the best known and most widely used in learning evaluations, which is unfortunate in view of the fact that interval and ratio scale data are so rarely found in education and industrial training. More appropriate test statistics, when an equal interval cannot be assumed, involve cluster analysis (including the so-called coefficient of belongingness) and clump theory using ranking correlation coefficients. Both methods are simple and dependable, but cannot, by their very nature, yield the invaluable tables of factor loadings associated with factor analysis.

Compared with such an array, the test-statistics available for use with data based on the nominal scale must seem very thin indeed. It is true that the techniques available are limited, but they still involve a great deal. For instance, analysis of nominal data can involve studying relationships by partitioning and cross-partitioning; frequency statistics, like chi-square, percentages, as well as coefficients of association and contingency, can also be used. A chi-square test can even be calculated to measure 'goodness of fit' and also independence.

Test statistics for use with the ordinal scale involve all those applicable to the nominal scale. In addition, rank order measures can be employed like Spearman's rank order coefficient of correlation, Kendall's Tau, and Kendall's coefficient of concordance; even a rank order of variance can be carried out. If there is any reason to believe that the data may approximate towards equal intervals, then test statistics, like r, t, and F, may be employed (Torgerson,

1958; Boneau, 1961). Some authorities even recommend that ordinal measurements are treated as equal interval (Bartlett, 1947), with the proviso that care is taken to ensure that no gross inequalities of interval are involved. However, the difficulties of interpretation are so troublesome that the advice may well be questionable.

Power Tests and Scales of Measurement

In measuring learning, transformations involving pretest, posttest, and retention test scores are commonly employed in evaluation studies. They are generally calculated by means of the formulae set out in Fig. 15.4, and it will be seen that five types of criterion power tests are commonly employed. These involve:

1. Basic scores.
2. Difference scores.
3. Predictive scores.
4. Ratio scores.
5. Modified ratio scores.

Basic and difference scores involve the ordinal scale of measurement, predictive scores involve the interval scale, and ratio and modified ratio scores, of course, the ratio scale. No one measure is entirely satisfactory, and all of them approximate in some way towards the ideal criterion. However, a basic rule of thumb is to use power test transformations based on the highest scale of measurement applicable to the data available.

BASIC SCORES

These are so commonplace in evaluation studies that no further comment is necessary.

DIFFERENCE SCORES

Basic scores take no account of the actual amount gained by a student, nor do they take account of what proportion has been lost after a known interval of time. Accordingly, it is sometimes useful to employ gain scores as an indicant of learning. A short-term gain score is simply the difference between posttest and pretest scores, whereas a long-term gain score is the difference between retention test and posttest scores. A loss score is the difference between a posttest and a retention test score.

Difference scores assume that equal gains or losses at different points on the scale represent equal increments or decrements of learning. For evaluation purposes, the criterion of success, therefore, is taken to be the amount actually gained (or not lost), implying that there *is* an advantage in learning beyond the minimum criterion level. For this reason, it is important that the examination or test that is used to measure learning actually measures well beyond a predetermined level of adequate performance.

No.	TYPE	CRITERION	FORMULAE	ASSUMPTION
1	*Basic scores*	Pretest Posttest Retention test	$C = P$ $C = A$ $C = R$	Any other scores are irrelevant.
2	*Difference scores*	Gain scores: (a) Short-term (b) Long-term Loss scores	$C = A - P$ $C = R - P$ $C = A - R$	Equal gains or losses at different points in the scale represent equal increments or decrements in learning.
3	*Predictive scores*	Residual gain Multiple residual gain	$C = A - bP - a$ $C = A - b_1 X_1 - b_2 X_2 \ldots - b_n X_n - a$	Pretest scores are valid predictors of achievement. Any variable can reasonably be used as a predictor, if it is found to correlate with achievement or retention.
4	*Ratio scores*	Short-term gain ratio Long-term gain ratio (a) Type one (b) Type two Loss ratio	$C = \dfrac{A - P}{100 - P} \times \dfrac{100}{1}$ $C = \dfrac{R - P}{100 - P} \times \dfrac{100}{1}$ $C = \dfrac{R - P}{A - P} \times \dfrac{100}{1}$ $C = \dfrac{A - R}{A - P} \times \dfrac{100}{1}$	Gains at higher points in the scale represent proportionately greater increments in learning than equivalent gains lower down in the scale. Similarly, loss ratios, imply that losses at higher points in the scale represent proportionately greater decrements in learning than equivalent losses lower down in the scale.
5	*Modified ratio scores*	Curvilinear measure	$C = N - N\dfrac{1}{\sqrt{qn}} \sqrt{n - \dfrac{An}{100}}$	The variance of the final levels of knowledge is much greater than the variance in the initial levels of knowledge. This high variance is concealed by the nature of the testing procedure.

C = criterion
P = pretest score
A = achievement (posttest) score
R = retention test score
a = regression constant
b = regression coefficient
Xn = other predictor variables
N = total number of units of knowledge
n = number of items on that test
$q = 1 - \dfrac{1}{\text{number of choices in question}}$

Note (i) A valid and reliable criterion measure should be assumed.
(ii) If criterion scores from different tests are to be combined, they should be standardized.

Fig. 15.4 A comparison of different criterion measures

PREDICTIVE SCORES

In many evaluation studies, it is relatively common to find low, zero, or even negative correlations between gain scores and other associated variables. For instance, gain scores ordinarily correlate negatively with pretest scores, and these usually correlate with general ability scores (Manning and Dubois, 1963). Most classroom teachers and instructors, however, would regard such results with grave suspicion, for their experience tends to support the hypothesis that students who are initially knowledgeable about a subject tend to learn more. If this really is the case, then the correlation between gains scores and preknowledge should not always be a negative one.

In order to eliminate this disadvantage, Manning and Dubois (1963) have suggested the use of a residual gain measure. Quite simply, this is a measure of improvement over (or failure to reach) an expected level of achievement. It involves calculating the difference between an actual posttest score and a hypothetical one, predicted by means of a regression equation using the student's pretest result.

The main advantage of the residual gain measure is that it always correlates zero with preknowledge. Furthermore, an important implication of residual gain is that students who fail to reach their predicted posttest scores (i.e., the low achievers) can be considered as in need of remedial teaching and guidance. High achievers (those who exceed their predicted posttest scores), on the other hand, can be regarded as a bonus to the instructional system.

RATIO AND MODIFIED RATIO SCORES

Ratio scores are particularly useful indicants of learning, since they measure the amount learnt (or retained) as a proportion of what could have been acquired. Gains at higher points on the scale are taken to represent proportionately greater increments of learning than equivalent gains lower down the scale. Similarly, loss ratios imply that losses at higher points on the scale represent proportionately greater decrements of learning than equivalent losses lower down the scale. Unfortunately, the measure can lead to anomalies when the student has a high degree of preknowledge.

Although high correlations may exist between pretest and posttest scores, it has been suggested that the best indicant of learning may still be posttest scores alone (Carver, 1966). In other words, the best system may be one which does not arbitrarily correlate zero with initial performance, but allows the relationship between initial performance and learning to be investigated empirically.

It has often been noticed by teachers and instructors that variance in posttest scores is usually very much greater than variance in preknowledge scores, although this fact can sometimes be hidden by the testing procedures employed. Subtracting pretest scores from posttest scores will not, therefore, appreciably change the relative ranking of the final scores. Furthermore, a gain from an initial score of 65 per cent to a final score of 70 per cent may, in every important sense, be greater than the numerically larger gain from 45 per cent to 55 per cent. Test performance, in other words, may have a curvilinear relationship to knowledge, rather than the linear relationship which is usually assumed. The existence of this curvilinear relationship may also help to explain why many research projects (which have assumed a linear relationship) have yielded results which seem contrary to logical expectation. Since residual gain measures, however, ordinarily correlate very highly with posttest scores, much of their success can be readily explained in terms of the curvilinear model.

Curvilinear measures, which involve an estimate of the number of knowledge units acquired by each student, are calculated from posttest scores. The measure assumes that there is *no* absolute or natural criterion of success in learning; rather there are different degrees of success. It may, therefore, be uneconomic to spend too much time and effort trying to raise the level of low achievers.

It is not necessary to assume that posttest scores are always the best indicants of learning, even within the confines of the curvilinear model. However, as long as the ratio of posttest or pretest scores is greater than one, then the model still holds – providing the correlation between initial knowledge and ultimate learning remains moderately high. As the ratio increases, so the size of the correlation becomes less and less important. In summary, providing that one or other of the following conditions are fulfilled:
1.   variance in posttest scores is greater than variance in pretest scores, or
2.   a moderately high correlation between initial knowledge and learning can be assumed,
then a curvilinear model can be employed by a teacher-manager as a means of measuring learning and evaluating the success of his organization.

Conclusion

Although many texts are now available on test statistics, usually little guidance is given on the methods of obtaining an adequate measure of learning and selecting appropriate statistical procedures. Indeed, the complexity of evaluation is not always appreciated, and the effects of gross departures from the underlying rules of measurement rarely understood. A scale criterion, however, offers a convenient model to the teacher-manager for the selection and interpretation of statistical procedures. Its use will ensure that not only appropriate test statistics are selected, but that the maximum amount of valid information is extracted from the available data. In this way, teachers and instructors are able to determine whether or not the learning objectives have been realized, and whether plans have been transformed into reality.

Posttest 15

ANSWER ALL QUESTIONS

1. Define the term 'measurement'.

2. List the three basic procedures that must be followed if sound measurement is to be obtained.

3. List, distinguish between, and write short notes on, the four scales of measurement.

4. Explain how the scales of measurement can be used to select appropriate test statistics.

5. List, and write short notes on, the five types of criterion power tests commonly employed as measures of learning.

6. State the relationship between the five criterion power tests and the four scales of measurement.

References and Reading List

ANDERSON, N. (1961) Scales of statistics: parametric and non-parametric. *Psychological Bulletin*, LVIII, 305–16.

ANDERSON, R. L. and BANCROFT, T. A. (1952) *Statistical Theory in Research*. New York: Wiley.

BARTLETT, M. (1947) The use of transformations, *Biometrics*, III, 39–52.

BERELSON, B. (1952) *Content Analysis in Communication Research*. New York: Free Press.

BONEAU, C. A. (1960) The effects of violations of assumptions underlying the 't' test, *Psychological Bulletin*, 57, 49–64.

BONEAU, C. (1961) A note on measurement scales and statistical tests, *American Psychologist*, XVI, 260.

BROWNELL, W. A. (1965) The evaluation of learning under different systems of instruction, *Educational Psychologist*, 3, 1, 53–65.

BURKE, C. J. (1960) Additive scales and statistics, *Psychological Review*, 60, 73–5.

CAMPBELL, D. T. and STANLEY, J. C. (1963) Experimental and quasi-experimental design for research on teaching. In N. L. Gage, ed., *Handbook of research on teaching*. Chicago: Rand McNally.

CAMPBELL, N. R. (1940) *Final Report, Committee of the British Association for the Advancement of Science on the Problem of Measurement*. London: British Association.

CARVER, R. P. (1966) The curvilinear relationship between knowledge and test performance. In K. M. Wientage and P. H. Dubois, eds., *Criteria in Learning Research*. Technical Report No. 9, Office of Naval Research Contract No. NONR 816 (14). Washington University.

COOMBS, C. (1953) Theory and methods of social measurement. In L. Festinger and D. Katy, eds., *Research Methods in Behavioural Sciences*. New York: Holt, Rinehart and Winston.

DANIELS, J. C. (1962) *Statistical Methods in Educational Research*. Nottingham: Institute of Education, Nottingham University.

DAVIES, I. K. (1967) The Management of Learning, *Training International*, Spring 1967.

DAVIES, I. K. (1969) Some aspects of measurement in educational technology. In A. P. Mann and C. K. Brunstrom, eds., *Aspects of Educational Technology, III*. London: Pitman.

DAVIES, I. K. (1970) Foundations of measurement in Educational Technology, *Journal of the Association for Programmed Learning and Educational Technology*, 7, 2, 93–112.

GUILFORD, J. P. (1954) *Psychometric Methods*. New York: McGraw-Hill.

GUILFORD, J. P. (1965). *Fundamental Statistics in Psychology and Education*. New York: McGraw-Hill.

HARTLEY, J. (1967) Some guides for program evaluation. In P. Cavanagh, ed., *Programs in Print*, 1966. London: Association for Programmed Learning and Educational Technology.

HILGARD, E. R. and BOWER, G. H. (1966) *Theories of Learning*, 3rd edn. New York: Appleton-Century-Crofts.

KERLINGER, F. N. (1964) *Foundations of Behavioural Research*. New York: Holt, Rinehart and Winston.

LORD, F. M. (1958) Further problems in the measurement of growth, *Journal of Educational and Psychological Measurement*, 18, 437–51.

MANNING, W. H. and DUBOIS, P. H. (1963) Correlation methods in research on human learning, *Perceptual Motor Skills*, 15, 287–321.

SENDERS, V. L. (1958) *Measurement and Statistics*. Oxford: Oxford University Press.

SIEGEL, S. (1956) *Non-Parametric Statistics for the Behavioural Sciences*. New York: McGraw-Hill.

STEVENS, S. S. (1946) On the theory of scales of measurement, *Science*, 103, 677–80.

STEVENS, S. S. (1951) Mathematics, measurement and psychophysics. In S. S. Stevens, ed., *Handbook of Experimental Psychology*. New York: Wiley, 1–49.

STEVENS, S. S. (1959) Measurement, psychophysics and utility. In C. W. Churchman and R. Ratoosh, eds., *Measurement: Definitions and Theories*. New York: Wiley.

TATSVOKA, M. A. and TREDMAN, D. V. (1963) Statistics as an aspect of scientific method in research on teaching. In N. L. Gage, ed., *Handbook of Research on Teaching*. Chicago: Rand McNally.

TORGERSON, W. (1958) *Theory and Methods of Scaling*. New York: Wiley.

WOOD, D. W. (1961) *Test Construction*. Columbus, Ohio: Merrill.

16 Managing by learning objectives

Learning Objectives

COGNITIVE OBJECTIVES

After carefully reading this chapter, you will be able to:

1. State in your own words what is meant by the term 'management by objectives'.

2. Draw a simple diagram of the management by objectives cycle.

3. State three basic requirements which should be met for effective learning.

4. Define, in your own words, what is meant by the term 'key tasks'.

5. List the four procedures involved in the cycle of managing by learning objectives, and write short notes on each.

6. Construct a list of the advantages and disadvantages of managing by learning objectives, and evaluate each factor in terms of its importance to the learning process.

7. Manage by learning objectives.

AFFECTIVE OBJECTIVES

After reading this chapter, the author intends that you will:

1. Be aware of, and value, the importance of management by learning objectives as a means of exercising the control function of the teacher-manager.

2. Incorporate the principle into your organization of managerial strategies, so that it is characteristic of your teaching style.

> Watch out when a man's work becomes more important than its objectives, when he disappears into his duties.
>
> *Alan Harrington*

The term 'management by objectives' was first used by Peter Drucker in 1954, and since then the principle has become widely known and practised as a system of management in industry and commerce. When Drucker first used the expression, he was referring to a prediction that future managers would be held accountable both for their results and for the quality of the human relations found in their organizations. Today, management by objectives is, '. . . a process whereby the superior and subordinate managers of an organization jointly identify its common goals, define each individual's major areas of responsibility in terms of the results expected of him, and use these measures as guides for operating the unit and assessing the contribution of each of its members'. (Odiorne, 1965). In the absence of such known precise

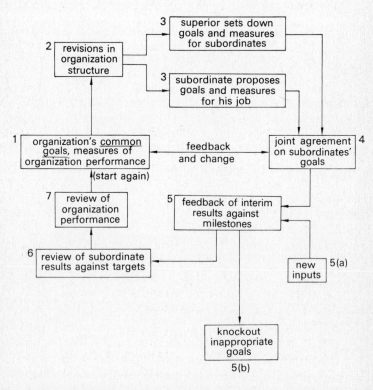

Fig. 16.1 The management by objectives cycle (Reproduced with permission from Odiorne, G. S. (1965) *Management by Objectives*. New York: Pitman)

and agreed standards, Odiorne goes on to argue that no amount of generalized motivation can produce satisfactory results based solely on personal responsibility. When standards have been made clear, and when the people involved have had an opportunity *both* to contribute to them and agree them, then the need to realize the standards will have a very strong motivating force upon the individuals involved.

As an overall system of control, management by objectives (MBO) commonly involves a complete cycle of operations. This cycle is illustrated diagrammatically in Fig. 16.1. It will be seen that MBO typically involves seven steps or procedures. First, the overall objectives of the organization itself are defined and agreement is reached on how performance will be measured – otherwise, it will not be possible to determine whether the objectives have been successfully realized. Subordinates' goals, together with their associated measure, are then decided upon and agreed. Any failures and successes in realizing the objectives are subsequently examined and analysed, inappropriate goals are removed, and each subordinate's performance reviewed in terms of the actual results that he has been successful in achieving. Finally, after everyone's effectiveness has been reviewed, the total performance of the organization itself is analysed, in order to determine weaknesses in its overall operation.

The Application of MBO to Education and Training

A management by objectives approach makes it clear that organization must be thought of as a total system. For this reason, the MBO principle can be very usefully applied to education and training, particularly as it capitalizes on the unique planning, organizing, and leading functions of the teacher-manager and training-manager. Such a system of managing by learning objectives (MBLO) helps to clarify, and does a great deal to resolve, the apparent conflict between:
1.   The overall aims and objectives of education and training, as determined and valued by society at large.
2.   The overall aims and objectives of an education or training organization or institution.
3.   The personal and professional aims and objectives of teachers and instructors working within a particular organization.
4.   The task and interpersonal relationship needs of the classes or groups making up an organization.
5.   The needs of individual students for self-development and responsibility, in terms of the learning results that they are required to achieve.
Managing by learning objectives also does a great deal to highlight the multiple managerial role of a teacher and instructor, with their many unique yet conflicting responsibilities.

If a student or trainee is to realize the learning objectives with which he has been tasked, then it is necessary to ensure that three basic requirements are met:

1. *He must know exactly what is expected of him.* Unfortunately, in most teaching situations, students are rarely given any precise and concrete information about what is going to happen to them, and what they are going to learn to do. It is not surprising, therefore, that a student's view of what is necessary, may be very different to his teacher's view of the same situation.

2. *He must be given an opportunity to learn.* This is just too obvious. Yet, some teachers and instructors *behave* in such a way as to make learning difficult, if not impossible. An opportunity to learn involves freedom to accept responsibility for one's own learning, freedom to exercise initiative, and freedom to work within the full limits of authority delegated to a student.

3. *He must know what progress he is making.* This means that his progress in realizing learning objectives must be constantly monitored, and the results *immediately* fed back to him in a form that is meaningful to both short-term and long-term action. The only really effective way of fulfilling this need is by means of regular and detailed counselling and guidance. This means that teachers are committed to discuss a student's successes and failures in realizing his learning objectives. There is little point in talking to students about such things as the need for hard work, the importance of trying, and the virtue of being interested; only effectiveness converts resources into results.

Hard work is futile when effort is directed at realizing unimportant or unnecessary learning objectives – particularly when it is done at the expense of objectives which are important.

In order to ensure that such a waste of time and effort does not occur, the importance of a teacher's role cannot be overemphasized. Not only must a teacher define learning objectives and ensure that they are indeed being realized, but he must also discuss them with his students in order to secure and maintain their personal involvement and participation in the learning process. It is possible to *talk* about the importance of student motivation. It is functionally more useful to *gain* a student's commitment to a set of agreed objectives.

KEY TASKS

Every teacher and instructor, of course, has many duties to perform, but management by learning objectives helps to establish priorities. Generally speaking, only a small proportion of all the myriad things that a teacher does are vital and crucial to his overall effectiveness, while the majority of the things that he does are often only marginally important. Indeed, the concept behind the well known 20/80 rule can usefully be applied to teaching:

20 per cent of the students tend to cause 80 per cent of the problems.

20 per cent of the objectives tend to cause 80 per cent of the learning difficulties.

20 per cent of the tasks tend to be responsible for 80 per cent of the results. Less essential or peripheral tasks can always, if necessary, be left, delegated, or assigned to the student. Key tasks, however, must always be accomplished under the personal guidance and supervision of the teacher. Nothing should be left to chance.

The recognition and realization of key tasks, and their associated performance standards, is the central concept of managing by learning objectives. This is where the greatest teacher impact can be made, since key tasks have such an extraordinary impact on learning – they can transform a student's entire performance – it is important to distinguish once more between accomplishment and acquirement. As we saw in chapter 4, achievement can refer to:
1. What a student has learned (acquirement).
2. The value of what a student has learned (accomplishment).
In terms of what a student knows, his acquirement can be very high indeed, but this knowledge will be of little use if his level of accomplishment is low. A small deficiency in acquirement, therefore, can make a great difference in accomplishment, hence the importance of recognizing these key tasks or areas of emphasis.

The Management by Learning Objectives Cycle

Management by objectives, as we have seen, is a simple, but complete cyclical procedure. In the context of education and training, however, it consists of a continuous process involving four main areas of action:
1. Setting organizational aims and objectives, and then deriving subject and topic objectives.
2. Writing a learning guide or prescription, which also includes information on key results and performance standards.
3. Agreeing a learning improvement plan with each student.
4. Systematically reviewing each student's performance, and then counselling him so that he can overcome his weaknesses, build on his strengths, and accept responsibility for self-development.
Looked at in this way, MBLO is an effective means of individualizing instruction, both as a strategy and a tactic, within the framework of traditional and modern patterns of organization for learning. Figure 16.2 both illustrates the characteristics of truly individualized instruction, and presents a decision table to enable teachers to assess the character of their own managerial style.

The first step in the cycle is for the organization or institution to define its overall aims and objectives. What does the organization hope to accomplish? Once this is known and agreed, it is possible for these aims to be broken down by the more senior teachers and instructors (i.e., heads of departments) into subject objectives for each member of staff. At the same time that authority, responsibility, and accountability are allotted, the necessary resources for realizing subject objectives can be broadly allocated.

Next, subject teachers must write detailed objectives and performance standards for each unit or topic, and these should then be given to students in the form of a learning guide or prescription. This key document should also contain progress tests, diagnostic tests, book and reading lists, assignments and the dates they are to be met, and suggestions on the ways and means of tackling the more important tasks. In order to ensure that the priorities are clearly understood and appreciated, key tasks should be boldly annotated and any constraints indicated.

CONDITION STUB		CONDITION ENTRIES	
Q1	Are the instructional objectives written on paper?	Yes	No
Q2	Are the content (lesson) objectives given to the student?	Yes	No
Q3	Are all students expected to achieve the same objectives?	No	Yes
Q4	Do all students use the same instructional material (e.g., texts)?	No	Yes
Q5	Arc all students expected to follow the same procedure while in the classroom?	No	Yes
Q6	Do all students work at each subject for the same amount of time?	No	Yes
Q7	Do students spend most of their time doing that which everyone else is doing?	No	Yes
Q8	May the student have any part in deciding which objectives he will be expected to achieve?	Yes	No
Q9	May the student decide which materials he will use in trying to achieve on objective?	Yes	No
Q10	May the student decide which procedures he will follow in attempting to achieve an objective?	Yes	No
Q11	May the student decide how much time he will devote to an activity?	Yes	No
ACTION STUB		**ACTION ENTRIES**	
Instruction is individualized		*	
Instruction is NOT individualized			*
Rules		(1)	(2)

Fig. 16.2 **A decision table for individualized instruction.** (Adapted with permission from Mager, R. F. (1968) Forward. In T. Esbensen, ed., *Working with Individualized Instruction: The Duluth Experience.* Palo Alto, California: Fearon, VII–VIII)

Teachers and instructors must now discuss this learning guide with their students. They should ensure that its purpose and content are understood, individual responsibilities recognized, and the importance of the target dates for assignments and projects appreciated. At the same time, teachers would do well to explain their role to their students, and indicate which particular topics they themselves will be formally teaching. Individual students should then be interviewed. The purpose of this interview is to select and agree one or two key tasks where emphasis and improvement are necessary; these should be recorded in the student's learning guide. At this stage, the emphasis is on helping a student to improve his performance, and this involves guiding him so that he learns how to isolate relevant problems, how to plan his work, study, and take notes, and how to identify reasons for any failures or mistakes. In this way, students can develop along broad educational paths, as well as along narrow specialist lines (see Fleishman, 1963).

The performance review is one of the most crucial steps in the whole management by learning objectives cycle, for its purpose is to review the progress students have made in realizing the learning objectives allocated to them. During the review, a student is faced with the reality of what he has achieved. It enables him to see what has gone wrong and where he needs help. His strengths and weaknesses can be isolated and identified. Teachers and instructors can then decide what special guidance and tuition are necessary, and how a student's performance can be improved and his potential realized by the time of the next counselling.

There is nothing, of course, in this fourfold cycle that is not already done, consciously or unconsciously, by good teachers and instructors. Management by learning objectives merely systematizes the whole process, and integrates the teacher's need for effectiveness with the student's need to contribute and develop himself. The philosophy behind the process is important and meaningful for the very simple reason that is personally rewarding to both teachers and students. Indeed, it is the best do-it-yourself hangman's kit that we possess at the present time.

The Proper Use of Human Resources

The application of management by learning objectives to education and training enables objectives to be related to the decisions that teachers and students make in a learning environment. However, the philosophy it generates is in marked conflict with the autocratic styles of leadership characteristic of some teachers and instructors. It will take some time before new attitudes and values evolve towards the role of the teacher and the student, for some are reluctant to make the necessary investment in time and resources that this approach demands.

One danger that is often voiced about such an approach is that managing by learning objectives could provoke antagonism, since its insistence on results and measurement could make students vulnerable to failure. Everyday experience in the classroom, however, runs contrary to this view. Most students prefer to be assessed against a set of clear criteria that they themselves have had the opportunity of influencing. They prefer:

> To control one's destiny and not be controlled by it; to know which way the path will fork and to make the turning oneself; to have some index of achievement that no one can dispute – concrete and tangible for all to see – not dependent on the attitude of others. (Whyte, 1956).

Posttest 16

ANSWER ALL QUESTIONS

1. State in your own words the meaning of the term 'management by objectives'.

2. Draw a simple diagram to illustrate the management by objectives cycle.

3. State the three basic requirements for effective learning.

4. Define, in your own words, what is meant by the term 'key tasks'.

5. List the four procedures involved in the cycle of managing by learning objectives, and write short notes on each.

6. State the characteristics of truly individualized instruction as presented by R. F. Mager.

7. Construct a list of the advantages and disadvantages of managing by learning objectives, and evaluate each factor in terms of its importance to the learning process.

8. Select a learning task, and state how you would organize it so as to utilize the principle of management by learning objectives. Justify your organization.

References and Reading List

FLEISHMAN, E. A. (1963) Some observations of industrial psychology: the USSR. *Personnel Psychology*, 16, 115–25.

GILBERT, T. F. (1964) A dialogue between teaching and testing. In G. D. Ofiesh and W. C. Mierhenry, eds., *Trends in Programmed Instruction*. Washington, DC: Department of Audiovisual Instruction.

HUMBLE, J. W. (1967) *Management by Objectives*. London: Industrial Education and Research Foundation.

HUMBLE, J. W. (1968) *Improving Business Results*. London: McGraw Hill.

HUMBLE, J. W. (1969) *Improving Management Performance*. London: British Institute of Management.

HUMBLE, J. W. (1970) *Management by Objectives in Action*. London: McGraw-Hill.

MAGER, R. F. (1968) Foreword. In T. Esbensen, *Working with Individualized Instruction*. Palo Alto: Fearon.

ODIORNE, G. S. (1965) *Management by Objectives: A System of Managerial Leadership*. New York: Pitman.

WHYTE, W. (1956) *The Organization Man*. New York: Simon and Schuster.

242

RAF photographers, job analysis,
63-64
Ratio scale, 219-220, 222-223
Realism theories, 110
Realm theories:
defined, 67
use of, 67, 68
Receiving, as a learning objective, 74,
75, 76, 80
Receptor processes, 48, 50
Record players, 5, 113
Reinforcement theory, 6, 7, 59, 98, 99
Relationships:
of association, 94-95
of discrimination, 94-95
Research in education:
role of in decision-making, 26
teachers' attitudes towards, 26
Residual gain scores, 225-226
Resistors, colour code, 59-60, 95
Resources:
allocation of, 25, 236
co-ordination of, 9
framework for managing, 4
human, 237-238
organization of, 4, 13-14, 206
pressure on, 128
Responding, as a learning objective,
74, 75, 76, 80
Responsibility, 24, 223, 235-238
delegation of, 25
and motivation, 152-154
Retention-tests, 212-214, 225, 226
Retrogressive chaining, 98, 99-100,
102, 103
Restructuring behaviour, 58-59
Revolution in education and training,
20, 24
Role-playing, 119, 168-169, 175, 176,
177
Rote learning, 10, 11-12, 99
Rules, 40-43
arrangement of, 41-42
characteristics of rules, 41
classification of, 94-95
examples of, 41, 42, 94
identification of, 40
patterns of, 95, 96
relationships between, 94
writing of rule set, 41
Rule set, 41, 94-97
example of, 42

Scales of measurement, 219-223
and selection of test-statistics, 223-225
Science of teaching, 15

Scores, power tests:
basic scores, 225, 226
difference scores, 225, 226
modified ratio scores, 226, 227-228
predictive scores, 226, 227
ratio scores, 226, 227-228
Screen size, 114n
Self-actualization, 150-151, 162
Self-fulfilling prophecy, 158-159
Sensitivity training, 173-174, 175,
176, 177
Sequence:
logical of learning, 190-191
rules for, 41
Shoe-laces, tying of, 60
Signals, classification of, 44
Signal structures, 92, 198
and AV aids, 114, 116, 117, 120, 122
characteristic matrix patterns, 95
definition of, 93, 96, 97
examples of, 93, 103
and learning objectives, 104-105
prerequisites, 93
teaching tactics for, 97-99
Signal tasks, and job analysis, 46-47,
63-64
Simple visual aids, 114-116
Simulators, 119, 198
Skill, 38, 58
aids in acquiring, 112
age and performance, 185
content of job, 198-200
function of, 200
learning phases in, 198-201
Skills analysis:
circumstances calling for, 50, 53
defined, 36-37, 48
example of, 51-52
objectives of, 49
overuse of, 37, 53
perceptual activities analysis, 49
sources of information for, 37-38
steps in, 50
writing skills analysis, 48-52, 196,
201, 202
Skills analysis training:
knowledge content, 197-198
objectives of, 197
skills content, 198, 200
technique, 197-200
Skill content, of job, 198-199
Skill, definition of, 49, 202
Slides, 114-116
Social requirements, need to balance
with task requirements, 25, 28
Socio-technical system, 43

Printed in Great Britain by
Clarke, Doble & Brendon Ltd, Plymouth